MASSACRE IN THE PAMPAS, 1872

Massacre in the Pampas, 1872
Britain and Argentina
in the Age of Migration

BY

John Lynch

UNIVERSITY OF OKLAHOMA PRESS : NORMAN

ALSO BY JOHN LYNCH

Spanish Colonial Administration, 1782–1810: The Intendant System in the Viceroyalty of the Río de la Plata (London, 1958; Buenos Aires, 1962)

Spain under the Habsburgs (Oxford, 1964–69, 1991; Barcelona, 1992

(ed., with R. A. Humphreys) *The Origins of the Latin American Revolutions, 1808–1826* (New York, 1965)

The Spanish American Revolutions, 1808–1826 (London, 1973; New York, 1986; Barcelona, 1989)

Argentine Dictator: Juan Manuel de Rosas, 1829–1852 (Oxford, 1981; Buenos Aires, 1984)

(ed.) *Andrés Bello: The London Years* (Richmond, 1982)

(ed.) *Past and Present in the Americas: A Compendium of Recent Studies* (Manchester, 1984)

Hispanoamérica 1750–1850: Ensayos sobre la sociedad y el estado (Bogotá, 1987)

Bourbon Spain 1700–1808 (Oxford, 1989; Barcelona, 1991)

Caudillos in Spanish America 1800–1850 (Oxford, 1992; Madrid, 1993)

Latin American Revolutions, 1808–1826: Old and New World Origins (Norman, 1994)

This book is published with the generous assistance of the Mellon Humanities Publications Fund.

Library of Congress Cataloging-in-Publication Data

Lynch, John 1927–
    Massacre in the pampas, 1872 : Britain and Argentina in the age of migration / by John Lynch.
        p.   cm.
    Includes bibliographical references and index.
    ISBN 0-8061-3018-0 (alk. paper)
    1. Immigrants—Argentina—Tandil—History—19th century.
2. British—Argentina—Tandil—History—19th century. 3. Massacres—Argentina—Tandil—History—19th century. 4. Argentina—History—19th century. 5. Tandil (Argentina)—History. 6. Argentina—Foreign relations—Great Britain. 7. Great Britain—Foreign relations—Argentina.   I. Title.
F3011.T28L94   1998   97-35259
982'.12—dc21   CIP

The paper in this book meets the guidelines for permanence and durability of the Committee on Production Guidelines for Book Longevity of the Council on Library Resources, Inc. ∞

1 2 3 4 5 6 7 8 9 10

In vain the sage, with retrospective eye,
Would from the apparent *what* conclude the *why*,
Infer the motive from the deed, and show
That what we chanced was what we meant to do.

Alexander Pope, Moral Essays

Contents

Illustrations

Tables

Acknowledgments

I am pleased to record my thanks for the help I have received from Samuel Amaral, María Alejandra Irigoin, and Juan José Santos, all of whom have generously shared with me their knowledge of the Argentine sources. I am also grateful to Joseph Smith, who pointed me towards comparable studies of frontier violence in United States history. I owe a special word of thanks to Andrew Barnard, whose expert research assistance helped me to document the British side of the story.

I wish to express my debt to the archives mentioned in the sources, especially the Archivo General de la Nación, Buenos Aires, where Miguel Unamuno was extraordinarily helpful, the Archivo Histórico de la Provincia de Buenos Aires, La Plata, and the Public Record Office, London. Particular thanks are also due to the British Library, the Institute of Latin American Studies, and the Library of University College London.

MASSACRE IN THE PAMPAS, 1872

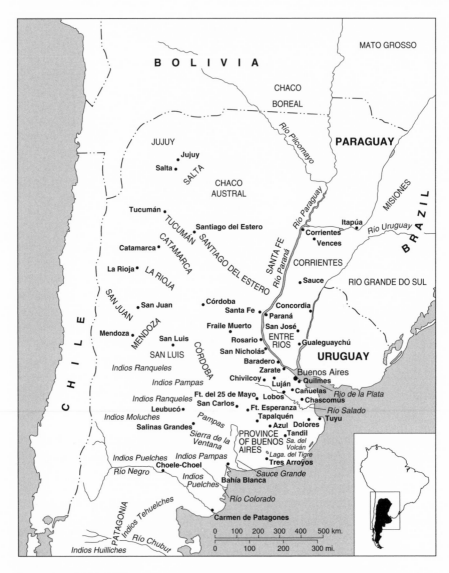

Argentina, 1862–1874

Introduction

On 1 January 1872 in the small town of Tandil, two hundred miles south of Buenos Aires, a band of armed men wearing red ribbons in their hats and shouting abuse against foreigners and Freemasons attacked the local courthouse, occupied the main square, and galloped off at dawn into the countryside on a rampage of murder and looting. Their first stop was a wagon train about a mile outside the town, where they killed the Basque drivers. Proceeding northwards, they killed, among others, a Basque storekeeper and a group of British settlers, hacking down a young Scottish couple as they took flight. They then approached a larger country store; there they stabbed the French owner, cut the throats of his wife and children, and killed the retainers. After moving on in search of further victims, they paused at a nearby *estancia* to take refreshments and examine their guns, swords, and lances. At that place the assassins were confronted by an armed posse, and those who were not killed or captured escaped into the hills and vanished from history. The victims, a total of thirty-six, were almost all foreigners: Spaniards, Italians, French, and British.

News of the massacre caused alarm and outrage. Local settlers armed themselves and demanded greater security. The Argentine press denounced the government, rural conditions, and religious fanaticism, according to political preference and the evidence available. Foreign governments protested to the Argentine authorities, who in turn harassed local officials. Immigration policies were denounced and defended, and Anglo-Argentine relations suffered. English newspapers, struggling to explain these events to their readers, compared them to "the massacre of Glencoe" and "the sepoy revolt in India."[1] No one produced a satisfactory explanation or discovered the identity of the prime mover.

The motive and meaning of the massacre were disputed then and now. Some insisted that it was a conspiracy among the local elite to frighten foreigners and check their advance. Others saw it as an expression of social conditions: a cry for help from oppressed gauchos and those marginalized by the expansion of private estates or, conversely, further evidence of the barbarism of rural society. Liberals and anticlericals detected the hand of the Church and the prejudice of Catholics whipping up blind fanaticism against all who did not conform. Others pointed to the messianic character of the rising, the doomsday predictions of its zealots, and the strange personality of its leader. Most agreed that it was in part a nativist reaction against the advent of the immigrant, who took land and work that should belong to Argentines. Few, except perhaps the British, were prepared to regard the massacre as an example of pure criminality.

Modern interpretations are also eclectic and seek to combine the immediate and the structural in a comprehensive explanation. "A bizarre melange of xenophobia, religious zealotry, superstitious fanaticism, and greed motivated these humble gauchos to embark upon their mission as exterminating angels. Deeper structural causes, including latifundism and legal oppression of the gaucho, also played a role."[2] A reasonable interpretation, but does each reason have similar force and equal relevance?

The massacre was not a solitary atrocity, and it had implications beyond immediate events. Violence and disorder were a way of life in rural Argentina. They had existed before and during the long dictatorship of Juan Manuel de Rosas (1829–52), who had, however, enough influence to control as well as to exploit the popular forces of the countryside. Since then the northern and southern frontiers of the Argentine littoral had become zones of agricultural settlement but also the prey of Indian raiders and gaucho rebels. For some ten years before the massacre British observers had documented the opportunities and the dangers for settlers in these empty lands and had drawn attention to the thin partition that separated order from anarchy. When the Argentine government failed to take measures to improve security, the Emigration Commission in London issued warnings to prospective emigrants that Argentina was not a safe country for settlers, while in Buenos Aires government ministers angrily defended their reputation and continued to encourage immigration as a national priority. To all parties the massacre of Tandil came as an untimely shock.

The evidence for reconstructing events in Tandil on New Year's Day 1872 comes from three sources. The first comprises the records of the trial and the official inquiry and is housed in the Museo del Fuerte Independencia in Tandil, a private institution not open to researchers.

However, the most significant part of this documentation has been published in recent years by the leading Argentine historian of the massacre.[3] The second source, the correspondence of provincial officials, can be consulted in the Archivo Histórico de la Provincia de Buenos Aires in La Plata. The third source consists of British documentation— Foreign Office reports, correspondence, and official notices—and is to be found in the Public Record Office, London. Each source is influenced by its own purpose. The prosecutors wanted a verdict of guilty, provincial officials sought to assign and to escape blame, and the British looked for action from the Argentine government. None of these documents, informative though they are, adequately explore the motivation of the massacre or its wider context, the depths as well as the shallows. This is left to the historian.

The following account opens with a description of Argentina in the age of national organization, 1852–74, gradually focusing on frontier society. Two particular problems of security are considered: hostile Indians and dissident gauchos, and the risks to foreign immigrants from both. The book then looks at social and economic structures in rural Argentina, with a view to locating the massacre at Tandil in the context of social protest. As the massacre was an expression of xenophobia, the inquiry leads to a scrutiny of Argentine nationalism, immigration policy, and the nativist backlash against foreigners. Having established the underlying structures of rural life, the book then describes in detail the onset and course of the raid, the nature of the killings, the identity of the killers, and, through comparative reference to vigilantism and lynch mobs in the United States, the character of the outlaw band. Liberals in Argentina condemned this gross encounter as another example of religious fanaticism; to address this question the book examines the massacre for signs of a millenarian message, for its background in popular Catholicism, and for echoes of past political fundamentalism.

At this point the story moves on to the fallout from the massacre. How did the local community react and the Argentine authorities respond? Were any lessons learned? Security on the frontier and in the interior was not noticeably improved in the years following the atrocity. The Argentine government refused to yield to the tide of indignation and rejected foreign intervention as an affront to its sovereignty. This further provoked the British authorities, who now came out frankly against Argentina as a country of immigration. As British outrage clashed with Argentine nationalism, relations between the two countries deteriorated, and in the process British representatives in Buenos Aires were ordered to supply detailed reports on Argentina and its prospects. These are a significant guide to foreign perception of an immigrant country and an illustration of latent conflict of cultures. They also complete the general framework with which the book began and within which the massacre at Tandil is enclosed.

1

Argentina, 1852–1874: Nation and Frontier

A NEW RULE OF LAW

Argentina emerged from the age of caudillos arguing over its history and disputing its future. From the past it inherited a nation of autonomies, a state without a constitution, and a territory open to invaders. The future became a battlefield of ideologies, each incapable of imposing its will. In any event the outcome was preempted by liberals, who alone had a clear national project: a constitution for all Argentines, death to the caudillos, and modernization by foreign capital and European immigrants. The decade 1852–62 saw tradition and modernity in uneasy coexistence. Rural society remained divided, as Sarmiento remarked, between *estancieros*, small farmers, and vagrants. The whole country was fragmented, provinces from each other, Buenos Aires from the rest, a scene of anarchy unattractive to investors and immigrants alike. Argentina consisted not of one state but of two: on the one hand the city and province of Buenos Aires, ruled by its governor and a liberal party, and on the other the Argentine confederation, ruled by a caudillo and his provincial allies. A combination of political leadership, economic resources, and military power enabled Buenos Aires to survive a decade of conflict and emerge, if not triumphant, at least in a position to launch a program of national organization.

The basis was the Constitution of 1853, an amalgam of native experience, the example of the United States, and the ideas of Argentina's leading political theorist, Juan Bautista Alberdi. There was an authoritarian streak in Alberdi which matched the interests of the political elite. He advocated a due balance between central power and provincial rights and signaled the way to modernize through immigration and education. But Alberdi's Argentina was fed only a minimal freedom; liberalism had to be prescribed, reforms imposed, and recalcitrants coerced, preferably by a powerful president. The constitution provided for a federal republic and incorporated the classic freedoms, civil rights, and division of powers. The legislature consisted of two houses, a senate to which each provincial legislature elected two members, and a chamber of deputies elected by adult males, voting in public. While granting autonomous institutions to the provinces, the constitution gave compensatory authority to the federal government and removed internal restraints on trade.

The president, who was chosen by an electoral college for six years, was given strong executive powers: he could introduce his own bills and appoint and dismiss his ministers without reference to Congress. The president was also empowered to intervene in any province in order to preserve republican government against internal disorder or foreign attack; to this effect he could remove local administrations and impose federal officials. The constitution was thus an instrument of compromise between unitarism and federalism. And Bartolomé Mitre, a *porteño* by birth and a hero of the provinces, was elected first constitutional president in October 1862. His prize? The Argentine Republic. His program? To replace the personal governments of the caudillos by the "government of institutions."[1]

A change in the form of government was not a panacea. National organization after 1862 was a theoretical construct rather than a real achievement, and words were more impressive than deeds. The political system remained primitive, and personalism prevailed at every level. Elections were no guide to opinion. Public voting under the eye of local justices and military commanders enabled them to manipulate voters by fraud and intimidation on behalf of their political bosses. Participation was low: in the Buenos Aires provincial elections of 1864, out of 130,000 qualified voters in a population of 450,000, only 13,393 bothered to vote.[2]

Ironically, stability owed less to institutions than to the political personality and the powerful regimes of two distinguished presidents, Bartolomé Mitre (1862–68) and Domingo F. Sarmiento (1868–74), intellectuals and men of letters as well as politicians and statesmen. Both had given years of service to the ideal of a greater Argentina. Both now stood for three objectives: national unity, liberal institutions, and modernization. But their enemies did not yield without a fight. In 1863 and again in 1866–68, Mitre had to suppress rebellions in the provinces, where caudillos continued to resist the new order. Underlying these insurrections were the depressed economies of the interior, slow to change and unable to sustain their populations in occupation or subsistence. Lack of work and food drove the rural peoples to the life of *montoneros*, to live in effect by banditry and booty and to rely on handouts from their personal leader.

No such conditions could explain Mitre's own reversion to violence in September 1874, when his followers attempted to overthrow the new president, Nicolás Avellaneda; this was a *porteño* separatist revolt, an old maneuver, and it was defeated by the new army conveyed to the front in the modern railway. But it was 1876 before the last caudillo, Ricardo López Jordán, was eliminated from Entre Ríos and Sarmiento's campaign came to an end. He fought caudillism not only with the gun, but also with the pen, in the schoolroom, and through development. The political elite of Argentina regarded economic growth by investment and immigration as an integral part of the modernizing process.

In spite of provincial traditions and caudillo resistance, central power and national organization survived and took root. They were not vigorous growths but were nourished by agencies with a national dimension, the press, the postal service, the National Bank, and the railway system, each a new piece in the construction of the Argentine state. Two particular institutions promoted national unity and identity: federal justice and the national army, both bitterly criticized by foreign observers and indeed badly flawed in their early days, but both an advance on previous institutions. By law of 1862 a national judicial power was established, and in 1865–68 the Argentine Civil Code was drawn up. The Supreme Court and the various lower courts completed the legal structure of the modern state. The Supreme Court had power to declare unconstitutional any laws or decrees, national or provincial, in conflict with the supreme law and thus became the interpreter of the constitution. The growth of federal power deprived the provinces of much of their traditional autonomy, though this was not entirely reflected in judicial relations. In practice federal law officers failed to intervene effectively against weak or corrupt provincial judges, and the criminal justice system foundered upon its inhibitions and its personnel, as British settlers discovered. Yet the executive had the right of intervention in the provinces, a right which became more effective once it was backed by a national army.

Mitre's reforms of 1862–64 made the command, the pay, and the supply of the army directly dependent on the Ministry of War, and new regulations were designed for recruiting and training officers and troops. By decree of 26 January 1864 the government created a regular army of six thousand men distributed among artillery, infantry, and cavalry. A military academy was established in 1869, and the formation of a professional officer corps was begun. The law of recruitment of 21 September 1872 anticipated national conscription. This was the institutional framework of the new army. It was not uniformly effective, and many of the reforms of the 1860s were purely theoretical. In the war with Paraguay (1865–70) the army was badly led and poorly motivated. In action against rebellious caudillos it was often made to look clumsy and brutal. But in 1874 it defended the constitution and saved the lawful government. Gradually it gave the president real power and enabled him to extend the executive's reach into the farthest corners of Argentina, though not as yet to the one area that mattered most, the Indian frontier. The verdict on national organization, therefore, is that the Argentine state still fell short of delivering two essential services of a state, jurisdiction over its territory and security for its citizens, but the first steps had been taken.

The political principles inspiring the presidencies of Mitre and Sarmiento were those of classical liberalism. Mitre led an identifiable Liberal party, and his strategy of national organization rested not only on the extension of federal power but also on the conversion of provincial governments into strongholds of liberal beliefs. Liberalism represented a political and intellectual elite, survivors and heirs of the opponents of Juan Manuel de Rosas, now free to apply their ideas; to promote political and material progress, the rule of law, and primary and secondary education; and to dispel the barbarism which Sarmiento abhorred. But they offered little to the mass of the people. Liberals disliked Indians, deplored gauchos, and turned aside from the rural poor, all wretches regarded as beyond the political pale. The federalists had once represented the traditional interests of provincial Argentina, but those of the proprietor rather than the peon, and federalism was now virtually extinct as a political force. The Liberals split into two groups during Mitre's presidency: the autonomists, conservative xenophobes who came to incorporate those federalists left leaderless by the death of the caudillos, and the nationalists, who continued to preserve pure *mitrista* principles of economic liberalism, links with foreign capital, European immigration, and railway expansion. But policy making in Buenos Aires and life on the distant pampas were two different worlds, separated by mutual incomprehension.

INDIANS OF HILLS AND PLAINS

Tandil, some two hundred miles south of Buenos Aires, deep in Argentina's grasslands, was founded on 4 April 1823 as a frontier post, a fortified settlement, and a stage on the military route to the Río Negro.[3] It took its name from an Indian cacique whose *tolderìa*, or camp, was in the vicinity, and its character from proximity to a dangerous frontier. The first settlers survived the hazards of frontier life, threw back the Indians, and, following General Rosas's expedition of

1833, gradually established a peaceful zone of settlement. South of Tandil, however, and west to Tres Arroyos and Bahía Blanca, lay Indian country, territory disputed by settlers and natives, dangerous for whites even in the 1860s, and not brought within civilization until Minister of War Adolfo Alsina established a new frontier in 1877. It was about 1880–83 before the Great Southern Railway reached Tandil and Bahía Blanca and the area was at last incorporated into modern Argentina. Meanwhile, between 1854 and 1869 the inhabitants of Tandil had increased from just under three thousand to almost five thousand, spread between town and country. They enjoyed a temperate climate and a green environment, looking out on a gently undulating plain covered with long, rough grass and surrounded by ranges of fine hills which relieved the monotony of the southern landscape. About three miles distant from Tandil was a famous landmark, the Piedra Movediza, a huge rocking stone so perfectly balanced that it rocked in the wind and so firm that, according to legend, even the massed horses and cattle of General Rosas had been unable to pull it down.[4] The stone was an object of gaucho superstition, and in 1872 the murderers of Tandil assembled at Peñalverde, a farmhouse nearby, and invoked its name. Tandil was overshadowed by its more substantial neighbor, Azul, the most congenial town in the south, though often besieged by Indians before the coming of the railway.

Indians did not participate directly in the life of Tandil or the politics of Buenos Aires, but they exerted a strong pull on the attention of government, the action of the army, and the lives of country people. National organization meant nothing if Argentina could not exercise jurisdiction over its own territory and defend its own people. This was the constant argument of Alvaro Barros, a leading soldier and politician of the new state; there is no security, he warned, "as long as it is possible for the Indians to invade and devastate our lands." The economic loss to the province of Buenos Aires was incalculable, though *La Prensa* attempted to calculate it: in the period 1820–70 the Indians had taken eleven million cattle, two million horses, and two million sheep; they had killed fifty thousand people, destroyed three thousand houses, and stolen twenty million dollars' worth of property.[5]

The Indians came in different guises, few of which were understood by contemporaries. They were to be seen in Buenos Aires and provincial towns, trading and negotiating. They were to be found, too, in their *tolderías*, huddled in primitive tents and planning the next raid against well-stocked *estancias*. The Indians of the plains comprised diverse tribes, displaying variations of a common culture and competing for territory among themselves as well as with the whites. They were all expert hunters, good riders, well mounted, and when they were on raids they ate, drank, and slept on their horses.

The ultimate source of Indian migration was Chile, from whose southern territories the Araucanians had been moving eastwards over the Andes for many years, taking with them their language, customs, and methods of war.[6] The first decades of the nineteenth century saw one of the largest movements of Indians from Chile as they lost space in the south to the new republic and its Chilean supporters. Numerous chieftains led their people eastwards to Argentina to settle or raid either individually or in group alliances. There they behaved not as nomadic tribes but as occupants of land which they regarded as their rightful inheritance and exploited not so much for cultivation as for cattle. The Indians needed horses for their own mobility and cattle for their trade with the Chilean market in their rear. Thus, in addition to the cultural unity of this new power in the Argentine south, there was also an Indian economic network in which various tribes and chieftains participated.

But territory was not infinite, and the Indians soon discovered that they, too, faced a hostile frontier, as settlers from Argentina, and ultimately the Argentine state itself, moved southwards in search of new land, resources, and sovereignty. The Indian response was to perfect the *malón*, the armed raid on white cattle estates, a source of grief for the owners, an agent of unification for the tribes, and a form of warfare vital for the Indian trading system. War or peace, pillage or pasture, it was all the same to the Indians; each was a tactical adjustment to their basic needs. In this way some twenty thousand to forty thousand head of cattle a year passed to the Chilean market.

This "Araucanization" of the pampas gave the Chilean Indians a vast reserve of land, cattle, and horses and posed for the frontier *estancias* and the Argentine government an almost insuperable problem of security. The only whites who wanted to see Indians were the missionaries in search of souls. When Colonel Lucio Mansilla's expedition to the Ranqueles encountered an empty Indian camp, the priests shouted for Indians: "'Indians, Indians, that's what we want to see!' cried the Franciscans, and I replied, 'Patience, Fathers, who knows, you may get a fright.'"[7] The missionaries were also mediators, and it was they who negotiated the return of those other victims of the *malones*, the white captives, especially the women, who were used by the Indians not only as concubines but also as items of trade.

The Andean foothills of western Argentina were the habitat of the Pehuenches. They were taller than the Indians of the plains, painted their faces, wore a cloak and a loin cloth, and lived on a diet of horse flesh and maize. They usually existed in peace with the whites, preferring trade to terror. This was not the case further east; the closer to Buenos Aires, the fiercer the Indians. On the pampas, from the frontiers of Mendoza and Córdoba to the Río Negro in the south, a group of nomadic tribes moved in search of pasture for their sheep and cattle. These were the Ranqueles and Auazes, a people prone to drunkenness and violence, implacable and unapproachable. But Colonel Mansilla approached them and was astonished at the sight:

> They all rode fine, stout horses. They dressed in the most fantastic clothes. Some wore hats, others bound their heads with a scarf, clean or dirty. Some wore hairbands of pampa weave, others ponchos, and yet others were as naked as Adam with barely a loin cloth to cover themselves. Many were drunk. Most had their cheeks and lower lips painted red. They all spoke at the same time, the air resounding with the word "Winca! Winca!" that is, "Christian! Christian!" and other effronteries, expressed of course in the best Spanish in the world.[8]

The Ranqueles had their *tolderías* at Leubucó, a settlement of some eight thousand to ten thousand Indians who could put thirteen hundred warriors in the field, and normally held six hundred to eight hundred Christians of both sexes in captivity. One of the three leading chieftains of the Ranqueles was Mariano Rosas, a former prisoner of the dictator Rosas, who had him baptized, gave him his name, and put him to work as a peon on one of his estates until the Indian took to flight and claimed his inheritance among his own tribes, without, however, losing his respect for Rosas or the dictator for him. The Ranqueles of Mariano Rosas had a powerful ally in the fearsome chieftain Juan Calfucurá, who in 1868 declared war on President Sarmiento over Argentine threats to Indian territory. His tribe, the Salinas, operating out of Salinas Grandes, consisted of some ten thousand Indians and two thousand active warriors. They were traders as well as fighters, importing into their camps many "white" consumer goods in exchange for Indian products such as hides, feathers, and handicrafts. In English eyes the Ranqueles were implacable enemies armed with spears and bolas and looking loathsome: "They were small wiry looking men, with very black hair falling over their shoulders, flat faces with high cheekbones, and no beard or whisker, and dark coppery complexion, with a repulsive expression of feature."[9]

The Huilliches, allied with the Puelches, established their dominion over the headwaters of the Río Negro and the Río Salado and to the north of the Río Colorado, spreading out into the pampas and highlands between Buenos Aires province and Mendoza; from their settlement of ten thousand Indians at Neuquén they could send two thousand warriors eastward. They were more peacefully disposed than the Ranqueles, possessing large herds and flocks of their own and manufacturing articles in demand among the whites—ponchos, skin cloaks, bridles— which they sold in Buenos Aires and at trading posts.

Penetrating further into the province of Buenos Aires were Indians known as the Pampas. They lived immediately south and west of Azul and were to be found also in the ranges of Tandil and Volcán, drawn there by rich pasture lands. Near Azul the cacique Catriel led a closely organized and well-mounted tribe capable of putting fifteen hundred warriors in the field. At Tapalquén a settlement of six thousand to ten thousand Indians could provide thirteen hundred fighting men.[10] The Pampas were regarded by the whites as the cruellest of all the Indians, irremediably savage, treacherous, and venal; perhaps they were all these things, though they were subject to growing provocation. Their way of life, it is true, was not an object of instant admiration. They exploited their women as slaves, kept them in filthy rags, and treated them as inferior beings who had to work so hard that they seemed to welcome polygamy as a way of sharing the burden. When not hunting or fighting, the men spent their time drinking, gambling, and sleeping. In each *toldo*, or tent made of hides stretched upon canes, lived five or six families, some twenty to thirty people, crowded together in squalor and disease. If fuel was scarce for cooking, they ate their meat raw. And they plundered the *estancias* not only for cattle but also for women. Whites had to parley very hard to secure the return of captive women, who, according to the laws of the Pampas, were the spoils of war and the sole property of the individual captors.[11]

Outside the tribal structure there were other Indians who lived independently and made war on their own account. Mansilla described such a group of some ten warriors who raided almost daily south of the Río Cuarto, sometimes alone, sometimes in alliance with larger parties. They were led by

the White Indian [*el indio Blanco*], who is neither cacique nor *capitanejo* [captain of an Indian band], but what the Indians call a gaucho Indian. That is to say, an Indian subject to no law or person, to no cacique, much less to any *capitanejo*; who strikes out on his own; who is sometimes an ally, sometimes an enemy; who sometimes takes to the mountains, and at other times shelters in a cacique's camp; who sometimes rides the ranges raiding, attacking, for months on end; and at other times trades in Chile, as has happened recently.[12]

The Indians on horseback were a highly mobile and elusive enemy whose weapons and tactics were perfectly attuned to their environment. The primary weapons of the Indians were the lance and the bola. The lances, which were usually fifteen to eighteen feet long, were lethal in the hands of a skillful horseman. The bola, small weighted balls on the ends of a leather cord, were used as either a club or a missile. In the relentless warfare against the whites—swift horseback raids on settlements and *estancias*—native weapons compared well with those of the enemy, and their horses were incomparable. Indians in Argentina took reluctantly to firearms, but by the middle decades of the nineteenth century they had acquired rifles, and soon they were familiar with the Remington.[13]

The expansion of the *estancia* economy in the course of the nineteenth century was a catastrophe for the pampa Indians. Whites began to push further south of the Salado; from the 1820s Tandil became first an advanced frontier fort and then a zone of agricultural settlement. Collision was inevitable. The whites regarded the Indians as invaders of Argentine territory, aliens who originated in Chilean Araucania. The Indians regarded this as past history and resented the spread of settlements on lands which they regarded as their ancestral property and now saw occupied by newcomers without any consultation. The more peaceable tribes retired to the mountains in the south, but the Ranqueles, the Pampas, and other migratory hordes retaliated by intensifying their raids against the intruders and their property.

In his Desert Campaign of 1833–34, Rosas extended the area of effective occupation by means of a double strategy: he struck hard at enemy tribes and made alliances with friendly Indians.[14] His idea was to coopt Indian groups into loyalty and to marginalize the nonaligned Indians. In a subsequent peace treaty the Indians bound themselves to keep to their own territory and not to cross the frontier, nor to enter the province of Buenos Aires without permission. In return, friendly Indians received rewards and supplies, the provision of which became a thriving rural business, from which *pulperías*, traders, and contractors made handsome profits.

While pacification served the nation well in the next twenty years, it also enabled the Indians to strengthen their position and in the long run to regroup under powerful leaders. The whole transaction, known as "Peaceful Commerce with the Indians," amounted to an Indian subsidy paid by the provincial government of Buenos Aires. The payments were made principally to allied Pampas and Araucanian tribes, while the recipients made their own deals with nonallied Indians. They also made their own preparations for the future, improving their leadership and strengthening their organization.[15]

The Desert Campaign was followed by rapid expansion of the southern frontier, and by 1850 *estancias* encroached once more on Indian hunting grounds. After the fall of Rosas, the annual subsidies petered out, and Mitre officially ended them in 1859 with the intention of replacing money payments by military action. In any event, the government continued to make deals with particular caciques. As for military strategy, it was flawed; it simply reacted defensively to Indian raids, never mounted a serious offensive, and in effect encouraged the settlers to collaborate with the Indians. Throughout the 1850s occasional punitive expeditions provoked rather than punished the tribes, and if *estancias* advanced, the effective frontier did not. In November 1855, following a series of lesser alarms, Tandil was the target of a great *malón*: three thousand Indians led by Yanquetruz surrounded the settlement and put many of the inhabitants to flight before attacking their property.[16]

Mitre was an honest imperialist: he defended British rule in India against its critics and denounced their attacks as "barbarous and antisocial, the equivalent in our war with the Pampas of someone wanting the victory of Calfucurá over the defenders of civilization and Christianity."[17] He warned Calfucurá in 1863 that he was determined to put an end to "these scandalous robberies" and to pursue the Indian plunderers "to the end of the earth." But there were always other priorities for the politicians in Buenos Aires, not least the war with Paraguay, Mitre's war, one of the least popular and most expensive wars in Argentine history, an opportunity for Indian raiders and a deterrent to immigrants.[18] Meanwhile, "foreign" Indians, such as the Araucanians, remained hostile, and the region between Tandil and Bahía Blanca continued to be dangerous for settlers and repellent for those country people who were conscripted for military service on the frontier.

The provinces most exposed to Indian attacks were those of Santa Fe and Córdoba. Among numerous *malones*, in November 1866 some five hundred Ranqueles led by a nephew of Mariano Rosas raided on the southern frontier of Córdoba, seized ten thousand head of cattle, killed twenty-five whites, and took seventy captives.[19] The national government was unable to provide adequate defense; in fact, some of the largest Indian raids were led by Calfucurá, who was one of the chieftains in receipt of a government subsidy but who after the fall of Rosas regarded himself as free from previous peace treaties and was clever enough to exploit the conflicts between unitarists and federalists.[20] The Indians were expert at probing defenses. When they sensed only weak opposition they were confident enough to bring in their families and encamp near large settlements before attacking, sweeping off cattle and sheep, and killing any owners who got in the way.[21] Colonel

Mansilla, who admired the Ranqueles, reported the "sad reality" of their constant threat to the property, homes, and lives of the Christians: "But what have Christians done, what have governments and civilization done for a disinherited race which is forced to rob, kill, and destroy, driven by the hard law of necessity?"[22]

Indian attacks increased throughout 1868, especially in the provinces of Santa Fe and Córdoba, and in response to the expedition of Colonel Julián Murga to Choele-Choel. The chieftain Calfucurá, a subsidy in one hand, a weapon in the other, led two thousand Indians against white settlements, taking two hundred captives and twenty thousand head of cattle.[23] The policy of Calfucurá was to establish a great Indian confederation. The institutions did not exist to realize this ambition, but in the years 1868–72 he led what amounted to a general Indian rebellion. In 1869, Indians attacked three colonies in Santa Fe province: California, Alexandra, and San Carlos, the showpieces of the foreign settlements, whose four thousand to five thousand colonists, mainly Swiss, Germans, and Italians, were supposedly destined to prosper. Sarmiento immediately ordered troops in, but the trouble lay with local government, which was indifferent towards protecting immigrants; central government might intervene in an emergency, but routine security was the responsibility of local agencies. According to *The Standard* of Buenos Aires, Indians from Sauce Grande attacked the San Carlos colony and murdered the entire Lefebre family. A posse of colonists found that the assassins were in the custody of one Denis, already known for harboring murderers. Denis was summarily shot. His son then led a reprisal raid on San Carlos colony, and there "this miserable band of cut-throats, half gaucho, and half Indian," was shot down by the colonists.[24] Self help was normally the only help.

In 1868, Indians were also stirring in Buenos Aires province, which for some years had been considered secure; a further cycle of *malones* began in which Indian hordes were often accompanied by white renegades. Military and political problems absorbed the government's attention, while security for frontier estates in the south and west of the province, many of them British-owned, was relegated to the provincial authorities. And in a classic tactic the Indians disposed of their spoils in Chile, thus completing the cycle of their operations. In June 1870 a strong force of Salinas Indians—one thousand according to one report—led by Calfucurá raided Tres Arroyos, a hundred miles southwest of Tandil and well inside the official frontier. The army detachment under Colonel Campos was unable to intervene, as one-half the troops were guarding the other half, who were confined to barracks for mutiny. The military garrison suffered sixteen killed and fifteen kidnaped, and the local *estancieros* took great losses, forty thousand cattle, according to most estimates.[25] In October 1870 a Calfucurá-sponsored raid on Bahía Blanca saw two thousand Indians invade the settlement; two Britons were killed and much livestock stolen. While the British minister reacted angrily, he also recognized, echoing Mansilla, that the Indians could not assume all the blame, since for them these raids were a legitimate form of warfare. Moreover, officers on the frontier had broken treaties by kidnaping Indian chiefs, raiding their camps, and stealing their livestock. He alleged, too, that the military had used "tame" Indians to direct the raids of the hostile tribes towards the farms of foreign settlers—in effect, making the immigrants pay for the arbitrary actions of the military authorities. Trade by officers with the Indians was responsible for many incidents. It was precisely the seizure of a local chief in receipt of an Argentine subsidy and a military raid on his camp which led to the Bahía Blanca invasion.[26]

Apart from mutiny and indiscipline among the security forces, the defenseless state of the frontier could be attributed basically to faulty priorities: the drain on manpower and money, including most of the British loans of 1866, for the Paraguayan war, then for the civil wars in Entre Ríos and Corrientes; the diversion of attention to the electoral struggle in 1867–68; and rival jurisdiction between national and provincial governments, the former repudiating the work of frontier defense, the latter neglecting it. Sarmiento raised the stakes: he promised in 1868 to give the Indian problem a higher priority and to recover land lost to the invaders.

Sarmiento sincerely wished to civilize the Indians as well as to tame them, to impose schools, police, and private property on these obdurate people.[27] But his views, influenced by policy of the United States, were largely unsympathetic to the Indians. He was on record as saying that the Spaniards "simply did what all civilized peoples have done with savages, and what colonization has always done, deliberately or not: absorb, destroy, exterminate. . . . It may be unjust to exterminate savages, to crush nascent civilizations, to conquer peoples who are in possession of a privileged land; but thanks to this injustice, America, instead of remaining lost to the savages, who are incapable of progress, is today occupied by the Caucasian race, the most perfect, intelligent, noble, and progressive race in the world."[28]

These views were representative of Argentine opinion; Argentines from top to bottom regarded Indians as beyond the nation, detestable neighbors, dangerous enemies, and people who stood in the way of economic development. Landowners and speculators wanted that territory in the south, and they demanded action from the government to conquer it.

A different view was expressed by Lucio V. Mansilla, nephew of Rosas, an awkward member of his class, an intellectual who once traveled overland from India to London, a convert from federalism. After service in Paraguay, he expected to be rewarded with the ministry of war; instead, Sarmiento sent him to Río Cuarto as military commander. In February 1870, Mansilla and a representative of the Indian chief Mariano Rosas agreed on a peace treaty, which Mansilla sent to Sarmiento for final approval. When the president suggested changes in the treaty, Mansilla reacted angrily, and the Indians lost faith. To show his commitment, Mansilla undertook an expedition into Indian territory and recorded his experiences in a journal which vividly re-created the world of the Ranqueles and quietly savaged Sarmiento's Indian policies and the concept of civilization that underlay them. He presented the Indian as a true Argentine, just as he saw the gaucho as a national prototype.

But Mansilla could not entirely escape his class or see the Indians from within; even he advocated a policy of civilizing and assimilating the Indians and putting them to work for the good of society, along lines not far different from those of Sarmiento.[29] During a long parley with Mariano Rosas he stated the government's position in answer to the question, "With so much empty land in the far south, why are you taking away this territory which rightly belongs to us?" Mansilla patiently explained that beyond the agreed frontier there had to be a stretch of no-man's land in the interests of security; that the fact of having lived in a place did not give right of property, and territory only belonged to those who made it productive; that the government would buy the land, not seize possession, and would leave some part for the Indians; and as for the railways, the Indians should trust the government to protect Indian interests. The cacique did not believe this and expected the Christians "to finish with us." Mansilla could only reply, "Some believe that; others think as I do, that you deserve our protection."[30]

The Indians preserved a profound distrust of the whites which nothing could move:

> Talking one day with Mariano Rosas, I said, "Brother, the Christians have done what they can for the Indians up to now, and they will do their best in the future."
> His reply was frankly ironic: "Brother, when the Christians have been unable to kill us they have not done so; and if tomorrow they could kill us all they would kill us. They have taught us to wear fine ponchos, to take maté,

to smoke, eat sugar, and drink wine. But they have not taught us either to work or to know their God. So, Brother, what exactly do we owe them?"[31]

Meanwhile, the Indian wars which formed the backdrop to Mansilla's journal continued with cruelty and savagery on both sides. Indians tortured their captives, and whites attacked Indian women and children. In 1868 the national congress approved raising four new cavalry regiments, each 450 strong, for service on the frontiers and in 1870 further approved the allocation of two million pesos to extend the frontier to the Río Negro.[32] In 1871 the Rural Society of Buenos Aires advised the provincial government that the Indians should be expelled to south of the Río Negro and offered its cooperation and resources in support. In the years 1869–71 army units of between 150 and 800 men made some ten expeditions into Indian territory in the region of the Río Colorado and Río Negro, most of them punitive raids. But the army was not winning the war; in 1871 Indian raids on the southern and northern frontiers cost many lives and much property, and in the second half of the year Indian attacks against forts and towns gave the impression of a great rebellion.[33]

This was confirmed in early 1872 when Calfucurá assembled an alliance of Salinas, Ranqueles, Araucanians, and other tribes normally regarded as "friendly" and with six thousand warriors quietly advanced on the western frontier of Buenos Aires. In March they launched a massive onslaught in the region of San Carlos, taking two hundred thousand head of cattle and five hundred hostages and leaving behind three hundred dead settlers amidst their burnt-out houses. British immigrants were among the victims. Indian raiders usually retreated as quickly as they attacked. This time they stayed and fought, unnerving *hacendados* and settlers by their numbers and confidence.

But for once the raiders miscalculated and the army resisted. General Rivas, having assembled a force of eighteen hundred, faced the Indians on 8 March in straight battle, and his superiority in firepower and bayonet force won the day. The federal government observed the victory with relief. Sarmiento was convinced that Calfucurá was not so stupid as to attack Rivas head-on had he not been misled by reports in the Argentine press on the weakness of frontier defenses, and the president continued to prefer negotiation to warfare in dealing with the Indian.[34]

The victory did not halt the *malones* or bring the Indian war to an end. Invasions of the northern and western frontiers continued without interruption, and Bahía Blanca was still threatened in 1872, while rebel tribes marauded throughout the southern and western pampas in the following years. The agrarian economy was affected, and settlers at 25 de Mayo asked the provincial government for a moratorium on land payments.[35] The second half of the year brought no reprieve. In an Indian raid near Rosario seventy settlers (non-British) were killed, thirty-two kidnaped, and four thousand to six thousand livestock driven off while the government looked on. Again, Indians were responsible when a Briton was robbed and murdered and an Italian boy wounded near the Alexandra colony. In an Indian raid on Colonia Tortugas on the Central Argentine Railway, sixty miles from Rosario, one Italian was killed, a number of captives taken, three thousand mares stolen, and several houses sacked. Once more the authorities could be accused of culpable inertia.[36]

Government policy, alternating between war and peace, was an encouragement, not a deterrent, to Indian advance. Sarmiento assured Congress in 1874 that "the savages are no longer a serious threat or a danger to rural prosperity. The Indians are virtually subjugated, and the time is near when their reduced and isolated tribes will be brought into reservations."[37] The analysis of Alvaro Barros was more realistic: "During war they seize the property of our rural inhabitants and barbarously destroy the wealth of the country. Then, having satiated themselves with atrocities and destruction, they make peace and are guaranteed a large subsidy, without even halting their raids and violence against our people."

The policy continued after 1872 with predictable results, culminating in the great rising of the Indians of Catriel at Azul in 1875 and the loss of two hundred thousand head of cattle in Buenos Aires province alone. It was now that Barros advocated an army of five thousand divided into three divisions, one advancing from Bahía Blanca, another from Río Quinto, and another from San Rafael, to operate in conjunction with the railways. The object would be to expel the Indians and destroy their resources and food supplies once and for all: "To systematically search out the Indians in their camps, not to exterminate them physically by force of arms but to deprive them of any safe refuge and thus to force them to surrender unconditionally, once they and their families have lost all means of subsistence."[38] And it was now that the national government decided on a major effort and a final solution, defeat and expulsion of the Indians. This was accomplished during the administration of Adolfo Alsina, minister of war, in 1874–77; in the first campaign of General Julio A. Roca in 1878–79; and in Roca's final campaign in 1880–85.

Indians had some friends among whites in addition to Mansilla. Military service on the southern frontier was not popular, and accommodation with the Indians was often seen as a better option than obedience to Buenos Aires. Indeed, Indian raiders were often joined by vagabond gauchos, deserters from the army, delinquents fleeing from the justices of the peace, and refugees from social or political conflicts, and from these the Indians learned the ways of the whites, the methods of the militia, and the use of firearms to add to their own repertoire of weapons. The alliance of Indian and gaucho was a frightening prospect, and it became notorious among settlers that if the Indian did not kill you the gaucho would.

GAUCHOS BY ANY OTHER NAME

The gaucho, a descendant of Indians, whites, and blacks, was traditionally a free man on horseback, as distinct from the peon, who in the pampas was a laborer or ranch hand.[39] The term was used by contemporaries and by later historians in a loose sense to mean rural people in general. Yet many country dwellers were neither gauchos nor peons; they were independent families living on small ranches or farms, or earning a living in a *pulpería*, a wagon train, or a village.[40] Greater precision would distinguish between the sedentary rural dwellers working on the land for themselves or for their patrón and the pure gaucho, who was nomadic and independent and tied to no estate. Thus, Mansilla distinguished between the *paisano gaucho* and the *gaucho neto*: "They are two different types. The gaucho country dweller has a home, a fixed abode, habits of work, respect for authority, which he always supports, even against his better judgement. The pure gaucho is the wandering creole who is here today and gone tomorrow; gambler, brawler, enemy of all discipline. He flees from military service when his turn comes, takes refuge among the Indians after a stabbing, or joins a *montonera* if one shows up."[41]

The *paisano* looked to civilization for his models; the gaucho preferred tradition and detested foreigners. "The *paisano* is always a federalist, the gaucho is nothing. The *paisano* still believes in something, the gaucho in nothing." Mansilla's *gaucho neto* comes suspiciously close to the type known to contemporaries as the *gaucho malo*, who lived by violence, would draw a knife upon eye contact, and was seen by the state as a criminal. Sarmiento established his own typology of the gaucho, the tracker, the pathfinder, the singer, the outlaw. Good or bad, the classical gaucho asserted his freedom from all formal institutions; he was aloof from government and its agents, indifferent to religion and the Church. Social marginality for the gaucho was an ideal rather than a condition. As Sarmiento observed, "He is happy in the midst of his poverty and privations," for what he most valued was independence and idleness.[42] Mansilla spoke of "the complete absence of a sense of duty in the gaucho, a horror of all discipline."[43] He did not seek land, for that would involve responsibility; he lived by hunting, gambling, and fighting.

If the gaucho hated gringos, they returned the sentiment. English settlers came to distrust the gaucho and to see in him the embodiment of all that was wrong in rural Argentina, where violence was a way of life and principles counted for nothing. From his *estancia* at Fraile Muerto, Richard Seymour poured scorn on the concept of the "noble gaucho." Superficially gauchos were more civil than English laborers, but when it came to essentials their moral character was inferior: "It seemed to me as if no kindness or confidence could excite any return of grateful feeling, and the utter want of morality is enough to call down a curse on any nation."[44] Seymour's own *capataz* (foreman), presumably one of Mansilla's *paisanos gauchos*, cheated him on every possible occasion and did no work he could avoid.

The image of the gaucho, part heroic, part tragic, has passed into folklore, and nostalgia has obscured reality.[45] With his face blackened by exposure and his long, matted hair reaching to his shoulders and mingling with his beard, he was an alarming rather than an alluring sight. He dressed in long, wide cotton drawers, a garment called the *chiripá* girdled around the waist, and the inevitable poncho, often made in England. A leather belt holding a long gaucho knife, a colored handkerchief over the head, and a felt hat completed the outfit, while a cured skin of colt's hind legs served for boots. Hunger, thirst, and exposure were never far from the gaucho. He rarely knew other food than beef, *asado*, and like the rural poor in general he ate no bread, vegetables, or milk, while for luxuries there was always maté and tobacco. His bed was his *recado* (saddle) stretched on the ground; his poncho and saddle cloths were his blankets. The gaucho was expert with the *lazo* and bolas and needed no other aids for catching the animals of the pampas. The lasso, known independently to the Araucanians as well as to the Spaniards, was about twenty yards long, made of a single piece of rawhide with an iron ring at one end to make a running noose.[46] Another way of catching animals—and men—was with the bolas, three stone balls on the end of thongs, flung round the rear legs of animals by a horseman at a distance of eighty or ninety yards. These, with the famous *facón* (long knife), were the weapons of the gaucho as well as his tools, and they were used in vicious fights, often near *pulperías*, where drinking, gambling, and feuds over women quickly flared into violence.

The nomadism of the gaucho was the enemy of settled work or occupation. Property, industry, land—these were alien concepts. So, too, was the gaucho family. Whereas the Argentine elite drew strength from family and kinship, the popular classes were much weaker institutionally. This was partly a cultural division between town and country, civilization and barbarism, landowner and laborer, but whatever its nature the disparity of family stability was a fundamental feature of Argentine society. Among gauchos and vagrants unions were temporary and the families only loosely joined together. Marriage was the exception, and it was the lone mother who formed the nucleus of the rural family and remained the only firm bedrock.[47] Even if the father was not wed to gaucho nomadism, he usually did not have the means to stay and sustain a family; he had to sell his labor where he could, or else he was recruited into armies or *montoneras*, to avoid which he became an outlaw. Lack of domestic instincts meant that the gauchos did not propagate themselves as family groups or preserve their identity through generations. Conditions were against them as they roamed the plains, homeless and hunted, prime targets for recruiting officers and outlaw hunters. The gauchos and the country folk in general were victims of government policy and economic conditions. As the English *estanciero* Wilfred Latham observed:

> Victims of the trimestrial levies for irregular warfare, they have no incentives to steady work and cannot, in fact, *root* themselves. At all times and by all parties they are hunted out, to fight or run away, disband or be disbanded, but to be hunted again; with none to share a home, with no home to be shared, driven to roam, they have no belongings and they do not propagate. What would it avail them to form homes or create surroundings as long as a press-gang incessantly dogs them, or they crouch and hide like hunted deer among dense scrub or thistle beds?[48]

There was, it is true, another life for *estancia* peons, one of economic incentives, labor mobility, and honest opportunity. But Latham's remarks were not mere impressions. The ruling class in the countryside had traditionally imposed a system of coercion upon people whom they regarded as *mozos vagos y mal entretenidos*, idlers and vagabonds without employer or occupation, a potential work force but one in need of constraints: imprisonment, conscription to the Indian frontier, corporal punishment, and other penalties. No doubt there was chronic lawlessness in the countryside and an identifiable criminal element. Robbery of *estancias*, murder, gambling in *pulperías*, illicit sale of hides and other products, traveling without a permit—these were not invented by the authorities but part of daily life in the pampas. Beyond this, however, legislation sought to identify *vagos y mal entretenidos* as a criminal class by definition and vagrancy itself as a crime. What is a *vago*? asked Sarmiento. "He is a native Argentine, born on the land from which he is now banished by those who have accumulated property through money or through service to the tyrant Rosas."[49] To be poor, unemployed, idle, and propertyless was a presumption in favor of being a *vago*, and in practice this was equated with being a gaucho. The first object of antivagrancy legislation, therefore, was to impose law and order in the countryside; the second, to provide a labor pool for *hacendados*; the third, to produce conscripts for the army. The only escape lay on the Indian frontier, the ultimate margin of Argentine society. Some gauchos took this route, drawn by a strange affinity: "Gauchos living near the frontier," remarked a French observer, "live a life very similar to that of the Indians, so if they are taken prisoner they soon adjust to their new existence." In Leubucó, Colonel Mansilla met Carmago, a gaucho fugitive from authority, companion of *montoneros* and Indians, a man to keep at arm's length. Carmago admitted to taking part in Indian raids against *estancias* but denied killing any whites.[50]

Coercive controls and the horror of life among the Indians drove many gauchos into the hands of the *hacendado*, but as hired ranch hands, wage-earners, *peónes de estancia*. They lost their freedom and anonymity in exchange for a wage, roof, food, and clothing, a life that had its merits: "Each man to his work," as Martín Fierro recalled, and even the poorest was rich. But it was an arbitrary regime. On the *estancias* a seigneurial order of private punishment and veiled coercion prevailed, and the countryside was ruled by an informal alliance of *estancieros* and militia commanders, who were often the same people.

By the 1860s the traditional *estancia* was under pressure, and the army had become a rabble. In a curious inversion of logic the victim of these institutions was made their wrecker, and it was argued that rural labor needed to be disciplined and the army freed from the levies. So there was no place for the gaucho in the new, liberal, and modern Argentina, though in a sense he was denied a place he did not seek. It was now that the gaucho acquired a spokesman, one of Argentina's cultural heroes, José Hernández, journalist, poet, and politician.

Sympathy for the gaucho came to Hernández in his youth on an *estancia* in the south of Buenos Aires province, where he learned the idiom and nature of the gaucho and acquired a lasting concern for his predicament. In Argentina identification with the rural poor usually meant support for federalism and provincial autonomy against the centrist liberalism of Buenos Aires, a policy which Hernández embraced with conviction, though not always with sound judgment. In his newspaper writings Hernández urged that to end the tyranny of the justices of the peace and democratize the countryside a series of basic reforms was necessary. He advocated popular elections for local authorities and equitable land distribution for immigrants and the rural poor, and he argued that the gauchos would only be debrutalized through education and political inclusion; he also criticized forced conscription of ill-armed gauchos to fight against Indians.[51] Hernández served a further apprenticeship in gaucho lore during his service in the forces of Ricardo López Jordán, the rebel caudillo of Entre Ríos, where he observed the gaucho soldier and the rural poor at close quarters. After a period of exile he was ready to write his masterpiece, *El gaucho Martín Fierro*, which he began to publish in 1872. His purpose was twofold: to record the grim reality of gaucho life and character and to present the gaucho as a victim of liberal values and government policy. Some historians have questioned Hernández's commitment to rural reform and have argued that he was complacent towards the *estancia* system.[52] Certainly his radicalism seems to have been tamed by time, and Part II of *Martín Fierro*, written seven years later, resembles a lecture rather than a protest and argues that with "houses, a school, a church and their rights" gauchos can become worthy members of the new Argentina. However, there were too many contradictions in the life of the gaucho to expect Hernández to resolve them all.

Yet for all the coercion, the sanctions, and the rough justice in rural Argentina, life on the southern frontier continued to be precarious. A system which guaranteed the power of *estancieros* within the older areas of settlement did little for the protection of immigrants on the margin of civilization. As Indians and gauchos continued to evade the security net, settlers asked with increasing insistence, "Where is the security for us?"

Peacetime Heroes

The presence of the regular army on frontier duty was not a serious deterrent. Indians could see the flaws and probe the gaps. The Argentine army lacked the elementary requirements of an army: a fair recruiting policy, a regular system of promotion, a training program for troops and officers, and adequate equipment. Terror took the place of discipline.[53] Army service was not popular, and throughout the history of the republic draft quotas had been denounced as the scourge of the countryside and a sure way to depopulate it. Reformers advocated an enlarged and reorganized regular army recruited from volunteers as the only fair and effective force for frontier defense. Given the right conditions, vagrants could thus be turned into useful soldiers. But conditions were never right: either resources were inadequate or they were diverted to other fronts. Native Argentines did not volunteer, and foreign recruits, being poor horsemen, were useful only in the infantry. In 1863 over one thousand miles of the southern frontier were guarded by little more than five thousand troops, 65 percent cavalry, 33 percent infantry, and the rest artillery, scattered in small detachments over immense spaces.[54] From 1865 the demands of the Paraguayan war took precedence over internal security, and the national government was hard put to stem the waves of Indian raiders and gaucho rebels in the provinces of Buenos Aires, Santa Fe, Córdoba, and Mendoza. The Paraguayan war was not a popular war, either among the elite or among the people; for southern ranchers it was a disaster, as peons became scarce either for work or for defense and Indians reappeared over the horizon.

In the absence of the regular army, rural security and frontier defense were assigned to the National Guard, a force of reservists which in 1852 displaced the old *rosista* militia but which, like the militia, was an ally and often the instrument of the local elites of *estancieros* and officials. As volunteers were scarce, in practice this became a conscript force and soon degenerated into a caricature of an army. The basic six months' service allowed insufficient time to train and post these cavalry troops where they were most needed. Conditions of recruitment encouraged evasion and desertion. Frustrated in their first aim of catching criminals and vagrants before they fled, the military by default often had to settle for industrious peons and reluctant gauchos, whom they herded into line like cattle, enforcing summary execution on any deserters. The system was condemned as oppressive and unjust by many reformers, not least by José Hernández:

> As a result of the measures adopted to govern the countryside compulsory service fell only on the laboring class, who had a family and home to keep, while the vagrant class escaped conscription, mocking the decrees which our governments apply to the countryside in their ignorance of the ills afflicting it and of the consequences they ought to prevent. The National Guard is an arbitrary and immobilizing institution, which can only be explained by the turbulent situation which brought it into being.
>
> If this applies to the institution in general, how much more so to the monstrous unfairness resulting from frontier service, demanded solely from the inhabitants of the countryside?[55]

The conscripts themselves were described by an English observer:

> The contingents thus formed were driven like cattle by mounted soldiers armed with lances, and woe to the wretch who from whatever cause lagged behind. They were often coupled in pairs and at night were folded like cattle "corrals," often ankle deep in mud and filth. . . . It is impossible to give an

adequate idea of the sufferings of these unfortunate beings—naked feet swollen by long marches on hard and stony roads, clothes scarcely adequate to cover their nakedness, parched with thirst, exposed to scorching sun during the day and to intense cold at night. They presented a scene of misery and wretchedness seldom seen in South America.[56]

Length of service, nominally six months, lasted as long as the military could hold them. As Martín Fierro complained:

> And before we went off, the Judge he up
> And made us a long harangue;
> He said they'd treat us like gallant men
> And he promised us over and over again,
> That we'd only serve six months and then,
> He'd send the relieving gang.[57]

But once on the Indian frontier they were forgotten by the law and left to the mercy of officers and sergeants. As in the regular army, corporal punishment was severe; the recruits were virtual prisoners, kept under guard until the actual moment of marching; and once in the field, the officers, army canteens, and *pulperías* robbed them of their small allowances. Mutiny was predictable, and many military personnel spent their time guarding mutineers rather than fighting Indians. Colonel Alvaro Barros reported in 1865 on the condition of his garrison on the southern frontier of Buenos Aires: "The garrison consisted of 400 men of the National Guard, whose condition was one of utter destitution, without sufficient arms, short of horses and trappings, in fact lacking everything needed for military operations and even for their own protection in that climate."[58] A force of this kind was unlikely to reach a high level of conduct or morale. The Danish settler Juan Fugl reported that following the Indian siege of Tandil in November 1855, "the relieving soldiers were not much better than the savages, for they robbed every abandoned house they came to, and helped themselves to everything they wanted." It was notorious that the National Guard usually arrived after the Indians had done their worst. A justice of the peace admitted to Fugl that he was "a brave soldier—in peacetime."[59]

Local interests at all levels, employers, the self-employed, and the unemployed, opposed military service of this kind. But the ultimate losers were gauchos and peons. Their immediate tormentors were provincial governors and local officials, while the victims were ignored by the national government. The key agent of control in the countryside was the justice of the peace, who was judge of first instance for most cases in his *partido*. The office had been established in 1821 to fill the gap left by the suppression of the colonial cabildo, but its original judicial and administrative functions in a given district were soon extended to include those of commander of the frontier guard, police chief, and tax collector. The justice administered the labor laws of the countryside; he pursued criminals, deserters, vagrants; he reported on properties and their owners, and also on their political affiliations; and he presided over elections. In short, the justice was the local representative of government authority, the agent of a distant state; for most of his constituents he *was* the state. Yet in general the local administration of justice was defective, and official lawlessness enjoyed an impunity denied to the gaucho.[60] Most justices of the peace were uneducated and ill qualified for office, part of a local patronage network, usually *estancieros* or caudillos, some of them totally illiterate. But these were not disqualifications, for they were political appointees selected by the provincial government for their loyalty, not their learning. The justices in turn appointed the *alcaldes de campaña* and the police for the smaller districts (*cuarteles*) into which the *partidos* were divided. Reformers demanded that justices be appointed in popular elections instead of by dictate of the provincial government, and this became one of the political issues of the time. But for many years local government remained the Achilles' heel of the new state.

A frontier society of sullen gauchos and hostile Indians was not a hospitable place for immigrant settlers. In default of good government and official protection, foreigners occasionally looked to their own defenses. In 1871, following an Indian raid at Fraile Muerto, some ten Argentine soldiers set off in pursuit; their "bad equipment and mounts," according to a British settler, "would have rendered them an easy prey to any body half their number." An English volunteer force put thirty well-armed and -mounted men into the field and recovered most of the rustled livestock.[61] But the British refused to serve in Argentine units, correctly claiming exemption. When the army attempted forcibly to recruit British subjects into a Foreign Legion, the recruits escaped on Christmas Eve while the officers were drunk. The British minister in Buenos Aires protested to the Argentine foreign minister, Marcelino Ugarte, who had to accept the complaint. Forced sale of British-owned horses to the army also met with strong opposition.[62]

IMMIGRANTS AND SETTLERS

Towards the end of the 1860s the combined effects of war in Paraguay, Indian raids, and provincial revolts generated a climate of violence in Argentina and posed urgent problems of law enforcement. Simultaneously, the national government was attempting to attract increasing numbers of immigrants, supported among others by British companies which made a business of colonization projects and by British residents who saw property values rise and the internal market expand as immigrant numbers increased. New settlers were particularly attracted by the cheapness of frontier land and were not at first deterred by the danger. They usually had little choice, for the best and most protected land was beyond their means. A new settler, such as Richard Seymour in 1865, was driven further and further out until finally he was "forced to go to the very edge of civilization" in search of his fortune, in this case to Fraile Muerto, west of Rosario.[63] Concerned that emigrants should not be led astray by false notions of their prospects, the British government issued a series of warnings in 1870–72 concerning the insecurity for life and property in Argentina.

Such concern was not simply foreign hyperbole. Before the British complained, Argentines with frontier experience were already criticizing official complacency. In the years from 1870, Alvaro Barros, soldier, politician, and frontier specialist, pointed to the incompatibility between immigrants and Indians: "To attract and increase immigration is the surest way to take possession of those deserts and make them productive. But first the immigrant needs to find there security for his life and property, a security which does not exist while the Indians are able to invade and devastate our countryside at will."[64]

Not all Argentine officials were as honest as Barros, and their testimony was often tainted. So the British looked elsewhere. The evidence available in London was derived from reports by the British envoys in Argentina, who closely monitored disorder in the countryside and attacks on British settlers; from the press in Buenos Aires; and from the writings of British settlers themselves. The British learned to be skeptical of statements made by Argentine ministers. When Seymour expressed misgivings over the presence of Indians at Fraile Muerto,

> these were represented to us by the people in authority, both at Rosario and Córdoba, as a trifling risk. We were about three hundred miles from the Indian settlements, and were told that they had the greatest dread of fire-arms, and never would dream of attacking well-armed Englishmen in a properly-built house, but merely scoured the country at one time of year in quest of any stray horses and cattle they could pick up.

On this assurance Seymour bought land and soon learned that he had been sadly misinformed.[65]

South of Buenos Aires one of the most vulnerable frontiers was Bahía Blanca. In response to the efforts of the British minister H. B. MacDonell to persuade the government to improve security against Indian incursions, Foreign Minister Carlos Tejedor replied that the government was doing all it could to protect the frontier and that, in any event, there were only thirty-two English colonists at Bahía Blanca and they all lived in town. Irritated by what he claimed was Tejedor's ignorance of the frontier and indifference towards settlers, MacDonell pointed out that in fact there were over sixty English settlers in the area and only two lived in town. "The English settlers are young men of means and education, and some of them possess large capital which they have laid out in lands for agricultural and farming purposes, or for the raising of cattle."[66]

The settlers themselves provided direct evidence of the dangers surrounding them and repudiated Argentine government assertions that the British exaggerated the extent of foreign exposure. A report from Bahía Blanca in 1872 calculated that foreigners, excluding children, constituted 19 percent of the frontier population, not 10 percent as asserted by Tejedor. Friendly Indians totaled another 13 percent. Tejedor asserted that most Britons lived in the town, that the amount of capital invested by foreigners was nil, and that the Italians were all *changadores* (porters and carriers). This was totally incorrect. There was much more foreign capital than Argentine, Italians owned businesses and paid most taxes, and out of twenty shops and businesses only three were owned by Argentines. Most rural establishments and farms belonged to foreigners.[67] The conclusion was that immigrants had much to defend.

Settlers were subject to two dangers. On the frontier they were vulnerable to raids by hostile Indians in search of cattle and captives, raiders who did not distinguish between the national origins of their white enemies. In rural communities settlers were at risk from *gauchos malos*, who instinctively hated foreigners and would kill any who stood in the way of money or booty. The risks to settlers were not confined to the province of Buenos Aires. On the northern and western frontiers, in Santa Fe and Córdoba, settlers were harassed by Indian raiders, gaucho rebels, and bandits, and reports of killings, damage to property, and official inertia multiplied throughout the 1860s.[68]

In 1865 a British sheep farmer was murdered by three Argentines (probably gauchos, but not identified as such) near Rosario. British residents joined forces and offered a reward for their capture. Taken near Córdoba, the accused were sent under guard to Rosario, where the *jefe político* made the British residents meet the expenses of the journey. One of those charged was eventually found guilty of murder and theft and sentenced to ten years' hard labor; his accomplice received three years' army service. The British minister in Buenos Aires considered these sentences inadequate and took legal advice. He was informed that according to the law code of Santa Fe there was no sentence between ten years' hard labor and the death penalty, and that the provincial governor had no powers to change the sentences.[69] In its outcome this case confirmed all the British complaints about Argentine justice: it was indulgent towards crime and failed to hold the criminals. Three years later the man sentenced to ten years' hard labor was involved in the murder of the Lefebre family.[70] Further confirmation was provided in November 1867 when a Briton working on an *estancia* was stabbed in a quarrel. He later died, and his employer and the local authorities attempted to cover up the crime. Pressure from British residents eventually led to the arrest of the criminal, but by mid-1869 there was still no news of a trial, and like many such cases it disappeared amidst official obfuscation.[71]

Meanwhile, Richard Seymour had experienced his first visit from the Ranqueles in 1866 when a band of fifty Indians with a large troop of unmounted horses appeared from nowhere and surrounded the *estancia* buildings. While Seymour posted his men to face them with firearms, the Indians insisted on holding a parley and produced a renegade gaucho as interpreter. They offered peace and friendship and presented themselves as destitute, in need of clothing, liquor, and tobacco. Having received some satisfaction, they departed amicably with an "adios amigo." Then, to the dismay of Seymour and his company, about a mile from the house they stopped: "Half their party rode towards our horses, and in a few minutes they had driven them up to their own troop of unmounted horses, and the whole body were off like the wind."[72]

This was a worrying experience for a new settler, a problem without a solution. Towards the end of 1867 Indian invaders returned and made a clean sweep of the *estancia*, driving off most of the horses, about one hundred, and all the bullocks and milking cows, amounting to over two hundred head of cattle. "Besides the actual loss of money, the want of horses and bullocks made us lose what was even more valuable—our time, it being impossible at once to replace them."[73] But Seymour had not seen his last Indian. On New Year's Day 1868 his horses, cattle, and flocks were attacked by a horde of Indians who were accompanied by a large band of gauchos from the south of Buenos Aires; in this raid he lost about twelve hundred sheep and had no means of pursuit, for his horses were already stolen. "This driving off of sheep was quite a new feature in Indian attacks and proved how large a body there must have been for them to venture on such a step."[74]

Fraile Muerto was virtually an Indian hunting ground. In 1866 raiders pounced on a settlement near the Seymour *estancia*, leaving three English settlers dead and their property in ruins. As Seymour and his party left the melancholy scene, they observed a local troop, armed with old swords and lances and led by the commandante of Fraile Muerto, approaching with exaggerated caution, supposedly in search of the Indians, "but they had taken very good care not to come out until the enemy had all made off" and kept their best horses at the ready to make good their escape should the Indians return. The British minister again urged the Argentine government to give more protection to settlers living inside the recognized frontiers. A memorial from thirty-seven British settlers describing the attack confirmed that three Britons had been killed, yet their lands were thirty leagues from the frontier; the soldiers who were protecting them had been withdrawn because of the war, and Indians had made three incursions in the last six months.

Fraile Muerto was becoming a zone of British settlement, and 520,000 acres were in British hands; but Indian raids were diminishing property values and preventing settlers from occupying their lands. The killing of the three British settlers left a powerful impression and checked for a time the influx of British immigrants. The British minister later reported that the government had finally sent troops under General Paunero to the area, and that if these were withdrawn he would make further protest. Meanwhile he pointed out that (1) the government was in great difficulties because of the Paraguayan war and internal insurrection, and (2) the settlers must have known the risks but were tempted by the cheapness of frontier land; they were thus partly responsible for their own plight.[75] These arguments, however, could not explain the violence endemic in gaucho society or the dangers lurking for British travelers in many parts of rural Argentina. In 1867 two English brothers traveling west from Entre Ríos with a troop of mules for sale were stopped in the vicinity of San Juan by a band of *montoneros* and invited to join them as they sat quietly around a fire drinking maté. The *montoneros* suddenly turned on their guests, and although the Englishmen put up a fight, they were brutally killed.[76]

According to *The Standard* of Buenos Aires, an English newspaper, a Briton taking care of stock for a friend in the region of Azul was murdered by thieves, a crime which the authorities attributed to Indians but which had the hallmark of gaucho violence.[77] In the same year a thirteen-year-old boy named Keegan, sent from a farm in Buenos Aires province on an errand to a nearby town, was murdered, to the horror of British consular officials, who insisted on a thorough investigation.[78] In Santa Fe, following a period of Indian aggression and government apathy, two colonists of an agricultural colony, Roberts and Eivers (one British, the other a U.S. citizen), were murdered not by Indians or gauchos but by provincial troops, an event which was reported to London with particular indignation. The outrage caused the emigration commissioners in London to issue a warning to prospective emigrants to Argentina on 22 February 1870: "Several British emigrants and other foreigners have recently been murdered. . . . No effectual steps have been taken by local government. . . . Under these circumstances there appears to be no sufficient security for life in that country."[79] The Argentine government angrily rejected the imputation and protested that its apparent want of energy in pursuing malefactors was the result of constitutional limitations on the national government's power to interfere in provincial affairs, but meanwhile it promised action. In the same year two Britons, Bold and Tait, were murdered on an *estancia* in Santa Fe.[80]

The tendency of atrocity cases to disappear into the Argentine legal system, or indeed never to reach trial, was a sore point with Foreign Office officials, who often faced demands at home for information or action on British subjects. In 1870 a query from the Foreign Office arrived at the desk of Consul Frank Parish. Parish was the son of Sir Woodbine Parish, the first British consul general in Buenos Aires, and like his father was experienced in the ways of the Argentine bureaucracy. London wanted information on the murder of a British shepherd named Scott and his native family in Buenos Aires province in March 1867. Parish reported that there was now little likelihood of the murderers being caught; the whole incident had been forgotten by late 1867, submerged by news of other crimes, "the natural consequence of the impunity with which these are committed." According to this view, local officials were too interested in politics to pay much attention to social conditions. Murderers were rarely caught and few were executed; indeed, there was a "morbid desire" to abolish the death penalty in Argentina, while many of those sent to jail either escaped or were deported to Patagonia, which was virtually the same thing.[81] An article in *The Standard* argued that the end of the war in Paraguay did not bring better prospects for peace, for the country was overwhelmed by widespread lawlessness: "In fact, the truth be told, all the vagabond gauchos of the country consider the gringos in the country good and lawful prize. A crusade of extermination has set in and foreigners must beware."[82]

Argentine outrage at the warning issued by the emigration commissioners in London caused MacDonell to send Minister Mariano Varela a list of the Britons murdered and wounded in Argentina between 1865 and 13 May 1870. The list, which MacDonell claimed was incomplete, consisted of fifty-six murders and sixteen woundings, according to Foreign Office calculations. Although the amount of detail in each case varied, it is possible to draw a pattern of sorts from the data given, though that pattern does not support the British case in every respect. (1) Murders of British subjects actually reached their high point in 1867 with seventeen killings; thereafter they decreased to six in 1868, nine in 1869, and four in the period to May 1870. (2) The city of Buenos Aires was becoming more secure: five Britons were killed there in 1865, none in 1868, one in 1869, and none to May 1870. (3) Most of the murders were committed in the frontier regions and rural towns. (4) Argentine nationals, probably gauchos, murdered far more Britons than did the Indians. (5) For all the frequency of insurrections in these years, only two victims were listed as having perished at rebel hands. (5) British immigrants could face death at the hands not only of Indians and gauchos but also of the police and *serenos* (night watchmen), who claimed three victims between 1865 and 1870. (6) Immigrants themselves were responsible for two of the murders listed.[83]

British complaints continued. *The Standard* of Buenos Aires alleged that assassins, although arrested and sent for trial, actually threatened their accusers with reprisals "when they are freed." Diplomats deplored the absence of capital punishment, criticized the moral condition of the Argentine people, and despaired of the judicial process in cases of murder.[84] Two more Britons were murdered in mid-1870, one by a well-connected psychopath with a record of three previous killings who announced, "I just feel like killing this gringo," before stabbing his victim, who had been quietly reading, and the other by a man in gaucho garb in the region of Mar Chiquita.[85]

A massive Indian raid on Bahía Blanca in late 1870 drew an angry reaction from the foreign community. The invaders, some two thousand strong, stole five thousand cattle and ten thousand sheep and killed several settlers, including two Britons, before riding off in triumph. MacDonell protested vehemently to the foreign minister, expressing his outrage at the "murder of Messrs Wilson and Bevrage at their estancia on the Sauce Grande, as well as the utter destruction of the estancia and cattle of five other Englishmen on the Naposta."[86] It was a raid recklessly provoked by the commander of the frontier, who in contempt of peace treaties put in irons a deputation of Indians seeking the monthly rations allotted to them by the government. An Argentine force then attacked a friendly tribe during the night and plundered its tents; the cacique and his family, together with other Indians, were taken prisoner and led to Bahía Blanca, while their horses and flocks were confiscated. Military folly led directly to Indian reprisal, and foreign settlers were the losers. The British colonists asked MacDonell to complain to the Argentine government on the unprotected state of the frontier. Basically there were not enough regular troops. The present force, they alleged, was composed of convicts "perhaps as dangerous as the Indians themselves." MacDonell headed a strong protest from the Swiss, Italian, German, and French ministers, but Tejedor remained aloof and indifferent.

MacDonell was convinced that had the Argentine government lived up to half its promises for protecting the colonists, "no other country could offer finer prospects," and he urged upon the Foreign Ministry the need for an army presence in Bahía Blanca. The reply? All troops were now needed for the civil war in Entre Ríos. The British chargé had his own analysis of conditions on the southern and northern frontiers: "The frequency of these invasions is solely due to the disregard of the Government for the security of its frontiers, its apathy and indifference for the losses sustained by settlers, and their policy towards the Indians."[87] MacDonell was disillusioned and daily more convinced that the Argentine authorities from the president down would do nothing to protect the life or property of the gringo or administer even-handed justice to him. His views were confirmed in reporting the list of Britons murdered during 1870, some ten or twelve cases, of which only one had led to a conviction. Most criminals were not even arrested. Recently in Santa Fe a colonist retaliated and killed a man for murdering his child, probably the only kind of justice that would restrain the gaucho.

The year 1871 ended with reports of further British victims of Indian invaders. In Santa Fe, Andrew Weguelin was killed by Indians in the Alexandra colony during a raid which had obviously been well reconnoitered and planned. Weguelin was actually inside the colony's stockade when the raiders were first sighted. As he rode to the aid of colleagues working outside the compound, he was cut off, speared in the forehead, and stabbed several times in the heart as he lay on the ground. An Italian laborer who tried to defend him was also killed. The raiding party, eleven mounted warriors, then drove off all the cattle and horses belonging to the colony. As for the Argentine authorities, they disclaimed any responsibility for those who settled outside recognized frontiers.[88]

British settlers in Bahía Blanca submitted a further complaint to the government after yet another Indian attack on the settlement and the killing of Thomas Jordan in Sauce Grande while he attended his flocks. The Indians who committed the murder were later seen in town trading in the skins of stolen beasts, but nothing was done. Indeed, they were escorted back to their camp to save them from the anger of the settlers. The complainants, eleven in number, went on to say that since they had no protection from the authorities, they would protect themselves by shooting any Indian they encountered. "We shall probably be reproached for taking this line of conduct; but what can we do, in a country where the authorities are utterly degraded, and arbitrary only in defence of the Indians?" They asked MacDonell to inform the Argentine authorities of their resolve, which was the only thing they could do for the legitimate defense of their lives.[89]

The Argentine foreign minister, Carlos Tejedor, rejected the settlers' position and maintained that they should have presented their complaints to the local authorities, not to the central government. He was scathing towards settlers who did not even contribute to frontier defense in the National Guard yet would shoot Indians on sight. This was not even a right enjoyed by Argentines.[90] The argument would have a long run. Tejedor regularly rebuffed MacDonell as a matter of principle rather than personality. Frontier violence was a fact of life in Argentina, and the courts had a tradition of adjusting to circumstances. Argentine liberals, moreover, opposed the death penalty and wanted to abolish it. Behind the heated debate between the British and the Argentines lay different perceptions of violence. Atrocities against foreigners in Argentina had a long and harrowing history. The British in particular were convinced that to farm near the Indian frontier or to travel in gaucho territory was to court disaster, a risk undertaken only from economic necessity. The years 1852–71, when Argentine governments were distracted by political conflict, state and nation building, war abroad, and insurrection at home, were a time of exceptional lawlessness, of progress in ideas but disorder on the ground. The events of 1872 at Tandil, therefore, were unique only in their dramatic concentration of violence. They had been preceded by two decades of discord, when the darker side of national organization revealed itself, atrocities mounted, and complaints multiplied.

2

A Land Fit for Landowners

RURAL BUENOS AIRES: GIFTS OF NATURE AND MEN

The massacre at Tandil in 1872 did not occur by chance. It came at a peak of economic growth during which Argentina multiplied its people, increased its production, and expanded its trade beyond the comprehension of the simple inhabitants of the countryside and beyond the expectations even of its leaders. The key to this transition was the province of Buenos Aires. In the period 1840–80, responding to international demand and the opportunities of comparative advantage, wool production and export became the main source of wealth; as sheep farms expanded and pushed cattle *estancias* southwards, the pastoral industry led the way in Argentina's first process of capital accumulation and its most dynamic participation in the world market.[1]

The exceptional growth of the sheep industry took place within a rural economy that still preserved familiar features from the past. The expansion of Buenos Aires was fueled traditionally by the export trade in hides, salt meat, and tallow, activities which drew increasing numbers to the countryside and enabled it to outstrip the city in population growth. The population of Buenos Aires, outside the capital, grew from some 32,000 people about 1800 to over 317,000 in 1869 and over 920,000 by 1895.[2] As new lands were occupied and opened to more people, the great plains of the interior and their animals ceased to be a resource open to all, gaucho as well as *ganadero* (stock breeder), squatter as well as *estanciero*, and became demarcated into great estates which appropriated cattle as well as land. By means of simple occupation, subsequently ratified with the government by leasehold agreements or outright grant, pioneers acquired large *estancias* whose further growth was impeded only by the Indian frontier. Gradually, and especially during the long regime of Juan Manuel de Rosas, public policy tended to favor a privileged few; to raise revenue and satisfy followers large tracts of public land were transferred in freehold or as outright gifts to private individuals, the power base of the dictator's rule.[3] Once these were in possession, commercial considerations and market forces took over without ever completely displacing the factor of favoritism.

Growing commercialization raised land values and created a market in land; private land sales and alternative rental agreements became common as new settlers moved into the pampas and previous occupants sought to maximize profits. Labor shortage became an opportunity as well as a problem. Ownership of land was made profitable through wage labor, sharecropping, and tenancy. Owners rented out portions of their *estancias* to a family that would cultivate the land with its own labor and relieve the owner of the burden of producing crops and foodstuffs with expensive farmhands.[4] Foreigners were preferred as tenants, just as they were welcomed as storekeepers and millers. The owners would depend on them for continuity, because the military drafts applied only to natives born in the province. Thus, Europeans, inspired by the will to acquire land, make a fortune, and become independent, moved into a social status of middling level denied to native-born Argentines. As farming gave the tenant an income above subsistence, immigrants enjoyed the prospect of eventually buying their own farms, despite the rising cost of land. The progress of the Danish settler Juan Fugl from peon to farmer and finally to mill owner and community leader became a classic of its kind.

Large estates established their roots at a time when ranching techniques were primitive and size took the place of efficiency. But when production became more intensive, as land was converted from cattle to sheep and sheep were accompanied by crops, the efficient unit of production decreased in size. This did not prevent the accumulation of numerous estates in the hands of entrepreneurs who combined land and commerce and found investment capital within their own network; the property of the Anchorena family, who by 1864 owned more than 1.6 million acres of prime ranch land, was a leading example of successful agro-business.[5] Land was a good investment, and the balance sheet was usually favorable; the main risks were Indians, droughts, and labor scarcity, while the profit margin came from expanding foreign exports. But the great ranchers were not the only pioneers and producers. The family ranch and farm were also among the prototypes of the pampas, working for the domestic as well as the overseas market. And even on the larger ranches, the foremen and *puesteros* (in charge of *puestas* or pastures) would be family men, living in separate huts with wives and children.[6]

How strong were these family units? Argentine women, the *chinas* of gaucho literature, were found in all parts of the pampas, fewer yet more durable than men. They raised families on the *puestas*, farms, and ranches and in small towns, often as single mothers when their men vanished into the army, the labor market, or delinquency. They also had working roles on farms and *estancias* and were indispensable in sheep shearing. Immigrant women were scarce but not unknown in rural society, and in Tandil some of them became the victims of xenophobia alongside their men. Immigrant settlers often returned to their own country to marry and bring out a wife on their second tour, thus reinforcing their home and their identity. Families, especially young families living near each other, provided a protective network amidst the hazards of the time, and also a base for advance to better things. Immigrant families profited from the constant turnover of land tenure. Business failures, trade recessions, the effects of drought, and increasing costs of rural production drove many Argentine landowners to the wall and caused the sale or rental of numerous rural properties. Often landowners rented out parcels of their property for the income needed to improve production on the rest of their land. Renting rural property offered newcomers, especially Europeans, the first opportunity to mount the ladder of progress, to operate ranches and farms in this era of growing markets.

By the 1850s, according to Sarmiento, the countryside of Buenos Aires was divided into three social classes: "*estancieros*, who reside in Buenos Aires, small proprietors, and *vagos*."[7] Another division identified three production zones, each specializing, though not exclusively, in one of the three main activities, cattle, sheep, and arable farming, and each containing a greater variety of social groups than Sarmiento's trinity. The zones had developed in accordance with nature and economic demand. In the north was the agricultural zone, close to the domestic market of Buenos Aires and populated by farmers, peons, and migrant workers, where *chacras* (farms) producing foodstuffs for urban consumers were often rented or owned by European immigrants. Next, to the south, was a mixed zone of farming and ranching, where large estates, further from the city, specialized in raising cattle and horses. It was here, north of the Salado River, that most of the sheep farms came to be located, occupying land originally belonging to the cattle *estancias*; the latter then moved further south as wool became a leading export business and competition for land drove up prices.[8] In the cattle zone of the south large *estancias* pushed up against the frontier in search of more and cheaper land, followed for the same reasons by the ubiquitous flocks. Thus, the frontier was occupied by a dual movement of people and animals, both ahead of the flag.

The variety of agricultural experience in Buenos Aires and the diverse rates of expansion attracted migrants of different origins and ambitions, some from the interior of Argentina, others from abroad. By 1854 some 25 percent of the rural population had been born outside the province.[9] Migrants tended to leave cattle raising to the natives and to specialize as sheep farmers, artisans, and retail merchants, occupations more likely to be found in the agricultural zone or in the agricultural sectors of the other zones. Arable farming had its own problems. Poor roads, bridges, and river transport meant that its freightage costs were high; it therefore needed protection against cheaper imports and depended on immigration to lower labor costs.[10] The immigrant might start as a laborer but would soon seek advancement as a tenant or landowner, renting or buying from large *estancias* whose owners were in difficulties or needed capital for improvements or for investing in diversification. Thus older cattle *estancias* were subdivided, rural production became more varied, and land was used more intensively. But the process did not modify the agrarian structure: "Sons of *estancieros* and immigrant Europeans usually benefited from the spread of landownership; native-born peons did not."[11]

The *estancia* was the center of a social as well as an economic world, and its owner was the heir of a distinctly Spanish system of values binding together family, clients, and retainers under his personal control. This enabled him to exert an exclusive monopoly over every activity on his land and in much of the neighboring economy, while through his ownership of *pulperías* and transport vehicles he dominated a wider countryside, especially in the sparsely settled frontier areas. During his first interview with Ignacio Gómez, the leading *estanciero* of Tandil, Juan Fugl observed a solemn and severe man, part potentate, part tyrant, accompanied by a large entourage of family and retainers and intent on assigning newcomers their correct status in the community.[12] An *estanciero* controlled his workers as a personal following, even as a personal militia, and no one doubted that he was the ultimate authority for law and order in his corner of Argentina. While a landowner would normally deal with his business affairs personally in Buenos Aires, on a large *estancia* he would leave daily management to his *mayordomo* (manager) assisted by *capataces* (foremen). These controlled the workforce of wage labor, some of it permanent, such as the *puestero*, who was responsible for his particular sector of pasturage, where he maintained a rude hut and a corral, and some of it seasonal, such as peons or *jornaleros*.[13]

Rural labor codes and vagrancy laws, together with the military levies, were permanent restraints on the freedom of the peon, designed in part to encourage peons to seek employment and in part to overcome the labor shortage in the countryside at a time of more intense land use. But they do not seem to have eliminated entirely the individual's ability to move from one employment to another. Since colonial times the *estancia* had attracted a paid peonage, laborers in search of seasonal or other work, aware of relative wage rates and coming and going according to the agricultural cycle and their own desires.[14] An active labor market coexisted with repressive rural codes, and collaboration between *estancieros* and army deserters resolved many of the problems of labor shortage.[15] Labor scarcity, in fact, gave the peon some advantage, seen in job mobility, short-term contracts, and maintenance of wage levels. The patrón-peon relationship was not entirely exploitative or unfair towards the worker, and on many *estancias* it provided a stable living and job security, if that was what the laborer wanted. Rural laborers, especially the Argentines, had a reputation for independence, indiscipline, and conceit; they were reluctant to perform any work on foot, such as plowing, digging ditches, or shearing sheep, leaving these tasks to foreigners. And if access to land and wild cattle was increasingly closed to the gaucho, forcing him to look for other subsistence, to rustle cattle, or to work for a wage, the cultural and social traditions of rural Argentina, closely associated as they were with work roles, as at roundups, endured and gave the rural laborer an identity and a living.[16] As the Argentine interior opens its spaces to the historian, a new image of the countryside and its dwellers begins to emerge, one that is less of a prison, more of a market.

Yet there is a limit to revision. The pampas were never a paradise for peons. Society was rigidly stratified, proof of identity often demanded, vagrancy still a crime, and the recruiting officer rarely far away. These were the daily realities for the majority of landless Argentines, who mutely watched the landscape change but not their condition.

PROGRESS AND PAUSE

The traditional economy of Buenos Aires province was a livestock economy, and the typical estate was a cattle *estancia*. This primitive structure underwent significant change in the period 1840–80, when sheep farming and wool export became the primary activities of the province, absorbing land and capital, improving production and marketing techniques, and introducing new jobs and greater profits to the rural sector.[17] The first period of expansion reached its peak in 1865: herds multiplied, production expanded, exports swelled. The boom was primed by international demand, especially from Belgium; by improvement of the financial and transport systems within Argentina; and by the increase of immigrant shepherds and farmers.

National organization was thus accompanied by a new model of growth, and from 1862 Argentina's elite adopted a modernizing program. Modernization meant diversification, growth through exports, investment in a new infrastructure, and accelerated immigration. Some local capital was employed in the primary sector, in cattle *estancias*, sheep farms, and sugar estates. But the required investment was beyond the resources and the mentality of the Argentine elite and depended essentially on the import of foreign capital, mainly from Britain. Up to the early 1870s British trade to Argentina was predominantly a trade in textiles, and British investment was confined to commerce and private *estancias*. But from 1860 new trends appeared.[18] First, several joint-stock companies were organized in 1861–65. These were established by British entrepreneurs with British capital and were applied to railways and banks. On 1 January 1863 the first branch of the London and River Plate Bank was opened in Buenos Aires, and in 1866 the Rosario Branch went into operation. At this point iron and steel, metal manufactures, and coal moved up the list of British exports to Argentina. The second stage took the form of investment in development, encouraged by Argentina for national reasons and promoted by the British in order to improve the market for their goods. In 1860 a loan of £2.5 million was marketed in London by Barings on behalf of the Argentine government. This signaled the beginning of a steady flow of capital from Britain to Argentina, much of it applied to the infrastructure, either as direct investment or as loans to the state. More substantial foreign investment had to await the period after 1870, when banks, factories, and public utilities became major recipients. But one area of investment was already established, the railways, and these were essential to economic growth, bringing out agricultural exports from the vast hinterland of Buenos Aires and carrying in imported goods.

The first track was opened in 1857; it ran six miles west from Buenos Aires and was built with private local capital. During the 1860s the northern and southern railways began to cut through the countryside from Buenos Aires. From its foundation in 1862 the Great Southern Railway penetrated deeper and deeper into the fertile lands of the frontier beyond Dolores, and in 1870 the Central Argentine Railway linked Rosario and Córdoba and opened up the great central plains. For this line the government contracted with British capital, guaranteeing a minimum return and granting adjacent lands, necessary concessions to attract capital to an empty territory whose value lay in future prospects rather than present performance. In twenty years 1,250 miles of track were laid in Argentina, through what Mitre described as "the happy partnership of English capital and Argentine progress."[19] The time came when English capital was ready to rely on market forces and dispense with the minimum guarantee and its accompanying restrictions.

The new Argentina needed more people, farmers, artisans, and frontier settlers. After 1862, immigration became a national policy and offices were set up in Europe, though the government did not finance the process, leaving passage and settlement to private enterprise. From the late 1850s about fifteen thousand immigrants a year entered Argentina. Sarmiento and others, influenced by what they saw of American frontier expansion, preached the virtues of agriculture and small farms, the importance of settling the immigrants in rural areas, and the need to provide land for colonization and to discourage speculation and latifundism. But the American model could not be so easily transferred to other frontiers, and reformers were unable to alter ingrained ideas and interests. The Land Act of 1867, which required the sale of rented land, settled the debate in favor of the large *estancia*, which was regarded as the most effective instrument of maximizing rents and responded to many interests. The government viewed land as a valuable resource which could be sold or leased for fiscal purposes. Cattle and sheep were basic natural assets. The *estancieros* formed a powerful group, linked to the commercial leaders of the city; they regarded access to land as a vital factor for stock raising. And land speculation, either by the purchase of public land to be sold later at a profit or by subdivision and subletting of holdings, was too lucrative a business to stop. By the 1880s, therefore, most of the public land of Buenos Aires province, by a series of inappropriate laws, had been transferred as private property to latifundists and speculators.[20]

The transition from old to new tested the nascent institutions of Argentina. In the mid-1860s the Paraguayan war coincided with monetary instability and a crisis in Europe to throw the economy out of gear. The markets for cattle products and for wool exports contracted and production declined; even sheep farming suffered depression.[21] The internal causes of the crisis lay in the land and derived from an excessive expansion of the flocks in the relatively restricted areas of soft grasses suitable for sheep raising. Overstocking coincided with a severe drought, which was a further setback to owners of cattle and sheep. The policy of the state did not help. The law of November 1864 decreeing the sale of all public lands available within the frontier—over two million hectares—and giving priority to the occupying tenants set prices which were considered too high at the time and were criticized by *estancieros* as another burden on the rural sector.

Recovery was rapid, and by 1871–72 the sheep industry was able to respond profitably to international demand and higher prices. But the experience caused a reappraisal of Argentina's problems and prospects.[22] Worried *estancieros* began to discuss the need for diversification of agrarian production, modernization of methods, greater capital investment, even abandonment of economic liberalism. There was talk, too, of combining agriculture and livestock, investing urban capital in the rural sector, incorporating new land, and establishing model farms. Was there even room for a rural manufacturing industry? Innovative ideas of this kind were characteristic of the group of *estancieros*, including sheep farmers, who in 1866 founded the Argentine Rural Society as a pressure group and a medium of debate. Rural labor, its plight and its supply, became a matter of increasing concern. The insecurity, impoverishment, and low status of the peon had often been attributed to the labor laws and military exactions of Rosas, but there were few signs of improvement after 1852, and the demands of the Paraguayan war became a new scourge of the pampas. The need for more people was urgent.

Tandil Society on the Eve of the Massacre

Tandil was a true reflection of rural society in an age of growth, an extension of the province of Buenos Aires and a product of frontier conditions. As sheep farms expanded north and south of the Salado River, so cattle estates were pushed further southwards and the frontier became a new area of settlement before it had been actually pacified. About 1870 the traditional type of *estancia* was still dominant, managed by owners who were not absentees and capable of defending itself in a hostile environment.

Public policy and private interest had combined to create these large estates, reproducing some but not all of the features of those in the northern part of the province. A few of the older traditions of the pampas still prevailed in Tandil. The taking of cattle for personal consumption by gauchos, as though they were free, was by now severely repressed in most parts of Buenos Aires. But not in Tandil: there it was still permissible to slaughter cattle for meat in the open range, as long as the hides were delivered to the owner. At the same time, Tandil was later than the north of the province in the adoption of wire fencing to mark the boundaries of private estates. But the concept of private property, the concentration of land, and the dominance of an *estanciero* class were all firmly entrenched. In the countryside of Tandil there were some immense *estancias*, suitable for cattle and sheep, watered by streams from the surrounding hills, and owned by the powerful families of the time: the Anchorenas, Aranas, Casaras, Gómezes, Machados, Velas, and Valientes, whose poor peons and gauchos inhabited a rural subculture and lived in mud huts. British settlers, too, had made their way to this wild frontier in the middle decades of the century, their names listed by Mulhall: Burnett, Butler, Coony, Crebbis, Eyler, Gebbie, Goodfellow, Harrow, Hinde, James, Lawrie, Leonard, MacAusland, and MacKinley.[23]

Public policy in this period, as in the time of Rosas, continued to favor the large private estate, and Tandil was no exception. Provincial politicians might pay lip service to a different model, the American homestead, and to speak of colonization of the frontier by immigrant settlers and their families. Indeed, individual colonizing projects were inaugurated from the 1850s, some of them, as in Santa Fe, attracting resolute settlers to the banks of the Paraná River. But in the south of Buenos Aires too much wealth was at stake; land was a source of revenue, rent, and profit, and it was never made available for a policy of settlement. No doubt cattle and sheep lent themselves naturally to large-scale enterprise. But this was not the only factor; a combination of political influence, greed, and speculation also favored land concentration in the hands of the few.[24] This did not preclude the emergence of vigorous arable farming in Tandil, and in the next decades miles and miles of wheat, oats, barley, flax, sunflowers, and maize would be sown in these fertile fields, many of them pioneered by immigrant settlers, and by the 1880s sheep breeding too would come to Tandil. But for the moment there were no threats to the cattle *estancia* and no obvious prospects for gauchos and peons. Immigrants too could be victims of land speculation, as when land had been bought cheap by speculators to be sold to the newcomers at a profit or when holdings were subdivided and sublet.[25]

As a frontier zone Tandil was well sited at the center of trade networks and merchant exchanges, legal or otherwise, and the social mobility of the time allowed the emergence of mercantile circuits not always controlled by the large *estancias*. While the major landowners marketed their own products, the smaller cattlemen and farmers depended on the development of a rural marketing system. In Buenos Aires were merchants who specialized in exchanging imported goods and consumer items for the pastoral goods of the countryside. Independent carters, drovers, and *pulperos* (storekeepers) in the rural areas collected the livestock, hides, wool, tallow, and grease for delivery to the stockyards and warehouses of the port. In the small rural towns which multiplied as the frontier was pushed back, builders, black-smiths, and carpenters formed artisan communities whose skill was needed for constructing the nearby *estancias* and farms. Small merchants collected export products and sold imported goods, alcohol, tobacco, yerba maté, hardware, and playing cards. In this way commercial and artisan establishments spread into the pampas at the same time as ranches and farms were founded. Migrants from the interior provinces came to rural communities to seek seasonal work in shearing and branding and to work throughout the rest of the year as cattle drivers and carters. Thus, a domestic marketing system came into being, and Tandil became part of an increasingly efficient rural economy.

After the fall of Rosas and the advent of more liberal governments, Tandil began to acquire a church and a school, a stage-coach service (only three times a month to Buenos Aires), a hotel, and other components of civilization.[26] Financial institutions kept up with the times. By a curious coincidence a branch of the Banco de la Provincia opened in Tandil on 2 January 1872, the day after the massacre.[27] Town and country also received more immigrants, some of whom were soon knocking at the door of local politics.

The political elite of the new Argentina came from families traditionally linked to the governing class.[28] Some of them inherited fortunes made by their ancestors or through past politics, but it was the family that counted, not the fortune. This political class was joined by an intellectual elite of philosophers, writers, and journalists, who came into their own in the decades after 1852 and were as representative of national reorganization as were the politicians. Social cohesion prevailed over political divisions. No doubt different economic interests and political factions competed for power at elections through the familiar networks of clients and caudillos. But no great political division emerged along socioeconomic lines; in Argentina public enemies were class allies. There was no alternative political class or movement. If the middle and lower sectors wanted to participate, they could do so as subordinates or supporters of the elite parties, or through local institutions. This meant that immigrants, too, were excluded from power. There was simply no political space for foreigners, no platform on which to express their complaints and concerns, no doorway to politics, either provincial or municipal.

The exclusion of immigrants from local office and electoral rolls was not absolute throughout Argentina; some municipalities were more open than others. But normally an immigrant had to possess exceptional talents to make his way in municipal government. Even Fugl, intelligent, ambitious, and successful though he was, made a slow start against the suspicion and hostility of local interests. "The local merchants always looked askance at me, suspecting that I would be a competitor. Nor did I inspire confidence among my near and distant neighbors."[29] He was visited by a justice of the peace who admired his wheat and his mill, material signs of success. Fugl demurred, pointing out the enormous work involved for an immigrant farmer, forced to be constantly on the alert against invasions of his crops by neighboring cattle and consequent conflict with ranchers. The justice appeared reasonable and declared he would order the ranchers to keep their cattle away from Fugl's farmland during the night. He instructed the local alcalde to see to it. But the alcalde "was a gaucho, a roughneck, a drinker, who did not sympathize with foreigners or with agriculture, and he had no intention of applying the instructions he had received."[30] In due course Fugl became a member of the municipal council, specializing in education, and his qualities of leadership made him a source of advice and support for foreign immigrants, especially in disputes between farmers and cattlemen over land use and ownership. He even made his presence felt in the Ministry of the Interior.[31] In 1869–70, Protestant though he was, he went to Buenos Aires as chairman of the committee to raise funds from the Ministry of the Interior for a new Catholic church in Tandil, in the event a successful mission.[32]

The local government of Tandil reflected these federal and provincial realities, yet it was not a closed corporation nor a mere appendage of the political class that controlled the national state. It is true that the offices of justice of the peace and commander of the National Guard could not be filled without the approval of the creole landowning class. So men like Juan Antonio Figueroa and Benito Machado, scions of the local elite, for many years occupied the offices of justice and frontier commander, respectively. Nevertheless, although the dominant groups in Tandil could not blame the ills of the countryside on the interference of Buenos Aires, neither did they find there the solidarity which they sometimes expected. The application of the *Código rural*, which defined the laws of property and labor in the countryside, could cause conflicts between farmers and ranchers. The ranchers did not take kindly to protective laws for farmlands. On the other hand, as Fugl discovered, the invasion of arable land belonging to *chacras* by livestock of large *estancias* in search of pasture, just at the time when the farmers were beginning to harvest their crops, was a persistent irritant and became a political grievance. Appeal to the provincial government by both sides received little response. Buenos Aires preferred to defer decisions, conscious no doubt of the need not to alienate groups whose support might be useful in elections. Meanwhile, Tandil was left to resolve its own problems.

OUTCASTS IN THEIR OWN LAND

As ranching was modernized, estates were defined, and cattle branded, so landowners preferred to employ a disciplined labor force listed on a payroll and deprived of traditional usages. The commercialized cattle ranch spread from north to south of Buenos Aires province, bringing with it various categories of workers: tenants, *aparceros* (sharecroppers), *puesteros*, and characteristically the *peón asalariado*. With it too came textbooks on estate management, in effect guides to monopolizing resources. The cattle *estancia* in turn moved on to make way for the sheep farm and to some extent for agriculture. Arable farming tended to be a family enterprise, but sheep farms employed herdsmen and shepherds, and every enterprise employed seasonal peons or *jornaleros*. The process, whether for cattle or sheep, marginalized the gaucho and deprived him of independent subsistence.

Public policy was not on the side of the gaucho. Shortage of labor and lack of labor discipline brought together proprietors and politicians in a concerted effort to prevent the rural population from having alternative means of subsistence other than wage labor, such as squatting on the borders of an estate, dealing with *pulperías*, or exploiting any rural resource claimed by the *estancia*.[33] At the same time, measures to control the movement of the rural population, such as certificates of employment and passports to travel, were favored by state and landowners alike; such measures reduced virtually everyone not on an *estancia* payroll to the status of a vagrant. And the penalty for vagrancy was army service. The military levy, however, divided the state from the landowner. For the state it was important as a penalty, a mechanism of social control, and a source of conscripts, but it was a double-edged weapon for landowners looking for labor. These views, prejudices, and animosities were incorporated in the Rural Code of 1865, which regulated the rights of property, relationship between employer and worker, and organization of rural police. In the same year a law was passed exempting *mayordomos* and *capataces* from levies and authorizing employers to pay substitutes in place of their workers. But the system itself continued, in spite of a chorus of criticism from social reformers and interested parties.

In an editorial published shortly after the massacre at Tandil, *La Nación* of Buenos Aires argued that the origins of rural violence should be sought not in religious fanaticism, as some publicists were implying, but in causes deep within rural society. The newspaper cited "the deplorable conditions of the gaucho" as the central motivation of the crime and specifically denounced the system of frontier defense. The government demanded six months' military service but held the gaucho for six years. Far from achieving frontier security, the system simply victimized a large part of the rural population. The gaucho, having lost his job, ranch, and family, reacted with violence and hatred against his oppressed social condition.[34] He could see, moreover, that the foreigner enjoyed favor from the government and protection from the law, was free of the threat of military conscription, and was not forced to go to the frontier to fight Indians, while the gaucho became an outcast in his own land, subject to responsibilities without reward and reduced to a nomadic and precarious existence.[35] Not all of these accusations, nor their acceptance by later historians, are justified by the facts. Foreigners were not automatically exempt from military service, though their poor performance on the frontier did not make them popular with their commanders or increase their prestige among the gauchos.

The fall of Rosas, the growth of new sectors in the rural economy, especially wool farming, and the greater competition for labor destabilized the old order and undermined the nascent alliance between the state and the *estancia*. The depression of the mid-1860s aggravated the mood of panic. The landowners, reacting from prejudice and ignorance, tried to restore labor controls at a time when these were no longer appropriate. The attempt to apply rigid regulation in the *Código rural* of 1865, harking back to old interests of the cattle *estancia*, came at a time when the economy needed more, not less, mobility of labor. The decline of traditional cattle ranching geared to primitive meat and hide production, the modernization of the *estancia*, the growth of sheep farming, the competition too of arable agriculture, all these created more demand for labor and a market for seasonal and casual laborers not permanently fixed to one *estancia*. This was recognized by attempts to increase free and mobile labor. In 1870 the Rural Code was modified to cancel the articles on vagrancy, and in 1873 the passport requirement was abolished.[36] Meanwhile, the country population reacted angrily to renewed constraints, and their resentment was expressed in rural unrest, cattle rustling, desertions, gaucho rebellions, and individual defiance of authority at the local level. Evidence from judicial records of arrests testifies to the long struggle of the gaucho to remain free and the determination of the elite to crush and control him.[37]

New tensions in rural society and economy in the 1860s were reflected in Tandil. Or so it is argued. A gaucho rebellion against the *es-*

tancia was difficult to imagine and to organize, and there were easier targets, foreigners and immigrants, substitutes for the real enemy. But how precisely did violence in Tandil conform to this interpretation?

The argument from rural conditions received its most eloquent expression in the appeal submitted by the defense attorney on behalf of the criminal band of Tandil. Martín Aguirre, a young lawyer from Uruguay, did not attempt to deny the crimes but reached directly for a sociological defense, referring to "the deplorable social situation of the wretched accused," which at once "explains and provides extenuating circumstances for their crime."[38] The sentences were excessive, granted the conditions prevailing in the countryside: "the religious fanaticism, profound ignorance, virtually nomadic lifestyle, lack of rights and welfare among the miserable inhabitants." They were denied any chance of justice or possibility of education, subject always to the tyranny of the justices of the peace and the military commanders, "citizens in name, slaves in reality." No one protected the gaucho of Buenos Aires; instead he was pursued to be sent to the war or the frontier. Society, argued Aguirre, was divided into two classes: the privileged, that is, the inhabitants of the city, the great landowners, and the foreigners; and the oppressed, that is, the laborers of the countryside. These unfortunates provided fertile ground for the influence of any scoundrel with a little more intelligence than they had. Such was the present case. The authors of the rebellion, Gerónimo Solané and Jacinto Pérez, had persuaded Aguirre's clients to believe with the utmost sincerity that one was God, the other Saint Francis. The two imposters worked on the imagination of ignorant and simple people and gained total control over them. "When all foreigners were denounced by Solané and Pérez as heretics and worthy of death, could my defendants, fanatics through ignorance and the example given them, resist what they believed to be the divine command? Could they fail to kill when they were told to do so under pain of death for themselves and their families in a great flood?"

RANCHERS' RESENTMENTS

Grievance was not a preserve of the gaucho. Landowners, too, harbored hatreds, and these were more difficult to contain, for they were symptoms of power. The alliance between state and proprietors, the support of the state for labor controls, and the collaboration of the *estancieros* in maintaining law and order were proof against most challenges but not against all. Changing conditions in the rural economy and the particular crisis of the mid-1860s threatened, if only temporarily, the stability of the ruling elite. The need for labor mobility caused problems for those who had to administer the rigid Rural Code and brought about conflicts of jurisdiction and power at the local level—for example, over military recruitment. Relations between *comisarios*, justices of the peace, comandantes, and *estancieros* were seldom smooth and sometimes tense.

Tandil on the eve of the massacre was a place divided by economic and social conflicts, some old, some new. The best land was in the hands of creole landowners. Distinguished among these was the Gómez family; originally from Santa Fe, they settled in Tandil in 1825 shortly after its foundation and came to acquire about six thousand acres. Later immigrants had to be satisfied with arable holdings near the town. They found that cattle land was difficult to obtain unless they were able to earn capital from commerce and storekeeping. Some of them did so and in the process reduced a number of *estancieros* to indebtedness, from which they could only escape by paying in land. A further source of friction derived from disputes over land use between ranchers and farmers. In their defense of arable land against cattle invasion farmers gradually began to receive protection from the state and the right to compensation for damage to their crops. But in practice this depended on the willingness of local authorities to apply the law. In Tandil farmers questioned the impartiality of the justice of the peace, Juan Antonio Figueroa, the chief local official at the time of the rebellion. Figueroa was married to a daughter of the Gómez family; of merchant origin himself, he had bought into land, adapted to the landowner mentality, and taken a position alongside the cattlemen. A third set of conflicts developed over National Guard duties and the evident favoritism shown to some employers. Farmers lost peons to recruitment, while the *estanciero* friends of the commander, who invariably combined landowning with military duties, were effectively exempt. The local commander of the National Guard was José Ciriaco Gómez, another member of the Gómez family and brother-in-law of Figueroa. Here was a closely knit network within the local elite in which a small kinship group brazenly enjoyed a monopoly of power and influence. They were not reticent in their opinions, making clear their resentment that foreigners enjoyed the privileges of Argentines without their obligations.

Juan Fugl, the Danish immigrant farmer and one of the leaders of the foreign community in Tandil, observed these trends as they developed in the 1860s. He was absent on a visit to Denmark in 1870–73 and so was not a direct witness of the massacre, but he had his informants and analyzed the evidence on his return. The driving force of the outrage, he concluded, was not simply the anger and xenophobia of ignorant gauchos; it stemmed instead from the invincible prejudice of the local elite. The *estancieros* "were of the opinion that immigration and arable agriculture were a disaster for the country, a usurpation of the rights of the landowners." According to this interpretation, the justice of the peace, Figueroa, whom Fugl had forecast would be "a justice of discord, not of peace," hated foreigners because their agricultural activities impinged upon the free movement of his herds and those of his friends.

> Figueroa nurtured a deep hatred of foreigners and of arable farming, which was spreading in the zone of Tandil. This was because he and his family and friends held lands and great *estancias* adjacent to the farmlands. They resented the laws which forced them to pay compensation for damage caused by their animals to the crops of the farmers, crops which now enjoyed protected status. At the same time, he allotted land to creoles and native Argentines, most of them simple people with no ambition to effect improvements, but not to foreigners who arrived poor but by dint of hard work and friendly adaptation soon acquired capital and lived comfortably.[39]

Fugl believed that Figueroa and the military commander, Gómez, headed a conspiracy of *estancieros* seeking to halt further encroachment by immigrant farmers. The massacre took place "with the knowledge and consent of Judge Figueroa." Gerónimo Solané, the manipulator of popular discontents and alleged leader of the rebellion, was protected by *estancieros*. "Ramón Gómez and Figueroa protected him, believing he would be useful for the realization of their plan of vengeance against foreigners: to strike such terror among them that it would check immigration, which was on the increase."[40] Another Gómez, Ramón Rufo, gave accommodation to Solané on his *estancia* La Argentina. Ramón Rufo was not a typical Gómez; he was a *rosista*, not a *mitrista* (codes for conservative and liberal), and he was his own man. But he was brother of José Ciriaco Gómez, the military commander, and a specific link to Solané.

The argument from social conditions, therefore, could lead not to gauchos but to *estancieros*; in this version it placed ultimate responsibility for the massacre on hostile Argentine landowners. Like many conspiracy theories, that of Fugl contained grains of truth scattered among groundless assertions; typically, it lacked specific links between these truths, and in particular between the conspirators and the crime. Yet the fact that it expressed a notorious immigrant suspicion, and that this preceded the massacre and was presumably known to native Argentines, added further weight to creole nativism, not only among lowly gauchos but also among the local elite and its allies.

The social interpretation of rural rebellion has been further developed by modern historiography, which scrutinizes the ranchers as well as the gauchos. The traditional *estancieros*, it is argued, who had acquired their lands in the time of Rivadavia and Rosas, had developed a particular network of power: on the *estancia* itself they had cultivated a paternalistic relation with their peons, while beyond the *estancia* they had established contacts with the military and the national politicians, especially those led by Mitre. Now these *estancieros*, no less than the gauchos, saw their traditional life at risk: incoming foreigners, a few of them *estancieros*, many of them farmers, and all exempt from national obligations, were accumulating land and forming a rival local elite. The invaders established contacts with merchants, many of whom had already bought their way into land, and forced some of the older landowners to become their debtors and clients. The newcomers included professionals and artisans, most of whom were also foreigners. In political terms they tended to be supporters of *alsinismo* (radical federalism) and determined to find a place in Argentina corresponding to their success in the local economy.[41] As soon as the established landowners saw their familiar *estancia* and political base threatened or diminished, they reacted. The gaucho band which rode into the pampas on 1 January 1872 was thus the instrument by which the traditional elite of Tandil sought to intimidate a "new middle class" of first- and second-generation immigrants.

The thesis has two weaknesses. It is essentially a variant of the original conspiracy theory, looking for hidden hands behind the action of the killers and arguing for collusion between two groups, traditional creole landowners and marginalized gauchos. These were unlikely allies: *estancieros* were not obvious protectors of peons, nor were peons willing agents of *estancieros*. Second, the argument relies for evidence on judicial and official inquiries that were more concerned with identifying the criminals than explaining the crime. The conclusion, that the massacre of 1872 opened a process of political change in which the subversives were subverted, is also speculative. "The middle class who were the targets of the conspiratorial blow had returned it and in the process taken power."[42] If this were true, and the old values were truly threatened, the historian would expect to see more evidence of it, if not in the mouths of the actors at least in the records of events.

There are further flaws in the conspiracy theory of the massacre. To argue that behind the criminals lurked the landowners supposes that there was a direct line of authority from the *estanciero* to the rural population, that the *estancia* was a secure base of social control. In the first half of the nineteenth century this may have been the case, but by 1872 conditions had changed.[43] The *estancia*, too, was affected by the political and economic transformation which the region was undergoing. Landowners now had to accept the shortage and indiscipline of labor as facts of rural life. Immigration, which Sarmiento and Alberdi believed would undermine the cattle *estancia* and lead to an agrarian utopia, was seen by the landowners in a different light, as a practical answer to their labor problems. In fact, neither of these hopes were fulfilled; while immigrants did not transform the rural landscape, they could develop economic activities rivaling those of the *estancia* and preserve their independence of the rural labor market. The traditional form of social control on the cattle *estancia*, expressed in Rosas's instructions for managers of estates, operated by means of the owner's monopoly of all economic activity; this in turn had been supported by a political and judicial structure enfolding the whole rural population except the Indians. These, too, were part of the equation; the needs of the *estancieros* coincided with the military needs of the state to expand and defend the frontier against the Indians, though at the expense of the marginal rural population.

This system of power was undermined by two things: the growth of sheep estates and the fall of Rosas. Now the provincial state ceased to be in the hands of direct representatives of the landowners and passed to a political class with wider interests than the cattle economy. The result was seen in the rural instability of the 1860s and 1870s, a situation constantly denounced by the Rural Society, and in the growing divergence between landowners and the provincial state. The state now recruited for frontier defense not simply among the marginals, who too often managed to disappear, but also among small landowners and *buenos vecinos* (respectable residents), a practice which worsened the labor shortage. The input into the Rural Code of 1865 came largely from the landowners. It reincorporated many of the old social and labor controls—prohibitions against hunting, carrying arms, establishing *pulperías*, and gambling—and it sought to control the movement of men and of cattle. But this attempt to revive past restrictions was ineffective. The new mobility of labor could not be reversed, and the movement of Argentine migrants from other parts of the province and from other provinces could not be halted. Any interpretation of the massacre, therefore, has to take into account the novel mobility of the rural population. It was not by chance that migrants from other provinces were predominant among the assassins. Some had only recently arrived in Tandil. Solané was from Entre Ríos and had previously resided in Tapalquén. Félix Juárez came from Tucumán, Mario Pérez from Córdoba, and José María Trejo from Santiago del Estero. The rest came

from other parts of the province of Buenos Aires and from the interior.[44] Few of the killers would have given Tandil as their first place of
residence.

The assassins of Tandil, therefore, were aliens. This adds to the mystery: Tandil society was mobile but defensive, open but reticent. For
this reason the massacre has remained a puzzle ever since that fatal day,
difficult to unravel and to explain. Answers have been sought in a re-
moter past, and social and agrarian structures of long duration have
been explored. More immediate causes have been invoked: xenophobia,
religiosity, superstition, utopianism, sheer ignorance and barbarism, all
combining to produce an irrational act. Was there an element of *rosismo* in that morning of horror, a political defiance of the new Argentina with its constitutional and liberal forms? Did the assassins
have personal scores to settle? Was this a campaign of vengeance? Or
did it express a simple hatred of foreigners? Immigration was the constant theme. The gaucho band swore to exterminate the foreigners and
Masons from Tandil. But not all foreigners were Masons, and some Masons were Argentines. Did the assassins mean to kill all foreigners, or
did they have specific targets in their sights?

3

Natives and Newcomers

AMBIGUITIES OF ARGENTINE NATIONALISM

A sense of national identity was slow to develop in Argentina. In the process of state building, the nation meant different things to different people. The new republic, like other former colonies of Spain, had its *americanistas*, whose sense of national awareness transcended individual nations to embrace a greater America and a common identity; but for most people these concepts were unreal and rapidly lost their credibility. In debating treaties and constitutions, politicians in the Río de la Plata were also asking who belonged and who did not, and they were seeking, even when they did not find, a particular construct of Argentina that would bring together state and nation. But what was Argentina? The great divide between unitarists and federalists, between liberals and conservatives, was not purely a constitutional struggle but also a dispute over the definition of their country, a dispute which lasted to 1852 and beyond. Was Argentina a union of federal provinces or a confederation of independent states?[1] The term Argentina itself was ambiguous; for some it meant not an inclusive nation but the old viceroyalty treated as a dependency of the city of Buenos Aires. Even the designation "Provinces of the Río de la Plata," united or otherwise, was too positive for many. The debate moved on, and gradually the debris of the past was discarded. But regional interests, suspicion of neighboring provinces, and distrust of Buenos Aires all made Argentina, whatever its definition, an assemblage of parts rather than a united whole.

These differences revealed widespread confusion in political objectives and terminology. They also meant that projectors or makers of constitutions in the period 1816–52 were either behind or ahead of national awareness at any given time. And national awareness as between an intellectual in Buenos Aires and a peon in Córdoba was impossible to define. While a few precocious Argentines such as Bernardino Rivadavia and General José María Paz already saw Argentina as a unitary nation with Buenos Aires as its capital, for many people the term *patria* referred to their native province, not to an Argentine nation. Esteban Echeverría, the young liberal and romantic, asked Argentines, "What does the *patria* mean for you?" His answer was a candid description of "Argentina" in the first half of the nineteenth century: "The fatherland for the *correntino* is Corrientes; for the *cordobés*, Córdoba; for the *tucumano*, Tucumán; for the *porteño*, Buenos Aires; for the gaucho, the *pago* where he was born." Everyone fought for his own corner, and larger national interests were an "incomprehensible abstraction."[2] Nation or province, it was all the same to the gaucho. He felt no pull of patriotism, no sense of allegiance, no obligation to any state, central or local. As W. H. Hudson observed, "The gaucho is, or was, absolutely devoid of any sentiment of patriotism and regarded all rulers, all in authority from the highest to the lowest, as his chief enemies, and the worst kind of robbers, since they robbed him not only of his goods but of his liberty."[3]

Writers, journalists, and intellectuals saw the practical inconvenience as well as the loss of morale caused by disunity and sought to inspire acceptance of a single nation, at least in the minds and hearts of the people. Between the establishment of an Argentine Confederation in 1831 and the beginning of a federal state in 1853 numerous Argentines, not least the Generation of '37, exercised their minds on the problem of identity. Who are we? In seeking an answer, they imagined an Argentina that could be a model of a nation.[4] Historians wrote to prove, or encourage, the existence of a nation. The colonial period was searched for traces of political consciousness. Liberation was interpreted as a struggle for a nation state. The history of independence in the hands of Bartolomé Mitre became a history of great men—Belgrano, San Martín—who laid the foundation of new nations. Argentina acquired its own mythology, built around national unity and national heroes, a myth, however, which was so disputed that it belied any real sense of unity. Nevertheless, by 1852 politicians had made some progress and were now familiar with the term *national* in an Argentine context. Representatives subscribing to the Acuerdo de San Nicolás defined themselves as "deputies of the nation," not as mere agents of the provinces. And in the Constitution of 1853 political arrangements and national awareness finally began to converge.

Yet there were still questions: Who and what were Argentines? Mitre, Sarmiento, and other exponents of liberal orthodoxy had no doubt what they *should* be: replicas of the peoples of North America and Europe. Alberdi was even more explicit: he argued that Argentines were already made in the image of Europeans. Argentina acquired its identity from

Europe: in giving us the concepts of order and freedom, the talents for creating wealth, and the principles of Christian civilization, "Europe has given us our native land."[5]

The elitist nationalism of Mitre and Alberdi was challenged by other thinkers, who sought to build a new Argentina by extending down to the whole people a belief in the existence of the nation. Lucio V. Mansilla, who called the Indians "the true children of the patria" and extolled the gaucho as the real national prototype, assumed that Argentina already had an identity, and it could be found in the inhabitants of the pampas, not in the foreign institutions, laws, and customs now being introduced. Mansilla treated the Indians as authentic Argentines, and, while mistrusting the antithesis, he placed them on the side of civilization rather than barbarism; indeed, he described their material culture as more civilized than that of the gaucho. When he greeted the court of the Ranquel cacique Mariano Rosas, he cried, "Viva Mariano Rosas! Viva el Presidente de la República! Vivan los indios argentinos!" It was an extraordinary gesture for an Argentine to extend national identity to Indians. He thought the barbarians were not so barbarous and had lessons for civilized republics. "They believe something that we refuse to accept: that principles are everything, men nothing; that there are no *hombres necesarios*."[6]

Mansilla was not a solitary voice. José Hernández made a national hero out of a gaucho outlaw; he denounced the exclusivism of the oligarchy and the banishment of the poor from the nation. Conservative nationalists accused the liberals of betraying the nation through their cultivation of foreign models, their subservience to foreign powers, and their collaboration with foreign capital.[7] Ironically, even the provincial caudillos, the living denial of an Argentine nation, were glorified by some as nationalists in contrast to the liberals' idolization of Europe and North America and what Mansilla called their "mania for imitation," which threatened to strip Argentines of their national identity and tradition.[8]

The Utopia of Immigration

While some Argentines were fiercely protective of their space, others wanted to open the country to new peoples and to encourage immigrants as providers of population and labor, models of the work ethic, and agents of Argentina's entry into the international economy. Immigration accompanied the rapid agricultural expansion of Argentina in the years 1850–1914, but it became an ideology as well as a process. Immigration was part of the national project of Argentine liberals, the uni-

tarists and centrists of Buenos Aires, who saw the immigrant as a pro-
ducer, consumer, and taxpayer and looked to Europe for the ideas, people, and trade necessary for modernization. The federalists, on the other
hand, the provincial caudillos and their landed allies, with support from
gauchos and the popular forces of the countryside, nurtured a more nativist and protectionist position, jealous of their national space.

Rivadavia actively promoted immigration and was the first politician
to make it part of a liberal program. He argued that the country ur-
gently needed new people who would be instruments of change as well
as of population: "the most effective way, virtually the only way, of destroying the degrading Spanish customs and terrible caste system and
of creating a homogeneous, industrious, and moral population, the only
solid foundation in any nation for Equality, Liberty, and therefore Prosperity."[9] From then on it was understood that immigration should be
white and European, though for cultural rather than racial reasons; it
should also preferably be non-Spanish and non-Catholic in order to
achieve a complete break with the past. These were the themes of liberal dissent during the regime of Rosas and its aftermath. The dictator
was not a promoter of immigration; while he allowed it and provided
some security for foreigners, he did nothing to encourage it. But the
ideas persisted and became part of the liberal project for Argentina. As
Mitre said in 1852, "Our social policy shall always be to promote European immigration, as a means of regenerating our society."[10]

Domingo Faustino Sarmiento, journalist, teacher, and statesman,
who employed the power of pen and presidency to change the course
of Argentina's history, saw immigration as a means of civilization, a
counterbalance to the creole and gaucho elements in Argentine society, a way of undermining the political and social power of the rural
elite, especially of those who had prospered under Rosas. He wanted to
populate the countryside with families of settlers who were committed to working the land; without a rural transformation the creation of
a nation was impossible. In 1856 he took the side of the farmers of
Chivilcoy in their conflict with the landowners in a case which he saw
as a test for the new Argentina. Were land titles given by Rosas for services rendered still valid? Could a few wealthy landowners establish
freehold at the expense of tenant farmers? Should their cattle be allowed to drive the grain growers from the land? Would landless laborers ever be able to become farmers owning land? In Chivilcoy, if not
elsewhere, legislation allowed occupiers to buy their land in spite of
the Rosas grants; thus, "the people of Chivilcoy have triumphed, and
tenants become owners."[11] Preconditions for a successful immigra-

tion policy were access to land, political reforms, and military changes. He wrote to a colleague in early 1853, "We can in three years introduce 300,000 new settlers and drown in the waves of industry the creole rabble, inept, uncivil, and coarse, which stops our attempt to civilize the nation."[12]

Sarmiento, then, had a social purpose: to challenge the cattle barons, protect the rural population, and encourage a new sector of small proprietors. In his message to Congress in 1869 he announced that thirty thousand immigrants had entered Argentina in the previous year, and the expectation for the current year was forty-five thousand. No other Latin American country received so many immigrants; no other paid such high wages. The colonies in Santa Fe, Entre Ríos, and Córdoba were distinguished for their agriculture and their example. But owing to "the most thoughtless system of colonization ever attempted by any nation," land was unavailable for immigrants precisely in those areas where they were most needed. "In the expectation of 100,000 immigrants a year, we should immediately undertake the task of making land easily accessible for them and regulating its distribution, in such a way as to prevent any individual from acquiring land the size of a European kingdom, and the present generation from depriving its successors of the right to own a home and piece of land which they can call their birthright." Unfortunately the existing agrarian structure ensured that the least populated part of the country was already in private hands or under private control, leaving no land for the immigrant except by purchase. "With an area of 800,000 square miles and a population of one and a half million, two-thirds of the inhabitants look in vain for a home and the immigrant for a hearth."[13] Sarmiento was backed by his minister of the interior, Dalmacio Vélez Sarsfield, who called on Congress for more funds to promote immigration and announced the reactivation of the Rosario Immigration Committee.

Sarmiento regarded the immigrant as the agent and the beneficiary of institutional change. The second of the necessary preconditions for immigration, political reform, would guarantee the immigrant full voting rights. Sarmiento would therefore grant Argentine citizenship on request; if the immigrants did not apply, they still had municipal voting rights. And to prevent peons from becoming voting fodder for *estancieros*, he refused to enfranchise illiterates. The third precondition was a reduction in the military power of the *estancieros* which they exercised through their role in the National Guard, the heir of the old militias. Sarmiento planned to professionalize the army, starting with the establishment of a military college and including reform of recruitment, in order to displace the local military forces and render frontier communities more hospitable to foreigners.

The liberalism of Sarmiento, his anger at the land monopolists, his dream of a new deal for small farmers and opportunities for immigrants, coexisted with a conservative view of society, a reluctance to challenge the basic structures of rural Argentina, and an assumption that Argentina needed an "aristocracy of patriotism and talent," by which he meant an aristocracy based on property as well as office.[14] Moreover, Sarmiento recognized the negative as well as the positive effects of immigration. He saw that not all European immigration was civilizing and that it had to be controlled by the state, otherwise Argentina would impair its prospects and punish its people. The greater risk to native Argentines, however, would come not from inferior immigrants but from those with educational, scientific, and industrial qualifications: "With the advent of new people and their greater ability to prosper, thousands of fathers of families who now enjoy a superior social position . . . will see their children soon descend to the lowest classes of society."[15]

Sarmiento did not want to replace one barbarism by another. Yet he also insisted that immigrants adapt to the culture of the host society, thus ensuring the survival of the best of Argentina's heritage. To contribute to cultural continuity in this way, Argentina's immigrants needed a certain level of education and political awareness, unlike the abject and ignorant people then flooding into North America, though he recognized that even inferior immigrants could be assimilated through education and religion, as they were in the United States. Sarmiento's view of the ideal society was informed by elitist and democratic values alike. The dilemma was never put to the test, for his political and military reforms were not immediately effective. Immigration, it is true, and the creation of new schools, had altered the face of the Argentine countryside; he rightly claimed that his administration had seen the increase of immigration from thirty-nine thousand in 1868 to eighty thousand in 1873 and that this great movement of people had become a significant agent of social change.[16] But landed proprietors continued to dominate political and military power, just as they still monopolized the best land. For these reasons, if there was mutual suspicion, there was no confrontation between Sarmiento and the landowners. The supposedly threatened elite never reacted against immigration; on the contrary, many of them considered it favorable to their interests.

Alberdi, author of the aphorism "To govern is to populate," was a more conservative thinker than Sarmiento, and his liberal instincts were controlled by deference to Argentine reality, which he believed made an "imperfect liberty" the only kind possible. So he never completely disavowed the caudillos and their gaucho followers, and he bitterly criticized Sarmiento for doing so:

> If we try to annihilate part of our population because it is incapable of constitutional order, tomorrow you will say it is better to destroy the entire population and replace it with foreigners, accustomed to living in order and liberty. Such a principle will then lead you to suppress the entire Spanish, Colonial, and Argentine Nation . . . and replace it by force with an Anglo-Republican Argentine Nation, the only kind that will never have caudillism. . . . The day you believe it proper to destroy and suppress the gaucho because he doesn't think as you do, you write your own death sentence and revive the system of Rosas.[17]

Nevertheless Alberdi still saw immigration as a means of bringing "the life-giving spirit of European civilization to our land," changing even the ethnic composition of the country. "Each European who comes to our shores brings more civilization in his habits, which will later be transmitted to our inhabitants, than many books of philosophy." He considered Americans as "nothing else than Europeans born in America," and he stated that "in America everything that is not European is barbarous." He urged the replacement of Indian elements by Anglo-Saxons, who were his model immigrants. "Do what you like with our *roto*, gaucho, and *cholo*, give him the best education available, and in a hundred years you will still not turn him into an English worker, who lives, works, and consumes in dignity and comfort."[18] The English people and the English language were the exemplars for Argentina. Let us encourage settlement from Europe, he urged, though not from Latin America.

Immigration was a policy of the political and intellectual elites.[19] No one thought of consulting native Argentines, much less rural workers. The answer would have been finely balanced. Many people asked what was being done to improve the lot of the native in the countryside. This was true of Martín Fierro, one gaucho who was resolutely antiforeigner. Elsewhere Hernández argued that Argentina did not have the infrastructure to absorb immigrants or the social system to give them a good life. First the government would have to correct the maldistribution of land in Argentina and guarantee new settlers basic rights in rural society. Then perhaps the immigrant could fulfil his promise; otherwise he would end up selling lottery tickets and become "a guest at the banquet of the poor."[20] Others argued that immigration should be promoted by the state for business reasons, in order to bring European capital and labor to Argentina, and that the interests of individuals did not count.

For these Argentines there were no democratic implications in immigration. The industrial worker and agricultural laborer did not need literacy; they needed only to know their jobs.

Immigrant Demography

In 1869, according to the First National Census, Argentina had a population of 1.7 million. By 1895 this had grown to 3.9 million, fed by foreign immigration. The years 1852–72 were not a time of mass migration into Argentina. This had to await the decades from 1880. Nevertheless, these years were the beginning of the trend, and by 1881—to focus down on Buenos Aires—immigrants accounted for almost a fourth of the total population of the province. Italians and Spaniards were the largest groups, followed at some distance by French and British.

In the last decade of the Rosas regime foreign immigrants multiplied in the city of Buenos Aires, not only in the ranks of large merchants but also among smaller traders, farmers, and artisans. Italians, Basques, and Galicians all identified openings and catered to the needs of local consumers. Immigration was also increasing in the rural sector. The expansion of sheep farming was made possible by Irish, Scottish, and Basque shepherds drawn to Argentina by an informal network of contacts, not by government sponsorship. These were able to employ their peasant skills and experience to secure work, often from their compatriots; from employment they advanced to contracts allowing them one-third of the increase of their flocks, and thus to a life of independent enterprise.[21] By 1866 there were twenty-eight thousand Irish in Argentina, out of a total British population of thirty-two thousand.[22]

Thus a new sector of rural labor, or some of it, was passing into the ranks of proprietors; they joined large merchants who had been investing in land since the 1820s, proprietors of middle rank, and yet others who were setting up as retail merchants in villages. As the immigrants joined a larger and more complex rural society, at all social levels except peons, so the image of the foreigner as a member of a wealthy and educated elite gave way to one of a competitor in the open market. At the same time, critics of the Rosas regime seized on the immigrant as a favored and protected species who had advantages over Argentines. He was not subject to militia service or recruited into the regular army and thus profited over natives in times of labor shortage, as a foreigner he had greater security of land tenure than natives, and in the last resort he was protected by treaties and consuls. Hard feelings did not end with the fall of Rosas. Seizure of native men and resources for war was no

Table 3-1. Immigration, Argentina and Buenos Aires, 1857–90

	Argentina	Buenos Aires	% Buenos Aires
1857–60	20,000	5,938	29.7
1862–70	159,570	52,558	32.9
1857–80	260,613	87,066	33.4
1862–90	846,567	278,508	32.8

SOURCE: Dirección General de Inmigración, *Resúmen estadística del movimiento migratorio en la República Argentina, 1857–1924,* (Buenos Aires, 1925); Dirección Nacional de Migraciones, *Estadística del movimiento migratorio* (Buenos Aires, 1956).

less severe in the 1850s and 1860s than before, with the result that resentment of the foreigner continued and became deeply embedded in rural life.

Yet the impression of a massive influx of foreigners was mistaken. In the 1850s Argentina received some 40,000 immigrants, increasing to 160,000 in the 1860s and 260,000 in the 1870s, most of them absorbed into productive occupations and helping to raise Argentine output of hides, wool, and cereals (Table 3–1). Yet foreigners, totaling 15,523 out of 140,000, accounted for only 11 percent of the population of Buenos Aires province in 1854, and this was the province that most attracted immigrants. Immigrants comprised only 7 percent of the province's 20,313 rural peons; but 45 percent of the 1,464 provincial merchants were foreigners.[23] At this point Spaniards were predominant (26 percent), followed by English (19 percent), French (17 percent), and Italians (11 percent). But these were early days and this was not the only migration. The cattle industry of the littoral attracted a substantial internal migration from the interior provinces, and many of the native population in the rural areas, though Argentines, were not locally born.[24] But the proportion of foreigners in the province rose steadily to 20 percent in 1869. And by 1870 almost half the population of Buenos Aires city was foreign-born.

In Tandil, too, the immigrant population grew between 1854 and 1869, though the rate of growth, like that of the dominant cattle economy, was modest. Out of a total population of 2,899 in 1854, 179 or 6.2 percent were foreigners. In 1869 foreigners numbered 767, that is, 15.7 percent of a total of 4,870.[25] Yet this was below the provincial average of foreigners in the population. Immigration to Tandil increased more rapidly in the 1870s owing to the expansion of sheep farming and the attraction of a moving frontier. But it was only from 1881 that Tandil's immigrants began to exceed the average, through its increased role as

Table 3-2. Immigrant Population, Tandil, 1854–1914

	Total Pop.	Native	Foreign	% Foreign	% Arg.
1854	2,899	2,720	179	6.2	93.8
1869	4,870	4,103	767	15.7	84.3
1881	8,762	6,389	2,373	27.1	72.9
1895	14,982	9,967	5,015	33.5	66.5
1914	34,061	21,331	12,730	37.4	62.6

SOURCE: Enrique Amadasi et al., *Estructura y dinámica de la población, evolución económica y empleo en el partido de Tandil*, 55.

Table 3-3. Nationality of Foreigners, Tandil, 1854–1914

	1854	1869	1881	1895	1914
Spaniards	47.5	31.8	32.6	26.8	43.9
Italians	0.2	13.1	29.1	40.7	33.7
French	19.6	27.3	19.0	14.2	5.0
English	13.4	5.6	3.8	1.1	0.4
Germans	1.7	2.4	1.1	0.5	0.6
Portuguese	6.3	1.3	0.3		0.9

SOURCE: Enrique Amadasi et al., *Estructura y dinámica de la población, evolución económica y empleo en el partido de Tandil*, 59.

principal supplier of goods and services for the whole of the south east to Bahía Blanca, and it was only then that immigrants could join a society which was becoming a shade more mobile (Table 3–2).

Foreigners were not the only immigrants. A 1862 census of Tandil's three thousand inhabitants showed a substantial internal migration from the interior to the littoral. Provincials comprised 28 percent of the rural male population and 31 percent in the town of Tandil. Tandil and Azul drew a number of foreign immigrants from the 1840s, but lack of security on the southern frontier was a deterrent to massive immigration. Native Argentines comprised all but 6 percent of rural males and all but 1 percent of rural females. Foreigners tended to congregate in the towns: immigrants accounted for 23 percent of urban males, and Spaniards and French were the most numerous (Table 3–3).[26] Tandil was primarily a cattle and sheep raising area, and livestock were the predominant employment. But it also attracted immigrant wheat farmers—several hundred Danes, as well as Italians, Basques, and others (Table 3–4).

Among the eight hundred or so foreigners in Tandil in 1870, details are known of only a few, and these are from the foreign elite. Ramón

Table 3-4. Population of Tandil, Occupational Structure

	1854	% of total employment	1881	% of total employment
Agrarian production	825	81.7	3,019	57.7
Manufacturing industry	62	6.1	616	11.8
Construction			107	2.1
Commerce and finance	123	12.2	646	12.3
Services			844	16.1

SOURCE: Enrique Amadasi et al., *Estructura y dinámica de la población, evolución económica y empleo en el partido de Tandil,* 148.

Santamarina was a self-made Spanish immigrant who worked his way up from ship's cabin boy, hotel porter, wagon-train peon, and then to independent carter. In Tandil he established his own store and transport business and began to buy land. In the 1860s he was the leading foreign settler and one of the few to obtain municipal office. His *estancia* increased at the expense of older landowners, from whom he bought property and some of whom became clients and debtors of his store. Upward mobility brought changing ideas. In 1870, Santamarina was a liberal, a Mason, hostile to traditional society. But as the family moved up, acquired more *estancias*, and established more stores, it became more conservative politically and returned to its Catholic roots.[27]

There were other types, some of whom became owners of *pulperías*. The country store had been a traditional goal of immigrants since the eighteenth century; no longer the primitive shack of the past or a simple retail outlet, it had become a means of social mobility, an essential trading link in the rural economy, and in some cases a source of credit and capital.[28] The Chapar family were French Basques who became owners of a warehouse and general store near Tandil and inevitably had dealings with landed proprietors. It was said that a number of traditional *estancieros* were heavily in debt to them, and many of those involved in the events of 1 January either at the front of the column or in the background were clients of Chapar. The young British couple, the Gibson Smiths, were immigrants of middle social rank who had made their way to Tandil via a London-based land company; they had up to two thousand pounds in cattle, sheep, and shop goods, and they owned the store that they managed on the *estancia* of the Thompsons, earlier immigrants from Britain.[29]

The career of Juan Fugl was perhaps the best example of what could be achieved by a talented foreigner and evidence that social and even political advance was open to those who pushed hard. He emigrated be-

cause as a poorly paid teacher he saw few prospects of a successful career in Denmark; a newspaper article convinced him that Argentina
was a good farming country where he could acquire land and become
independent. After working at various trades such as carpenter and as
a farm peon, he acquired enough capital to establish a stagecoach service and, more importantly, to obtain a piece of land in Tandil for agricultural production aimed at the regional market. His success depended on fair treatment from the local authorities, though he had to
confront some officials and hold his own, too, against ranchers, whose
cattle often destroyed farmers' crops. On his arrival in Tandil in 1848,
Fugl was subjected to a lecture by the leading landowner, José Ignacio
Gómez, who told him exactly where power and influence lay: "My
lands border on the territory of Tandil. If you wish to slaughter some of
my animals, take what you need, and if you do not wish to keep the
hides you can hand them over to my storeman in Tandil. If you are
short of money, let me know. I have influence here and can say yes or
no." Most of this was normal practice in Tandil and not a sign of special favor to Fugl. In the same interview he was assigned his place in the
social structure of Tandil: "If you have come to settle in this country,
rely on yourself and on no one else. You must respect and obey the local
authorities, namely the justice of the peace, Felipe Varela, the alcalde,
Daniel Arana, the comandante, Rosendo Parejas, the lieutenant alcalde, Rómulo Zabala, and me, a former alcalde. And you must respect
and honor the Argentine people, who are the owners of this country.
You must keep peace and friendship with your neighbors, and not cause
trouble or offense to anyone."[30]

Fugl had mixed feelings on his experience at the hands of Argentines
and found that he could not drop his guard. If he encountered few permanent obstacles to successful farming, he found that political influence was a distinct advantage.[31] He participated in municipal government from the 1850s, service interrupted only by a return visit to
Denmark to recruit more immigrants. But politics were confined to nationals. And the fact remained that Argentine legislation did not encourage foreigners to take nationality or to participate in federal or
provincial politics.

Yet foreigners were encouraged to come to Argentina. Laws and pro-
cedures favored immigration, especially when, in the words of the Constitution of 1853, it was "directed towards working the land, promoting
industries, and inaugurating the teaching of science and the arts." Specific laws authorized the establishment of agricultural colonies, partly
by granting lands, partly by subsidizing promoters. Working examples
could be seen in Santa Fe and Chubut. General legislation, on the other

hand, and action by the state in assimilating immigrants tended to lag behind their actual arrival, partly because of strong political opposition to the idea of artificial support for immigration. The first law of immigration and colonization, in 1875, authorized the government to grant lands and advance the costs of passage. A year later a more extensive law empowered the government to establish an immigration service and created the Department General of Immigration and the Office of Lands and Colonies, which were intended to help the arrival and establishment of foreigners.[32] The constitution guaranteed foreigners the same treatment as nationals, with the exception of political rights and military obligations, from both of which foreigners were excluded. Yet the Argentine government did little to encourage immigrants to acquire rights of citizenship by taking Argentine nationality.

Foreigners could acquire Argentine nationality at the age of eighteen and after two years' residence in the republic. Yet there was no rush to apply. Immigrants had little confidence in the institutions of Argentina, as distinct from its economic prospects. The Argentine state lacked credibility, and in the minds of many immigrants it was much weaker than the state they had left. Better to look to their local consul for protection than the Argentine government. The diffidence of Argentina in developing a policy to encourage the extension of nationality only confirmed these opinions, especially among immigrants who had no previous experience of political or electoral activity. The most powerful motive of immigrants was economic; they came "to make America," and having done so many preferred to return home rather than integrate into the local community. As the English settler Richard Seymour explained, immigrants were short of money back home. They came "to make a rapid fortune by sheep farming," and they found by experience that their hopes were frustrated by the Argentine government when requests for security and protection against Indians and gauchos were ignored.[33] These were powerful deterrents against political integration.

While immigrants experienced the silence of distant government, they faced the closer scrutiny of their immediate neighbors.

THE NATIVIST BACKLASH

In the years about 1870 the demographic picture of Argentina, Buenos Aires, and Tandil signified underpopulation, not overcrowding. The southern frontier was not swarming with immigrants; foreigners were not obviously pushing out natives. But perception was more important than reality, function more relevant than numbers. The immigrants were visible signs of change in the Argentine countryside, the messengers of a new order.

Nativism has not been exclusive to Argentina. Most peoples of the world have resented the arrival of large groups of foreigners in their midst and seen them as a threat to their position and prospects. Resentment is fed from various sources, economic, social, cultural, and religious, and is aggravated if the native peoples see immigration as a policy imposed from above by a ruling elite while they themselves are forgotten and their interests ignored. A process of mutual estrangement then takes root between natives and newcomers. What immigrants see as protection, natives regard as privilege. What immigrants welcome as employment, natives resent as loss of opportunity. When immigrants acquire property, natives become conscious of their poverty. When immigrants express their culture and religion, natives believe they are abandoned and their identity is diminished.

These tensions are increased in countries of mass immigration. In the United States, Protestant opposition to Catholics and nationalist hostility to foreigners were strong in the 1830s and 1840s. Xenophobia was rekindled in the 1850s when fraternal societies of the American-born affirmed their exclusivity; labeled as Know-Nothings because of their secrecy, by 1853 they were organized nationally, affirming the supremacy of native-born Protestants.[34] After the demise of organized nativism about 1860, xenophobia continued in attacks not only on Catholics but also on Jews, Chinese, and immigrants from Southern and Eastern Europe. After 1880 more overtly racial and cultural arguments were used to defend Anglo-Saxon America and its perceived identity. The experience of the United States suggests that xenophobia of this kind usually erupts in times of crisis and is "the product of a loss of national confidence owing to internal stress of one kind or another."[35] Beginning as a reaction to Catholicism, criminality, electoral power, labor competition, and epidemics, in the decades after 1885 it was related to industrial strife and economic depression when social divisions were alleged to have been introduced by foreigners into what had been a homogeneous society.

Argentine nativism was not as precisely focused as that of the United States. Religion was weaker, the Church was more thinly spread, and targets were not so easily identified. Foreign Protestants in Argentina did not display the high profile adopted by Irish Catholics in the United States. Immigrants in Argentina were not politically active enough to join a struggle for power or to demand their own schools and access to public office. North American nativism was a middle-class movement that appealed to native industrial workers in towns, where the immigrant presence was more obvious; true, it eventually spread to rural areas, but it rarely became a feature of the frontier as it did in southern Argentina.

While Argentina did not reproduce the conditions of the United States, nativism presented similar features. In the province of Buenos Aires, the shift from cattle to sheep and the expansion of arable farming generated friction between different activities and interests. In the agrarian sector immigrants tended towards particular functions. In Buenos Aires province some became peons on cattle estates which were producing and exporting, and they enabled landowners to keep their labor costs low in times when international prices were depressed; this was why the landed elite in general supported immigration. But the *estancias* could not retain immigrants, who had their sights on better careers than *peonaje*. Many went into sheep farming and through accumulation of shares gradually joined the ranks of landowners themselves. But perhaps the most characteristic occupation of immigrants was tenant farming and grain production, especially in provinces such as Santa Fe. Buenos Aires, a traditional cattle province, was less open to agriculture, and there immigrant farmers had to compete with *estancieros* for land and resources, and competition led to collision.

Immigrants and gauchos, on the other hand, seldom competed directly for employment. This did not mean that they lived in peace. The foreigners always seemed to be one step ahead, and when they owned *pulperías*, as they sometimes did, they became creditors of the gaucho as well as competitors. The mere presence of the immigrant seemed to pose a threat and personified rapid, bewildering changes that altered the pampa way of life; the landscape itself marked the changes as fences were erected and plowed fields replaced grasslands. Strange languages, accents, and cultures further signaled the presence of people alien to Argentine tradition. Nationalism is frequently a response to foreign pressure, cultural as well as economic, which is perceived as a threat to national identity and interests. In this sense the clash of cultures on the southern frontier was a stage in the growth of popular nationalism in Argentina. It was one of the ironies of the age that the gaucho, who had little awareness of an Argentine nation, reacted instinctively to the presence of non-Argentines. Much of the rivalry was perceived rather than real, but it was enough to arouse the latent xenophobia of the natives. As Martín Fierro complained, referring apparently to Italians:

> I'd like to know why the Government
> Enlists that gringo crew
> And what they think they're good for here?
> They can't mount a horse or rope a steer,

And somebody's got to help them out
In everything they do.[36]

José Hernández argued that if foreign agricultural colonies were necessary, how much more urgent it was to establish agricultural colonies of
native Argentines which would give work to "vagrants" and keep the
police off their backs.[37]

Xenophobia had a history in Argentina. The Rosas dictatorship, if not
the dictator personally, tended to encourage nationalist susceptibilities.
Conflicts with France and Britain made the foreign immigrant vulnerable to the charge of collaborating with the national enemy, while he
was simultaneously suspected of partiality towards unitarians, whose
preference for foreign ideas and models was notorious. Popular hostility was aroused when the foreigner was thought to be exempt from national obligations such as conscription and forced loans. Some of the
principal collaborators of the regime were extreme nationalists. Propagandists insulted "gringos" and denounced aliens as enemies of creole
values and interests. Tomás Anchorena, relation and associate of Rosas
and like him strongly influenced by Hispanic values, an ultra-Catholic
who would have liked to restore the Inquisition, regarded all foreigners
as heretics, liberals, and thieves; he had particular contempt for lower-
class immigrants and the "foreign rabble," as he called them, and he
advocated rounding up any to be found in Buenos Aires, branding them,
and sending them into the interior. And he admonished Rosas, "The
excessive generosity which you have shown to the gringos makes me
very angry.[38]"

Many *rosistas* survived the fall of Rosas and kept alive the prejudice
and mythology surrounding foreigners for many years to come. Juan
María Torres complained to Mitre in 1862 that if foreigners continued to
enter Argentina in their present numbers, they would soon realize that
they were more numerous than the traditional ruling groups and would
end up by displacing them.[39] These were fantasies, but nationalism
feeds on phantoms as well as facts. At ground level mutual fears were
real enough, and Sarmiento himself envisaged a time when children of
the elite would compete unsuccessfully with the new Argentines.

One of the first violent manifestations against immigrants occurred
in 1854 in Paraná, capital of the Confederation.[40] A group of Italians,
some fifty in all, disembarked to have a night on the town, with money
advanced from the English agent of their colonizing company. They
split into groups in bars and taverns, and two revelers became separated
from their fellows to end up half drunk and singing in the street; there
they encountered a police patrol of five men, who ordered them to be

quiet. The Italians ignored the order, perhaps not understanding the language, and continued singing in spite of further warnings. They were then seized by the police and threatened with jail, but they resisted arrest, and the noise of the affray brought to the scene other Italians, who surrounded the police and demanded they release the prisoners. The police reacted by taking out their swords and viciously attacking the crowd. An Italian with a knife killed one of the police, but the rest of the group were too unnerved by the bloodshed to respond. More Italians arrived, but also more police and military; these dragged Italians from the bars and with club and sword beat and slashed them, finally herding them into jail. When the count was taken next morning, five Italians had been killed and nine wounded, and one policeman was dead.

The rest of the Italians, who had remained on board, were outraged when they heard of the atrocity against their compatriots and were only held in check by the British agents of the colonizing company supported by a British warship in the port. The immigrants had received not a welcome but a warning that law and order were scarce commodities in Argentina and that a hatred of foreigners lurked not far below the surface. The carnage was obviously a setback for immigration and for the reputation of Justo José de Urquiza, its patron. The incident contained a number of features that British envoys and emigration officials were to hold against Argentina throughout the following twenty years: the absence or inertia of the police in face of real criminals and, when the police were present, their failure to apply the law if it meant favoring foreigners against nationals. The outrage was also, for the moment, a lesson to the rival government in Buenos Aires, as distinct from that of Urquiza in Paraná. As a report on the incident to the governor of Buenos Aires made clear: "On account of this the Government of the State of Buenos Aires, acting wisely and profiting from experience, resists all temptations to contract for immigrants and to acquire ill-considered obligations which turn out to be difficult if not impossible to fulfil."[41]

The government of course never prohibited immigration, nor was it able to eliminate abuses. Latent tensions surfaced whenever there was competition for power or resources. Azul was the scene of confrontation in 1856, when an agricultural colony established along military lines by Colonel Silvio Oliveira, an Italian army officer, erupted in violence. Oliveira named his colony New Rome and included in it Argentines as well as Italians, a recipe for disorder. In August 1856 he imprisoned sixteen Argentines in a cave which served as the colony's jail. When negotiations failed, more natives rebelled, killed the colonel, and freed their compatriots.[42]

In the popular mind immigrants carried disease as well as subversion. They were blamed for epidemics, and natives backed away from them as from the plague. The principal epidemic was smallpox, which in 1861–62 became endemic in the countryside; from 1867 deaths from smallpox rose, reaching 3,271 in 1871. Other diseases such as cholera and yellow fever were also killers, though their effects were felt mainly in the city of Buenos Aires. The yellow fever epidemic of 1871 closed offices and workplaces throughout the urban area and confined the majority of people to their homes. The chaplain to the British legation, the Reverend T. E. Ash, wrote a pamphlet on the epidemic; he calculated that it started in January and climaxed in April, killing some twenty-six thousand people, including about six hundred Britons.[43] These epidemics were linked in the public mind with the increase of immigrants, and they played their part in stirring rural rebellion. There were moves to stop the arrival of foreigners in Buenos Aires and to encourage those who came to move on into the countryside. This only created further problems, for the rural infrastructure was not ready to receive them, and the unpopularity of foreigners increased.

One of the complaints most frequently voiced against foreigners, and invariably accepted as valid by later historians, was that they were exempt from military service and did nothing to protect the frontier. This was not entirely true, for foreigners could be persuaded to take the place of natives for a price. The commander of the southern frontier complained to the Ministry of War and Navy in 1872 that he had been sent far too many foreigners for frontier service in the National Guard:

> Half of the men in my forces are foreigners (Neapolitans), who are completely useless for service on the frontier, for half of them are sick and none of them are capable of mounting a horse.
> I have complained about this deficiency to the Sub-Inspector of the South, who has replied that the Provincial Government cannot deny the right of citizens to nominate a proxy to do their service.
> Meanwhile, the units made up of these types are a liability on the frontier. In the event of rapid advance it is necessary to leave the foreigners in the forts, because they are incapable of keeping up with a column at full gallop, and they invariably render the horses they are riding ineffective, because they have not the slightest idea how to saddle them.[44]

Attempts were made to coerce British settlers. In June 1872 two Britons near Fraile Muerto were arrested for being in possession of cattle which did not belong to them. They were given the choice of a fine or two years' service in the frontier forces. They alleged irregularities in their trial. The British minister intervened and arranged for the fine to be paid, making the point that their "crime" was a common occurrence, an attempt to recoup something from the havoc wrought by successive Indian raids.[45] British settlers normally refused to submit to service in Argentine units, though they were willing to organize their own groups of volunteer or vigilante forces in frontier or lawless territory.

Life among Argentines, therefore, was hard for immigrants, who were caught between unyielding *estancieros* and unfriendly gauchos. Many were victims of popular resentment as waves of xenophobia, often expressed in physical harassment and violence, made daily existence dangerous in the "camp." Throughout the 1860s foreign criticism of the treatment of immigrants, emanating from the press and consulates of Buenos Aires, was too insistent to ignore.[46] The massacre of Tandil, following a series of lesser outrages, was exceptional only in its ferocity, its concentrated cruelty, and its organization by a large band of outlaws. Death on the pampas was a serial, not a singular, outrage. Yet it has been argued that these atrocities were exceptional and that most cases of violence against foreigners could be attributed to local officials, who did not select their victims exclusively among immigrants but among the lower classes of the countryside in general, where immigrants were most likely to be found. It is further claimed that diplomatic intervention over Tandil and other cases of violence caused the federal government to concede more attention to foreign than to Argentine victims.[47] The arguments are not convincing, and the evidence, at least that from the British consuls, points the other way. The majority of immigrants soon climbed above the lowest rung of rural society, a process which raised their profile and attracted their assailants. Nor is it clear that the Argentine government overreacted; on the contrary, it tended to repudiate foreign intervention and drag its feet over British complaints.

While at the popular level immigrants felt the force of native hostility in violence and terror, some of them also suffered from economic pressure from Argentine landowners. Cattle ranchers still dominated the countryside of Buenos Aires province, challenged but not displaced by the increase of sheep farmers. Agriculturalists were the weakest group of producers, with smaller holdings, fewer rights, and less protection from the government than other rural interests. Their commonest complaint was the intrusion of cattle into their arable land. In Tandil in 1869 a conflict flared between a number of immigrant farmers and neighboring *hacendados*. The justice of the peace, Juan Antonio Figueroa, who had been appointed in spite of his exclusion from the municipal short list, was an *estanciero*, linked by kinship to the Gómez

family and through them to Colonel Benito Machado, the frontier commander. Figueroa did not disguise his bias towards the *estancia* elite,
with whom he also shared political affiliation to the *mitristas*. The
Danish immigrant Juan Fugl, who as a local councillor had already
crossed swords with Figueroa, assumed the defense of the farmers, foreigners as well as natives, and took the case to the provincial authorities. There it disappeared without action on the part of the government.[48] Immigrants could be excused for concluding that there was
collusion among the local elites in defense of their political and social
supremacy. Conditions favored them; as Argentine nationality was a
requisite for voting, it was not surprising that natives dominated local
politics. Moreover, the traditional structure of rural life was too rigid
to allow foreigners easy entry into the patron-client network.

In spite of the reflex reaction of traditional families against new ar-
rivals, local government posts were not entirely closed to immigrants,
some of whom managed to integrate into the local community at a
minor level. In Tandil it was notorious that the same group of people
invariably appeared in key public offices—Ciriaco and Ramón Gómez,
Juan Antonio Figueroa, Carlos and Juan Carlos Díaz—all members of
old creole families. Nevertheless, from the 1850s foreigners such as
Ramón Santamarina, J. M. Dhers, and Juan Fugl participated actively in
municipal affairs, proving perhaps that immigrants could pass for established leaders as long as they had achieved some economic status.
They could not challenge the elite's control of municipal government
and the informal channels of power, and they had no hope of becoming
justices of the peace, but they benefited from reform of the system during the process of national organization. In 1854, *comisiones munici-
pales* were established; these consisted of four members elected by native inhabitants of the municipality and were presided over by the
justice of the peace. One of their functions was to propose a *terna* (short
list of three) from which the provincial government appointed the justice. Towards the end of the decade the commission became a *corporación municipal*, and foreigners were allowed to vote for members
(though not to be a member) if they had two years' residence in Argentina and one year's in the municipality. These were the rules, but
the informal process was often more decisive, and it did not exclude
Fugl and others. When Fugl arrived in Tandil in 1848 he depended on
the good will of the local authorities. By 1850, in spite of municipal law,
he was an active member of the *comisión municipal*, specializing in the
promotion of primary education, transport, land distribution, and religious affairs. But Fugl was an exception. Foreign participation in municipal government was small; the town hall continued to be domi-

nated by native Argentines. Immigrants had to be wealthy and successful before socioeconomic status would take precedence over national origins as a determinant of political power.

Modest political progress could draw attention to the immigrant, and this in itself might be risky. But there was another layer of protection to be found in personal relations. Marriage ties were possible: a niece of Ramón Gómez, a man presumed to be implicated in the events of 1872, was married to Emilio Delpech, a prosperous wool merchant from France and purchaser of land in Tandil.[49] At a popular level feelings of mutual respect could overcome ingrained suspicion, even in the massacre of 1872. One of the gaucho band, Melchor Miranda, had worked on the farm of a Danish miller, Pedro Nielsen, and got on well with Danes. Miranda was specially appointed to begin the slaughter of the Danish community. On the night of 31 December he went to Nielsen's house, and after loitering rather shamefacedly he left without saying a word. He then got helplessly drunk and was incapable of acting the next morning, with the result that the Danes were saved.[50]

Argentina was not the only country in the Americas to experience a nativist backlash against immigrants. During the rise of mass immigration in the United States, 1815–65, when migration was seen as a safety valve for the Old World and a necessary addition to the New, there were also warnings against the menace of foreign influence and outbreaks of burnings and killings.[51] But 1 January 1872 in Tandil was unique in many ways, a day to remember. British opinion in Buenos Aires had no doubt that this was primarily an act of terrorism against foreigners. "If there be any truth in the doctrine of metempsychosis, the soul of the Sepoy has passed into the mortal coil of the Tandil gaucho. The Sepoys of Tandil have risen to murder the foreigner. His blood alone can slake the thirst of gaucho fanaticism."[52] In less dramatic language Consul Frank Parish reported to the British government on the gauchos' "natural aversion to the foreigner, to whom they have to give place as civilization advances in their country."[53]

4

Massacre at Tandil

DIVINE DOCTOR

In November 1871 the townspeople and settlers of Tandil became aware of a stranger in their midst, a *curandero*, or folk doctor, called Gerónimo de Solané. His past was vague, no doubt by intent, and he had only recently come to the southern frontier. But his powers of healing and prophecy seemed real enough to the people of the countryside, and they were soon persuaded that a new Messiah was among them.

Solané's vocation was common in rural Argentina, and as a *curandero* he practiced medicine and other mysteries, reassured people, gave warnings of dangers and promises of better things. He was a more imposing figure than most of his type and became widely known as Tata Dios (Father God) or Médico Dios (Doctor God). Many people thought of him as tomorrow's savior as well as today's healer. Others saw him as a charlatan. To middle-class thinking he was "one of those folk healers who unfortunately plague our countryside, and his followers make him out to be a prophet."[1] He looked like a prophet. Aged about 45–50, he was tall and dark complexioned, with a penetrating gaze, a white beard, and long, lank hair. His full-length pampa poncho added to his stature as he moved majestically among his followers, taciturn, rapt in thought, and extending his hand to be kissed. His cures consisted largely of laying on of hands, reassuring words, and hypnotic gestures rather than traditional medicine and treatment, though these were not excluded, usually taking the form of herbal remedies. He charged nothing, asking only that his patients make offerings to the Virgin of Luján, whose statue he kept in his room. Inevitably tales circulated of his magic powers and his ability to improve nature as well as men; others thought that his extraordinary knowledge of prospective patients was derived from information gathered in advance by his aides.

Solané's background was obscure, and he was variously held to be a Bolivian, a Chilean—a "Chilean Zambo" according to *The Standard*—

or from the interior of Argentina. It was also rumored, more credibly, that he came from Entre Ríos and had been expelled from that province as a troublemaker and for stirring up hatred of foreigners. More immediately he had lived in Tapalquén, and before settling in Tandil he had spent some time in Azul, where his activities gained popular acclaim but official disapproval. The authorities harassed him for practicing medicine without a license and jailed him in early November 1871. According to the report of the police doctor, Alejandro Brid, "He is committing scandalous abuses, not only by practicing medicine illegally but also by encouraging superstitious beliefs and deceiving ignorant people, who unfortunately comprise the majority of those living in the countryside."[2] Solané appeared before the magistrates of Azul and stated in his defense that he provided remedies for those who came to seek them, but he did not claim to be a qualified doctor; he added that he did not charge fees, but his patients left small contributions in honor of the Virgin of Luján, which he distributed "in expenses and grants to the poor who came for cures." He also admitted that he was virtually illiterate, being able to read a little but not to write. His defense appeared convincing, and there were protests that he was unjustly imprisoned; he had to restrain some of his followers from offering resistance to the authorities. The justice of the peace in Azul, Botana, strongly criticized Dr. Brid for making groundless accusations, and Solané was released.

From Azul, Solané went to Tandil, apparently at the invitation of Ramón Rufo Gómez, who sought him out because his wife wanted treatment for headaches. His new patron, a member of the well-known Gómez family and brother-in-law of the justice of the peace, allowed the *curandero* to settle on his *estancia* La Argentina next to the Chapar store and in mid-November allotted him the work station La Rufina as his base. His presence on an *estancia* of the Gómez family would later raise the suspicion that he was protected by *estancieros* and partner in a conspiratorial movement. Meanwhile, with three assistants he established himself at La Rufina, which became part clinic for his patients and part camp for some fifty followers. There he worked miraculous cures, communicated with the spirits, and prophesied events. By late November 1871 he was attracting crowds of men and women variously estimated at two hundred, four hundred, or five hundred, some traveling from Azul, Tapalquén, and Arenales and some from Tandil itself.[3] He appeared to magnetize the countryside. As horses, carriages, and bullock carts came and went, tents and shelters appeared, and people set up camp in the vicinity, La Rufina came to resemble a place of pilgrimage or a mass meeting.

Did Solané plan these developments? Was he deliberately creating a following, inciting fanaticism, and encouraging devotees to call him Tata Dios and Médico Dios? Why did so many people gather around him? According to his assistants and his protector, Gómez, the reason was no more sinister than a search for help and cures. Gómez found nothing suspicious in the behavior of the crowds; he had heard no one say that Solané was divine, but "among country folk he was regarded as a holy man and a person of mystery."[4] Even so, the numbers seemed excessive, and he appeared to be gaining some kind of ascendancy over the multitude. Neighboring landowners became alarmed and complained about the crowds, and eventually, after two months, Justice of the Peace Figueroa ordered the *curandero* to close his establishment, suspend his activities, and disperse his followers. Solané complied with the order, though he continued to treat individual patients who came for further care. Figueroa reported: "The success, more or less, of his remedies and the apparently organized propaganda on behalf of this man had brought together for about two months a sizeable crowd of people, men and women. As soon as I knew, I ordered them to leave, and the local alcalde saw that they did; at the same time I forbade further gatherings. My order was obeyed. Solané continued to live in one of the quarters of this district and treated only a few country people who came to him with their complaints."[5]

Solané, therefore, gave an impression of reason and compliance, and for the moment the authorities were satisfied. His patron Gómez saw him as a person with strong ideas but not a man of violence: "I occasionally heard him speak of foreigners, saying that he did not like them because they exploited the country; as for the Masons they were an evil society who had no religion. But I never heard him say that they should be killed or incite anyone to do so."

According to another witness, people went to Solané for cures, not for conspiracy; he did not claim to be a saint or divine, but he accepted the popular titles of San Gerónimo and Tata Dios and allowed people to kiss his hand: "Only once did I hear him speak in general terms of foreign immigration, when he said that it took work from the Argentines; the occasion was a visit he made to treat two foreigners. I never heard him say that foreigners and Masons ought to be killed."[6]

The judicial inquiry, when it came, was slipshod, and vital evidence was allowed to pass without comment. An *estanciero*, Faustino Lara, claimed to have seen a written proclamation attributed to, but not signed by, Solané "in which the people of Tandil were told to mend their ways, and it was said that the enemies of religion were the foreigners and Masons, who ought to be punished." The judge accepted the evidence, which was not produced, in spite of the fact that Solané was well known to be unable to write.[7]

Many distant observers in Buenos Aires jumped to the conclusion that Solané was the author of rural unrest and the prime cause of Tandil's tragedy. "The bloody drama of Tandil had its roots in the brutal exploitation of ignorant countrymen by a perverse individual. . . . There is no idea what his objective was unless it was to rob the nearby towns and then join up with hostile Indians."[8] But beyond his outward appearance Solané was not an outstanding figure capable of raising a rebellion. He lacked distinction of character and personality. In addition to his vocation of *curandero*, he expressed a few crude political ideas common to many Argentines, including the elites and the clergy. But his presence in Tandil, if not conspiratorial, raised some questions. Did he use his gatherings and contacts to preach against foreigners and Masons? Justice of the Peace Figueroa alleged that he had "fanaticized" the masses and persuaded them that he was a superior being, thus constituting a threat to "the basis of our social organization."[9] Was this confirmed by other evidence? Witnesses testified that he railed against Freemasons and denounced them as irreligious; he also criticized foreigners and blamed them for unemployment and epidemics. But no one said he advocated violence or issued calls to arms.

As the end of 1871 approached, his utterances, as reported by his henchmen Jacinto Pérez and Cruz Gutiérrez, became more apocalyptic. He foretold sensational events: the guilty would die, prisoners would be freed, Tandil would suffer a catastrophic storm, and the people would drown in a great flood. From the hills a new people would rise to exterminate the enemies of God, the foreigners and Masons, and heaven would punish those who did not partake of this holy work. These rantings were relayed by his principal assistant, Jacinto Pérez, a man more violent than his master, a wild gaucho who called himself San Francisco and San Jacinto el Adivino (the Fortune-Teller).

In the last days of December 1871, Pérez and his accomplices scoured the countryside for recruits, quietly calling a meeting for the night of 31 December. Over forty people assembled in a place called the "rancho Peñalverde," where Pérez lived with his wife; they were a mixture of rural types—peons, gauchos, vagrants—some of whom had done frontier service in the National Guard and were known in the community and to each other. The mood induced by Pérez was menacing. Claiming to speak in the name of Solané, who had come to bring happiness to the people, Pérez harangued the group, predicting the end of Tandil's world and a last judgment, after which a new settlement would rise in that very place. He called on "men of good faith" to unite against the forces of evil and exterminate the enemies of God and religion. He gave out scarlet ribbons for their hatbands, raised a red and white flag, distributed rudimentary arms—lances made of metal-tipped bamboo, knives, sabers, and carbines—and with cries of "Long live religion!" "Death to Masons!" and "Kill gringos and Basques!" he urged the band into action.[10]

THE KILLING TRAIL

Tandil was a small hillside town situated near a river with numerous waterfalls shaded by willows and poplars and powering flour mills. The houses were solid but stark; single-story and mostly built of bricks and whitewashed, they had flat roofs, though some were thatched or roofed with tiles or zinc. The town contained a full range of trades—smithies, carpenters, and coach works—most of which belonged to French, Italian, and English owners. It had a church, a hotel, and a bank, but otherwise there were few services or amenities.

In the early hours of New Year's Day, while the town was still asleep, the rebels entered Tandil, encountered neither guards nor police, and promptly occupied and sealed off the main square. Meanwhile, a smaller detachment broke into the guardroom of the courthouse in search of more arms, spared the unresisting sergeant and guards, all native Argentines, and freed and recruited the only prisoner, an Indian named Nicolás Oliveira, before rejoining the main group. Amidst great clamor and shouting, like "a horde of savages," according to one observer, the whole band of forty-five to fifty men rode out of town, pausing only to deal what proved to be a mortal blow to the head of an Italian, a forty-five-year-old musician out for the New Year who happened to be crossing the square as they left.[11] They then took the Buenos Aires road northwards into flat, open country.

About a mile from town they encountered two troops of bullock carts owned by Domingo Lasalle and Esteban Vidart and surprised their drivers as they slept. They killed nine of these, including Vidart, all Basques, lancing, stabbing, and cutting throats, and they mortally wounded three others. Still moving northwards, they came to a store owned by another Basque, Vicente Leanes, who desperately tried to shut his door on them. But they burst through and shot him and his servant, the son of an Italian; his young wife, Tomasa, an Argentine, they spared.

The gaucho band next came to the *estancia* of Henry Thompson, a British establishment containing a country store owned by a recently married Scottish couple, William Gibson Smith, aged twenty-five, and his wife, Helen Watt Brown, aged twenty-three. Their assistant, William Stirling, also a Scot, heard the horses coming up and on opening the door of the store was immediately shot down and stabbed and his throat was cut; he died of his wounds six days later. Meanwhile Smith and his wife, alerted by the noise, fled out the back window, hoping to make their escape into the countryside. They were overtaken a short distance from the house and killed in a frenzy of violence: both had their throats cut and received several stabs to their bodies.[12] All these assaults were accompanied by robbing and looting.

The assassin band then rode on to the business premises of Juan Chapar, which they reached sometime before 10:00 a.m., six hours after the attack on the courthouse. Chapar, or Chaparro, was a thirty-four-year-old French Basque, a storekeeper well known in the locality. Facing the intruders in his corral, he dropped his guard when they claimed they only wanted to change horses for a murder hunt; they then surrounded him, overcame his resistance, and speared him to death. The assassins turned on the rest of the family. They killed two daughters aged four and five and a five-month-old son, pulled from the arms of his screaming mother before she herself was killed; all had their throats cut, and the five-year-old was shot. A number of employees and retainers, too, were killed, including a girl of sixteen; they forced her legs apart, raped her, and cut her throat. Some passing customers and travelers who found themselves in the wrong place at the wrong time were comprehensively slaughtered. The Chapar killings totaled eighteen men, women, and children, of whom fourteen had their throats cut, their heads almost completely severed; two were shot. One of the victims was first tied to a cartwheel before his throat was cut. The Indian Oliveira excelled himself as a killer, racing after a victim who tried to escape on horseback, pulling him down, and knifing him. The assassinations concluded with four more killings, bringing the total number in the morning's rampage to thirty-three. The raiders then sacked and robbed the house of its merchandise and destroyed the store's account book with its vital record of debts.[13]

Leaving the *pulpería*, the raiders turned towards the *estancia* of Ramón Santamarina, the wealthy Basque immigrant whose execution would be the climax of the operation. Finding no sign of their prey, they paused to take maté and change horses. Behind them they left a trail stained by the blood of thirty-six bodies: sixteen French, ten Spanish, three British, two Italians, and a number of Argentines, victims of mistaken identity.

Pursuit and Capture

News of these gruesome events began to filter back to Tandil within an hour or so of the first outrages. The justice of the peace had already been alerted by the sergeant of the guard while the outlaws were still in town and had heard their noisy exit. He knew something was seriously wrong when he was brought the wallet of the stricken Italian.

Figueroa then sounded the alarm on bells and drums, aroused the sleeping citizens, and posted armed men in defensive positions. By 5:00 a.m. José Ciriaco Gómez, commander of the National Guard at Tandil, was leading a troop of guardsmen and other citizens in pursuit of the assassins, following the tracks left by the corpses of drivers and store-keepers, Britons and Basques. The posse increased to thirty with further reinforcements from the National Guard, and at 10:00 a.m. they caught up with the killers, then numbering thirty-two, at the *estancia* of Santamarina. Gómez was a typical frontier officer who shot first and asked questions afterwards. One of the bandit leaders tried to explain, "We are killing gringos," and seemed to expect negotiations. But in a brief and clumsy encounter violence prevailed. "Kill them! Kill them!" shouted Gómez as he urged his troop into action. The assassins charged at the posse and opened fire. They then made good their escape in the direction of Chapalcotú, leaving ten of their comrades dead and eight captured.[14] Among the dead was the leader, Jacinto Pérez, while his second-in-command, Cruz Gutiérrez, was taken prisoner. Search parties were dispatched into the countryside and sierra; on 13 January two escapees were taken, one in Tres Arroyos and the other in Juárez.[15] Meanwhile, just as the bodies of the Chapar family arrived in Tandil, the prisoners were escorted into town and had to be protected from the fury of the mob before being jailed. Soon, those suspected of involvement numbered twenty-eight in all.

Among the men arrested was Solané, yet he had taken no part in the action and denied all knowledge of it. The first he knew of these events was on arrival at his clinic at La Rufina in the early morning of 1 January, when he was told that an assassin band was invoking his name. In a confrontation with officials he showed shock and dismay and was taken into custody under protest.[16] By now foreigners were adopting measures of self-defense and, lacking confidence in the justice of the peace, insisted on mounting guard at the jail. They were convinced that Figueroa was partial to the assassins and might be tempted to free them, especially Solané, who, though not actively involved, presumably knew more than he was saying. Figueroa reported to Buenos Aires, "I have him in my power, shackled and guarded."[17] It was an empty boast. Solané refused to make a statement until a senior judge took over the case. In fact he never testified. Five days later, on the night of 5 January, he was found shot in his cell in mysterious circumstances, having remained silent on the whole affair. Some believed that the justice of the peace was the assassin. But this was not the only view, as Fugl explained: "Others were convinced that the foreigners were the killers out of fear that the one most guilty of the assassinations would be freed. This seems to be the truth, according to the account of one of my closest friends."[18]

The judicial process was promptly begun and rapidly concluded. Dr. Tomás Isla, judge of the supreme court of the province, was appointed by the provincial government to conduct the trial and inquire into the conduct of local officials. Isla took the first statements on 17 January and pronounced sentences on 7 February. The trial was concerned only to establish guilt, not to investigate causes, so the evidence was narrowly focused. Insofar as responsibility was established, it was all laid on Solané; the wider context was ignored, motivation left obscure, social and economic background unexplained. Even as a judicial process the investigation was hurried and careless; suspicion remained that there had been a cover-up over the Chapar account books with their lists of debtors. These were official documents as well as private records, but they either were destroyed or went missing before or after the arrests. One prisoner, Juan Villalba, died in prison on 14 May of wounds received at the time of capture. Before his death the authorities had intercepted a letter to his wife showing that the criminals had made a plan of escape, taking advantage of the fewness of the guards.[19] In any event, justice was spared this particular embarrassment. Of the twenty-nine brought before the court, three—Cruz Gutiérrez, Esteban Lasarte, and Juan Villalba—were condemned to death; seven were sentenced to fifteen years' imprisonment, two to three years' imprisonment, and two to one year's.[20] The remaining fifteen were acquitted.

An appeal to the Supreme Court was allowed, and Dr. Martín Aguirre, a Uruguayan lawyer practicing in Argentina, was appointed defense attorney, funded from legal aid. He never met his clients, though he spoke eloquently on their behalf.[21] The appeal failed, and the Supreme Court confirmed the sentences on 29 August 1872. The death sentences were carried out on 13 September, when the two surviving guilty, Cruz Gutiérrez and Esteban Lasarte, were executed by firing squad in the square of Tandil. "The plaza was full, about 800 people, and natives of the country were notable by their absence."[22]

The Supreme Court stressed the need for condign punishment, "above all at the present time when unfortunately crimes of this kind are committed all too frequently."[23] Whether the investigation or the sentences satisfied these sentiments was a matter of dispute then and since. Many foreigners cited the trial as further evidence that the Argentine authorities were by European standards soft on crime. The massacre ended in a confused encounter during which ten bandits were killed and some twenty escaped. The commander of the National Guard felt obliged to explain not why twenty bandits had escaped, but why ten had been killed: "It was necessary to take the offensive and act in this way because of the horrible murders they had committed."[24] The judicial authorities were more lenient. Of the original forty-five to fifty bandits only fourteen received sentences, while five were acquitted.

The virtual immunity granted to local officials was the subject of much comment, and the upper classes of Tandil were spared the embarrassment of even being called as witnesses. Local British opinion was convinced that the trial was a cover-up. "It is notorious that Judge Isla has exculpated the *Juez de la Paz* and Alcalde Gómez even though the late Medico had gathered around him for 4 months great crowds of over 400—the scum of the district—on Alcalde Gómez's farm. . . . Gómez gave his permission for this on 8th December 1871, [and] the *Juez de la Paz* ordered Gómez to disperse these gatherings, which he said he would do on January 1st, the very day the massacre took place."[25] These allegations were not entirely accurate, but they pointed to matters of public concern which were not ventilated in court. The Danish community leader Juan Fugl was also convinced that there had been a whitewash. The massacre, he wrote, "was done with the knowledge and consent of Justice Figueroa." As for Solané, he was protected by Figueroa and Ramón Gómez, who planned to use him in their campaign to harass foreigners and halt immigration.[26]

The justice of the peace reported to the provincial government in a long-winded, pompous, and self-justificatory missive, dated 2 January, which gave his version of events and his own actions. Before this reached Buenos Aires, the provincial government knew unofficially of the massacre—"by a band of outlaws numbering more than fifty persons"—and the information was immediately circulated around the various departments. Minister of the Interior Antonio E. Malaver promptly ordered the local units of the National Guard to be called up to improve security and pursue the outlaws.[27] Malaver instructed Juan L. Somoza, subinspector of the National Guard in the south, to assist the local authorities in their search for the criminals and, in the name of the government, to urge the justice of the peace to initiate legal action before the criminal court of the department of the south as soon as possible. At the same time, the Supreme Court was alerted. The provincial government was evidently worried by the perceived inertia of Figueroa and intervened to raise its own profile and rally local officials.[28] On 5 January, Malaver sent the justice of the peace of Tandil a rebuke for his silence and ordered an immediate report on events and on the measures taken. The government was anxious above all lest the massacre have a demoralizing effect on the local population and noted that many families were already threatening to leave. In the age of migration depopulation was the last thing the Argentine government wanted.

By this time the press in Buenos Aires was also reporting the atrocity. Newspaper accounts were not objective, nor were they based on verifiable evidence. The Argentine press was strongly influenced by patrons and proprietors, and its pages were vehicles of opinion, not of record. Each newspaper had a political position which colored its reporting of Tandil. *La Nación* was the voice of *mitrismo; La Tribuna* of *porteño* autonomism and support for the national policy of Sarmiento; *El Nacional* of the minister of the interior, Vélez Sarsfield; and *La Prensa* of the opposition to Mitre. Only *La República* preserved a shred of independence and support for political principles, though its reporting was not uniformly objective. Outside the Argentine media stood *The Standard*, a high-quality English-language daily founded by Michael G. Mulhall in 1861, a British voice certainly and one which stood on the British side of Anglo-Argentine relations, though normally from a reasoned position. On the subject of the massacre the Argentine press sought to explain and blame rather than inform. Three trends can be observed. First, the massacre was viewed according to the political bias of individual newspapers. Second, in the search for causation writers targeted the Church and the clergy and blamed rural violence on ignorance and fanaticism. Third, the press produced evidence to show the unpopularity of the frontier defense system among the rural population and cited social conditions in the countryside as the principal source of violence and disorder.

It is not surprising if the press, and public opinion in general, were confused about Tandil. Once the event was over, there was little further evidence, and none from the government side. As for the rebels, they issued no statements, wrote no memoirs, and left nothing in writing.

INCITER OR INNOCENT?

The massacre was a mystery. The trail of killings could be traced and the corpses identified, but the causes were confused and the authors remained in the shadows. Agrarian structure could be invoked and rural discontents linked to social and economic conditions. Tandil was part of a regional economy that favored *estancias*, and its people were divided by class, culture, and national origins. But the actions of the assassins, while no doubt conditioned by their environment, did not conform precisely to social and economic imperatives, nor was their attack an obvious reaction to oppression. It is a moot point whether crime rates increase under growth or under recession. In any case this was no ordinary crime, a mere stage in serial statistics, even if these existed. Whatever the role of Solané, a *curandero*'s vocation functioned outside the limits of the regional economy. Structural conditions and the rural situation were not enough in themselves to explain the actions of his followers, the collective violence, the targets chosen, and the discourse of the actors. The killers did not kill officials. They did not molest *estancieros*. They did not harass the native poor. If disorder originated in social divisions, how can we explain these priorities? If indiscriminate militia levies were the cause of the revolt, why were officials, and above all the justice of the peace, not targeted by the assassins? If agrarian change marginalized a large part of the rural population, rewarded some and penalized others, why was the violence not directed at the winners?

The structural argument is relevant in explaining gaucho conditions but not sufficient in itself to pinpoint immediate motivation or the dominant desire on the fatal day. Immigration was the irreducible factor, the foreigner the focus. The prime targets seem to have been the Chapar store and the Santamarina *estancia*, the secondary objective to kill known foreigners on the way. The itinerary is the clue to the motive: it was a nativist rising. This still leaves the question of responsibility. Who conceived the crime? Were the healer and his henchmen the guilty men?

Solané denied all knowledge and responsibility for the massacre. On the morning of 1 January he attended his clinic at La Rufina and heard of an assault by some men who said they were acting in his name. This disturbed him, and he immediately returned to the *estancia* La Argentina. When the bandits were confronted, and before they were attacked, one of the leaders, Sergeant Rodríguez, came forward and declared that the killings had been done on the orders of Médico Dios, who had ordered them to finish with the foreign Masons; they had no quarrel with the posse, who were Argentines. Solané denounced this statement as a lie and denied that he had ordered any killings. Various witnesses testified to his shock and distress on hearing of the assassinations. Yet, on the orders of Commandant Gómez, he was arrested along with the others and imprisoned in solitary confinement in the

Tandil jail, guarded by a unit of armed foreigners.[29] On the night of 5–6 January he was assassinated, shot three times through the window of his cell.

Investigation by the justice of the peace was perfunctory, and he found no evidence to identify specific assassins. This did not prevent him from airing his opinions on the *curandero*, and he had no hesitation in identifying him as the principal murderer:

> The origin of these unhappy events is attributed by public opinion to the iniquitous propaganda of one individual, the so-called Médico Dios. He has appeared in this district and attracted men and women from far and wide who have flocked to him in search of remedies which he has dispensed. . . . On the evidence of public opinion and of most of the criminals it is clear that Gerónimo G. de Solané, known as Médico Dios, took advantage of some people's ignorance and of the popularity which he was gaining among the unthinking masses and spread certain ideas with the intention of perverting religious beliefs and thus corrupting the basis of our social organization. In this way he gained ascendancy over a considerable number of people, whom he fanaticized to such an extent that they regarded him as a superhuman person.[30]

Figueroa's report need not be taken at face value. Most of it was hearsay, based not on evidence obtained from Solané himself, who refused to be interviewed, but on statements taken from those accused of the massacre. Most of the witnesses admitted that they had never spoken to Solané. Figueroa argued that many of the criminals now accused of the massacre had previously been of good character, working men and heads of families; this he took as proof that Solané had corrupted them.

These were not conclusive arguments, and the verdict on Solané remains unproven. His camp was not a place of conspiracy or rebellion or of hostility to any particular people. It was a place for the laying on of hands, for medicine and cures, for prayer and meditation, or, as the press of Buenos Aires would say, for superstition. Nevertheless, rumors of impending doom emanated from the camp; there was going to be a catastrophe, a flood, an epidemic, and these calamities were attributed to the presence of Masons and foreigners. Solané did not go around explicitly repeating these warnings, but the message was powerful, and people looked to his leadership for protection. He was a leader by selection rather than character; he had no angel tongue, and his discourse was not memorable enough to be recorded. On the other hand, while he presented no principles of action, he helped to create a climate of terror and unleashed a tiger which he could not control. He inaugurated a movement that started as revivalism and ended in massacre. In this sense he bore some responsibility for the events of 1 January 1872.

THE ASSASSINS

Who were the assassins? In the press and other organs of opinion they were variously called *bandidos, malhechores, bandas fanáticas, degolladores,* or simply *gauchos de caballería.* In fact, the majority were not hardened criminals or people with a history of delinquency. Two of them used pseudonyms, as though they had something to hide, and two had criminal records in other places. Marcos Barraza was a recent deserter from the frontier, and Francisco Rodríguez had been previously detained for causing an affray with menaces. As Tandil was a zone of recent settlement, it was not surprising that many of the bandits were natives of other places who had been attracted by opportunities for cattle work or agricultural labor during the harvest season. A few were farmers and foremen of *estancias.* The majority were plain characters from the most vulnerable sector of the rural population, heads of families whose income did not meet their obligations, and were thus ready recruits for action. Some had military experience, though this would not be exceptional in a society near the frontier and already semimilitarized since the days of Rosas. They had been brutalized and alienated by injustice and mistreatment, perhaps on an *estancia,* perhaps on the frontier. In their view immigrants lived a different life, one of immunity and privilege. To kill a few immigrants was not a great sin. Were the assassins, then, violent by nature, through experience, or as a result of the environment?

Violence was everywhere intrinsic to frontier culture and not exclusive to Argentina. In the United States, robbery, fistfights, and gunfights were daily events, and deaths from gunshot or knife wounds were frequent. Much of the violence on mining frontiers in California stemmed not from specific disputes over property claims or arguments between neighbors but from what has been described as "reckless bravado," an instant response to insults, challenges, or irritations, often encouraged by alcohol and the habit of carrying guns. Killings in frontier settlements and mining towns in the American West were endemic and usually treated as justifiable homicide, one delinquent killing another, while the majority of citizens went about their lawful business. But when innocent people were gunned down in cold blood or were the victims of attacks on stagecoaches and banks, then the local reaction was different, and the gunmen were pursued by the law or, where the law was deficient, by vigilantes. Vigilantes were regarded by local opinion in Nevada as "our best, most substantial and law-abiding citizens," who took the law into their own hands to rid the community of badmen and "to assert the right to self-preservation and the supremacy of natural law over defective statutory forms and tedious tribunals."[31]

In the United States there was a further level of conflict. Frontier communities were often divided by violent struggles for control of the local economy and in some cases lapsed into virtual civil war. A prime example was the Lincoln County War in New Mexico in the 1870s.[32] There an English entrepreneur was shot and killed by bandits backed by the sheriff, a scenario that proponents of conspiracy theories in Tandil would have readily understood. In other respects the dimension of conflict in New Mexico went far beyond the experience of the people of Tandil.

While the incidence of killing was greater on the North American frontier, the Argentine variety had a quality of its own. The distinctive feature was throat-cutting; this was the favored form of killing in Argentina and the most valued skill of the gaucho. Gauchos fought to display their masculinity, defend their honor, and claim a place in their social group.[33] The knife was the gaucho's weapon of choice and to cut a throat his delight, as Hudson recalled: "The people of the plains had developed an amazing philosophy, they loved to kill a man not with a bullet but in a manner to make them know and feel that they were really and truly killing."[34] In Tandil some of the victims of the assassins were almost decapitated. Sarmiento described decapitation as "another Argentine trait."[35] Inexplicable violence was inherent in the nature of the gaucho. In Indian territory at Leubucó, Colonel Mansilla met Rufino, a *gaucho malo* and well-known bandit:

"They say you are a thief, a rustler, a murderer."

"That's right."

"But what do you think?"

"I am not a bad man."

"What are you then?"

"I am a gaucho man" (*Soy hombre gaucho*).[36]

Gaucho morality was *sui generis* and gaucho violence a way of life, as Martín Fierro showed. Was the composite character of the Tandil band that of a Martín Fierro? Hernández admired but did not idolize the gaucho: his story was infused with realism as well as sympathy. Dragged from his home by the press gang, victimized on the Indian frontier, and outlawed by society, Fierro turns to the life of a deserter and criminal. At a dance he insults a black woman, compounds the outrage with racist remarks, and provokes a fight with her black boyfriend. Fierro knifes him; the victim kicks and twists a few times and then expires.

> Like a she-wolf there she began to howl
> When she saw her mate was dead.
> I had half a mind to give her a whack
> To make her shut her jowl.

The incident occurs in a moral vacuum, where reason and responsibility have no place. Fierro calmly departs, indifferent to the hatred he has aroused:

> I cleaned my knife on a clump of grass,
> I untethered my nag from the rail,
> I took my time to mount, and then,
> At a canter I hit the trail.[37]

Fierro could turn easily from innocent victim to callous killer. He seemed to need violence to retain some belief in himself; it was part of his identity and a way of expressing resistance to the world. Like Fierro, the assassins of Tandil acted as though their only defense against injustice, their only means of keeping some control over their lives, lay in violence and personal defiance, expressed with no sense of pity or remorse. Buried deep in their consciousness was the cult of the knife, brought to life at the call of a leader or the conviction of a wrong.

Was such a group representative? Would others in similar conditions—and there were many—behave in the same way? Possibly, given leadership and opportunity. But the fact remains, they did not do so. Does this mean that the bandits were exceptional? Only in their adoption of a final solution. In other respects they were representative of local society. Solané's horde of followers, the famous "400" attending his clinic, were rural people similar in type and motivation to the outlaws. This could be one reason why Solané was assassinated, in case his followers attempted to free him.

If the leadership of the outlaws was not exercised by Solané himself, then who provided it? In the judicial proceedings one name emerges in various statements, together with a number of henchmen. These were Jacinto Pérez, chief assistant to Solané, followed by María Pérez, lieutenant in the National Guard; Pedro Rodríguez, sergeant in the National Guard; and José María Trejo and Juan Molina, gauchos. Jacinto Pérez, Pedro Rodríguez, and Juan Molina were killed in the stand-off, while María Pérez and José María Trejo escaped without further trace. Vital evidence, therefore, was lost, and the trial itself disclosed little of the leaders and only a minimum of their action. There was no judicial investigation into Jacinto Pérez and his origins, activities, and links with Solané, nor was his wife questioned. The judge was seeking instant culprits, not wider motives. The story that emerged was simple and unadorned: for some days before 31 December there was talk of an impending catastrophe, of action against foreigners and Masons, and of a rendezvous in Jacinto Pérez's house. Pérez himself seemed to be known to a few of the band but by no means to all; even so, he was recognized as the leading actor in the events of New Year.

The subordinate members of the band were even more obscure than the leaders. Cruz Gutiérrez, whose real name was Crescencio Montiel, was described as forty years old, of Argentine nationality, with an open but threatening expression and the bitter look of a man who expected nothing from life. There is little doubt that he was one of the killers, being captured with his knife still gory and his clothes stained with the blood of his victims. Character witnesses described him as "an honest and hard-working peon." He was married with seven children, the eldest fourteen years old and the youngest seven months, and he had no previous convictions. According to his own testimony at the trial, he had never met Solané but had been recruited by Solané's assistant, Jacinto Pérez, El Adivino, and persuaded to attend a meeting on the night of 31 December at Peñalverde. There Jacinto had announced to the assembly "that they had come to fulfil the duties assigned to them by Tata Dios," and they would meet the following day to speak to the priest, the doctor, and other people. Next day they met in the plaza, but Jacinto made no attempt to arrange a meeting with the priest or with anyone else; instead, they attacked the courthouse and then took the road to Urraco under orders from Jacinto to kill foreigners. After the killings they made for the *estancia* La Argentina, where Jacinto said "they were going to seek the blessing of Tata Dios, who would distribute what they had seized." Gutiérrez swore that he had attended no other meetings, though there were always crowds in search of remedies at the home of Tata Dios on the Gómez estate.[38] At his execution Gutiérrez wept for his family but faced the firing squad defiantly: "This is how a poor Argentine gaucho dies."[39]

Esteban Lasarte, thirty-three years old, was described as "*simpático*" in appearance, with the bravery of a gaucho; other witnesses alleged he was covered in blood from the morning's killings. In the stand-off he fought desperately and was left for dead with five bayonet stabs and a bullet wound, but he recovered in prison. He was unmarried, a *peón de campo*, and he, too, had a reputation of an honest and hard-working man. He stated in evidence that while looking for a house in the country he had met some men and joined them on the way to a meeting organized by Jacinto, also known as "San Francisco." "Having given them all a scarlet ribbon for their hats—presumably so that they would all know each other, for he knew no other reason—he told them they were going to kill the Masons."[40] Lasarte denied knowing Solané or having any knowledge of previous meetings. At his execution he drank a glass of champagne and smoked a cigarette; he died impassively, refusing to be blindfolded and demanding to be buried only by "natives of the country, not by any Italian"—Argentine to the last.[41]

Pedro Torres was thirty-five years old, married, and employed as a ranch hand. He was sentenced to fifteen years as a participant in the massacre, but no proof was adduced that he had killed anyone. He stated that he was collected by a group of men on the night of 31 December and taken to a meeting at Peñalverde, where fifty people were assembled. On the following morning an older man whom he did not know organized them and distributed "a scarlet ribbon for their hats, telling them that with that sign they would have to win or die; he also told them that they were going to invade Tandil in order to kill the foreigners and the Masons." Torres, too, denied ever having spoken to Solané, though he had seen him at the house of Ramón Gómez and observed that he eventually became reluctant to give treatment or advice.[42] None of these men were criminal characters. Pedro Rodríguez, on the other hand, a sergeant in the National Guard, who was killed in the final encounter, had been previously charged with robbing a hacienda.

Most of the band were poor peons, many from the interior provinces, people whom Sarmiento would have regarded as barbarians. The age group seems to have been thirty to fifty, years when hope had turned to despair. Rural officials circulated descriptions of some of the escapees: Félix Juárez, black, bearded, aged forty-five to fifty, from Tucumán; Mario Pérez, tall, swarthy, with Indian features, aged fifty, from Córdoba; José María Trejo, short and stout, with Indian features, aged forty, from Santiago del Estero; Gerónimo Navarro, short, stout, flat-nosed, from Buenos Aires province; Leandro Quevedo, black, aged thirty, from Buenos Aires province.[43]

The paucity of information on the assassins led to the creation of conspiracy theories, some of them starting in the newspapers of Buenos Aires. *La Tribuna* used the opportunity to blame its political opponents and therefore attacked the *mitrista* appointees in the local government of Tandil, authorities who had welcomed Solané to the area and ignored the warnings of the danger posed by his large gatherings. And it was these officials—Commander Machado and Justice of the Peace Figueroa—who were cheered by the bandits. The newspaper also blamed the provincial governor, Emilio Castro, who was responsible for ill-appointed justices throughout the province.[44] This trail of evidence, continued *La Tribuna*, had led to speculation that the massacre was deliberate. The assassins were hired killers, manipulated by hidden hands among the landed and governing elite of Tandil. These were the real instigators of the massacre, the paymasters, who then turned denouncers, accusers, and judges. And having planned the operation, they had to take steps to conceal any contact with their agents and destroy all clues pointing to themselves. According to Teodoro Lezina, a resident of Tandil and witness to the assembly of the band: "About thirty to fifty country people on horseback had gathered in the plaza and from there proceeded to the courthouse, raising a red and white flag and shouting: 'Long live Machado and Figueroa, death to Masons and gringos!'"[45] The theory was plausible but lacked proof.

Rebels might feel the need for legitimacy and appeal to their own community leaders for support. But this does not prove the existence of a conspiracy. Enough outlaws escaped imprisonment and execution to make leaks of a conspiracy, had it existed, only too likely, but in fact no subsequent evidence emerged.

A Mob or a Movement?

The classic vigilante committee as it developed in the United States was an organized movement outside the law, intent on taking the law into its own hands. The group could consist of fifty to one hundred members and operate for a short period of time, perhaps weeks or months. It was normally a response to the absence of effective security in a frontier region. Pioneers acted on their own initiative to establish law and order in newly settled areas or to secure persons and property against outlaws and other marginal types.[46] In Lincoln County, New Mexico, so-called Regulators intervened to supply justice where the existing legal system was corrupt.[47] Because the prime object of vigilantism was to establish or restore the received values of society—property, law and order—vigilante movements were usually led by the frontier elite, either landowners or the judiciary itself or local businessmen, as in the case of the San Francisco Vigilance Committee of 1856.[48] In many cases they were a young elite, anxious to assert their leadership in a new community where traditional standards were threatened by lawless incomers and the law itself ignored the victims.

There were over three hundred vigilante movements in the United States, the majority in California, Montana, and Texas, and in the course of the nineteenth century vigilantes were responsible for seven hundred executions and thousands of corporal punishments. While the details of vigilantism varied from region to region, certain common features emerged. Vigilantes were prepared to use violence, they organized themselves with military precision and discipline, and they could count on noninterference by lawmen. They claimed a kind of legitimacy, tending to proceed not by instant killing but by trial, judgment, and execution by hanging. Vigilantism in its purest form was indigenous to the United States.

The southern frontier of Argentina had obvious similarities to the western frontier of the United States. Ineffective and corrupt local government, a weak criminal justice system, and inadequate military presence in support of government policy were notorious features of the Argentine south. But there were also differences. The Argentine frontier was a virtual desert; lacking the extensive mineral resources of the United States, it also lacked the violence and vigilantism characteristic of mining towns. An Argentine landowner could defend his property against Indians and Indianized gauchos by deploying his own peons or summoning the local militia, without the need of vigilantism. The nearest approach to the North American model was the response of British settlers to Indian attacks and gaucho violence. In the absence of government action they provided their own protection and organized mounted patrols from the British community. On the Bahía Blanca frontier, to the indignation of the Argentine authorities, they announced their readiness to use force to defend their property. At Fraile Muerto an English volunteer force could put thirty armed and mounted men in the field.[49]

The Argentine frontier, in spite of differences, was populated by many villains of the type targeted by vigilantes. But these were not the targets of the Tandil bandits. The band did not conform to the vigilante model. They were not a paramilitary group, intent on defending property and enforcing law and order in the absence of legitimate government. On the contrary, they attacked people who had broken no law and seized property whose ownership was not disputed; bandits of this kind were normally the objects of vigilante justice, not its authors. And unlike vigilante organization, the leadership of the Tandil band cannot be traced to the frontier elite unless the conspiracy theory of hidden direction is accepted.

Spanish America had its own informal enforcers. The bandit gang, assembled by a local strong man, driven by experience of injustice, living for booty, and operating alongside or outside rural communities, had a long history in Spanish America.[50] In the nineteenth century rural impoverishment, absence of a rural police force, and personal delinquency combined to keep bands of robbers and criminals in business. The Argentine south was a perfect frontier of settlement, where land and cattle were commercialized, communal usages eroded, and the gauchos pushed into poverty and peonage. These conditions encouraged the formation of bands organized for subsistence and plunder under natural leaders who assembled a client network and proved themselves by their success. The gauchos were historic victims of social conflict, outcastes in their own land, as the authorities enforced the interests of powerful ranchers, deprived the gauchos of traditional usages, conscripted them for Indian wars, and left them with few alternatives outside the *montoneras*.

The typical bandit of the southern pampas was a loner, and larger bands such as that of the Barrientos brothers, Pedro and Julio, who ambushed, robbed, and killed in the region of Tandil and Lobería, were the exception. A more heroic outlaw, at least in popular mythology, was Juan Moreira, who lived by the knife in defense of his rights and his family, fought with sheriffs, storekeepers, and anyone who insulted him, outstared politicians, and was finally cornered and cut down in the Star Hotel in Lobos.[51] But whatever the style, lone bandit or gang member, many gauchos turned to the life of the outlaw, often driven by a particular incident of injustice or oppression at the hands of the military or civil authorities. The Tandil bandits, however, did not belong to this tradition. The massacre at Tandil was committed neither by an established band under a local caudillo nor by a gathering of professional outlaws. It was mobilized exclusively for this particular action, to terrorize the foreigner.

The Tandil outlaws looked more like a lynch mob than a vigilante committee or a group of *bandidos*. Outlaws of this kind killed people by illegal group action; they applied an unofficial law to punish people who were perceived to be acting outside the norms of the community. Lynch law, like vigilantism, was an invention of the United States: it already existed in colonial America and was practiced in Virginia during the Revolution. The lynch mob, as identified in the American West, attacked rustlers, murderers, and other villains. After the Civil War, lynch mobs were active in the Southern states, where they attacked blacks for alleged murder, rapes, and lesser crimes, or for no crime at all but simply for being black. The lynch mob was an organized, spontaneous, ephemeral mob which came together briefly for a specific action and then broke up, as distinct from the more regular vigilante movements, which were engaged in systematic forms of law enforcement.[52] Southern lynching acquired its own ritual of torture, burning, and spectator attendance, features which were not reproduced in Argentina. Race hatred is by no means unknown in the history of modern Argentina, but it was not a prime motivation on the southern frontier. There men took the law into their own hands out of jealousy, revenge, sense of injustice, and other primitive urges. Reporting the case of a colonist in Santa Fe who lynched a man for killing his child, the British minister in Buenos Aires expressed his conviction that only lynching will stop the "murderous propensity of the gaucho."[53]

The Tandil band possessed rudimentary organization and a paramilitary formation. The band was assembled over a period of two days, chiefly by Jacinto Pérez; the command group included Pérez's immediate associates, José María Trejo and Juan Molina. Two others were also associated with the leadership because of their military rank in the National Guard: Sergeant Pedro Rodríguez and Lieutenant María Pérez. Jacinto Pérez, Trejo, and Molina had seen service some months previously in Fort Tres Arroyos, where Ramón and Ciriaco Gómez of the *estanciero* family were officers.

It would seem, therefore, that these were not a mysterious group, a band of men in hoods, appearing suddenly on the southern frontier. Some were well known to each other and in the local community. They were not a random collection of individuals. They had a group identity and were motivated by a common object. Under questioning at the trial, some claimed that they had been recruited by deceit and they were made to believe that it was done in the name of authority. Others declared that their reluctance was overcome by threat of divine punishment. Yet others pointed out that they had been unwilling to join, and Jacinto had accepted this. No one had been forced to participate. Collaboration had been sought by appeals to solidarity of interests and ideas.

Once assembled, the band was divided by Jacinto Pérez into three groups: one to occupy Tandil, the second to attack the courthouse, and the third to remain on the outskirts. The attack on the courthouse was well organized; the attackers burst in, demanded keys for the arms room and prison, and left without confrontation or violence. Meanwhile, another unit had occupied the square and blocked all entries. The various groups then united into a single column to search out their victims in the countryside. From that point violence was applied systematically and selectively. The band was not allowed to rampage indiscriminately, and the victims were not selected at random. As Justice Figueroa reported, the victims were foreigners: "Apart from the feeling of outrage caused by these unprecedented events, it is also unfortunately true that they have fallen only on persons of foreign nationality, who form the majority of the population in these parts."[54] He made two mistakes in one statement. Foreigners, while numerous, were by no means a majority of the population, and in the madness of that New Year morning a few Argentines were caught in the net. Nevertheless, Figueroa was more or less correct.

The assassins targeted foreigners, but not just any foreigners. It was an effective tactical decision to attack foreigners in the countryside, where they were isolated in small groups, rather than in the town, where they were concentrated and capable of resisting. As *The Standard* reported: "The Chilean hyena and his band of cut throats did not try to sack the town. . . . It might have been better had he tried because most of the artisans and hotel keepers are French and there is a large Basque population . . . ; these would have made short work of the villains had they dared anything of the kind. . . . But the Zambo was too cunning for this."[55]

Of the thirty-six victims, only one, Antonio Ledesma, could be positively identified as Argentine, though a few other natives may have been mistaken for foreigners. The bandits made efforts to distinguish between allies and enemies, and they refrained from killing anyone they recognized as a native. One of the Basques in the wagon train that was attacked hid under some hides in his wagon and heard the assassins shouting, "Kill them, they are gringos and Basques."[56] Then they robbed the victims. According to a witness, Honorio de la Canal, owner of a nearby *estancia*, he observed a band of horsemen—thirty-three in his estimate—making for the commercial house of Chapar, all wearing red ribbons on their hats. One came forward sword in hand to kill him, but another, called Rafael, stopped him with the words, "Don't kill that one, he is native of the country and I know him." The swordsman took him to Jacinto Pérez, who told the prisoner he could go: "We have orders from Médico Dios to kill only gringos and Masons."[57] Another witness, Avelino Coria, a peon of the wagon trains belonging to Antonio García camped next to Chapar, was approached by two of the rebels. One of them, known to him as María Pérez, told him, "Friend, your boss is dead," and the other said, "All the Masons are dead over there." The evidence, therefore, indicates a measure of control by the leadership; in a number of encounters the Argentine witnesses were not attacked. And at the end there was an apparent reluctance on the part of the bandits to fight with the posse that overtook them, because they were not seeking to kill their compatriots.

Was the action at Tandil confined to one corner of the southern province, or was there a wider dimension of protest? In the weeks before and after the massacre there were rumors of other movements in preparation or in being. Risings of Indians, preachings of *curanderos*, rebellions of gauchos, murmurings of malcontents—each had its report and its messenger.

The Tandil movement, it was said, had contacts in Luján, Cañuelas, and Zárate, where other *curanderos* were active, and Solané was known to have had dealings with the Indians. The press, too, speculated that the Tandil band would collaborate with other rural dissidents for rapine and robbery and then join up with hostile Indians.[58] Speculation was a measure of ignorance concerning rural security and bewilderment over events at Tandil. But it was also a sign of tension in the countryside and convulsive reactions in rural society. Government inquiries found no evidence of a general rebellion but failed to penetrate the hidden subculture of life in the pampas.

According to a report of the justice of the peace some days after the events of 1 January, when he was able to question the prisoners in greater detail, this was a movement with pretensions:

> Among the cheers raised by the band was the cry "Long live the Argentine Confederation!" They also had emissaries spread out throughout the countryside of this province and particularly in the districts of Villa de Luján, Cañuelas, Chascomús, Azul, and Tapalquén, who had gone out expressly to recruit people to come and join the group which had been organized here. In addition to the one styled Médico Dios there were three others, called San Francisco, Santo Domingo, and a name I do not know; the first an inhabitant of Cañuelas, the second thought to be of Baradero or Sarate, the third unknown. The one known as Médico Dios, also called San Gerónimo, has resided for some time in the district of Tapalquén, where he was in continuous contact with the Indians of that place. He left there and moved to this district. Here, as in Tapalquén, under the pretext of practicing medicine he has spent his time making subversive and harmful propaganda. And leading citizens who were designated to be assassinated included first, Colonel Benito Machado; second, the parish priest; third, myself; and fourth, the Commander of the Fort. . . . I tell you all this so that you may appreciate the character and aim of the movement, for all the bandits agree that they planned to extend the campaign up to the Río Salado, and they reckoned also to incorporate into their movement other groups of various strengths in the north and center of the countryside.[59]

Hold a mirror to the Tandil massacre and it shows a group of gauchos wild enough to kill people, impoverished enough to plunder property, and resentful enough to mark out foreigners. The killers were probably representative of malcontents throughout rural Argentina, in their motivation if not their action, though speculation about their contacts inside and outside their own community remains unproven.

Whether the massacre was linked to a wider movement or not, outside observers saw it as an extraordinary example of an ordinary situation: insecurity on the frontier. Foreign settlers had two things to fear, the knife and the lance, the gauchos of Tandil and the Indians of Bahía Blanca. Foreign consuls raised their complaints about both and demanded protection for their nationals against the two enemies of civilization.[60]

Horror was accompanied by censure. The massacre was denounced not only for its cruelty but also for its depravity; it was seen as an example of the superstition, fanaticism, and cultural inferiority of the rural poor. Argentine liberals and foreign observers alike were convinced that morals and mentalities, no less than rural conditions and agrarian structure, were at the root of the Tandil tragedy.

5

Millenarian Message

A New Messiah

The mystery of Tandil was not resolved by economic, demographic, and social analysis alone. Deprivation, it is true, was a prevailing factor and resentment of newcomers a powerful motive, discontents which were not impossible to articulate. Theoretically Argentina was a constitutional republic which allowed its citizens free expression of grievances. But federal, provincial, and municipal elections were so controlled that only the elite had a voice, and no one seriously believed that the common people of the countryside could plead their cause or determine their fate. The gauchos were politically defenseless and lacked any legal means or encouragement to express their concerns; direct protest emerged in default of institutional and other outlets.

There was a further institution in Argentina, the Catholic Church. In another time the people of Tandil would have flocked to a Franciscan friar preaching at Mass, but the age of evangelization had passed. While gauchos and their families were not deliberately neglected by the church, they neither received nor emitted a strong religious message. The outrage at Tandil, therefore, was not only a response to economic and social adversity but also a reflection of spiritual emptiness in the community. This was the reason why so many people—some four hundred in a population of five thousand—assembled at the camp of Solané: they were seeking religious assurance as well as medical treatment. While there was no overt talk of politics or rebellion, religious revivalism was fertile ground for agitation. Moreover, flickering through events at Tandil were signs of a messianic cult whose followers have been described as "the only millennialist movement in modern Argentina."[1]

Belief in the millennium remained alive in the Christian world even when the promise of Christ's second coming was not literally fulfilled. The apocalyptic tradition survived as a belief in a second advent which would herald the establishment of the kingdom of God on earth. This belief was variously interpreted. The millennialists believed that the kingdom of God would come gradually through Christian-inspired human progress, while the more popular millenarians looked for divine intervention and cataclysmic action to establish Christ's kingdom on earth.[2] A common millenarian scenario prophesied a time of trial and tribulation, after which the world would be purified; calamities in nature—floods, famines, and earthquakes—would herald a new era of peace and prosperity, terror would be followed by joy, discord by goodwill. According to these beliefs, the millennium would come suddenly in the form of group salvation, destroying the old world of sin and replacing it by a new and perfect society. Divine agency, not human effort, would be the instrument of change. A prophet or messiah would appear, who would lead and instruct the faithful and would shine by acceptance rather than personal qualities. He was not a priest but stood outside the normal religious structure. His qualifications were established by healing and counseling; these were the powers which attracted and held his followers. Around him gathered an inner band of disciples and beyond these a wider circle.

Millenarian movements, as they developed in England and the United States in 1750–1850, occurred in response to particular social and economic conditions, often a time of crisis, when distress, anxiety, and feelings of relative deprivation caused ordinary people to look for a leader and to follow a radical social programme.[3] In Spanish America belief in the millennium first appeared in the sixteenth century, when Franciscan missionaries, drawing on the prophecies of the Cistercian Joachim of Fiore (1135–1202), interpreted events in New Spain as living proof of the advent of a new age and the creation of a new society. The friars Motolinia and Mendieta proclaimed that the Indians would be freed from their tribulations through baptism; secure in the expectation of the second coming of Christ and the last judgment, they would vindicate the policy of mass conversion and give Mexico a leading place in Christian history before it climaxed in the end of the world. Many popular rebellions in the colonial period expressed apocalyptic beliefs as well as social grievances and echoed the language of the friars. The millenarian tradition was still alive in the eighteenth century. The Chilean Jesuit Manuel Lacunza, writing from exile in Europe, spoke of the coming of the Messiah in glory and majesty to establish a reign of peace and justice in the Old World and the New, a message which was heard in Mexico, if not in Argentina, and which responded to the anxieties of a revolutionary age.[4] Later in the nineteenth century popular religion in Mexico added further chapters to millenarian history.

The rebellion of 1 January 1872 approximated to the millenarian model, while not entirely reproducing it. The social significance of millenarian convictions was conspicuous in Tandil. This was a period of crisis and change in the southern countryside; feelings of anxiety and insecurity notoriously affected gauchos and peons; and rural conditions had long made them a deprived and oppressed class. The religion of millenarians and the vision of a new age can also be identified in Tandil, though the evidence is indirect and can only be glimpsed in symbols and slogans. "Viva la Patria y la Religión," "Death to gringos and Masons." Kill them all, this is a "holy war." The cry "Kill Masons" was a religious slogan aimed at a composite demonology of liberals, Protestants, and atheists. To kill in this cause had a redeeming quality. Cruz Gutiérrez, bloodstained from the morning's slaughter, pleaded with his captors, "Spare my life, Captain. We have done this for the sake of religion, because we are Christians." This was the chilling message the assassins had been given.

> At daybreak on 1 January the whole band assembled in the plaza headed by Jacinto, who raised a cheer for the Argentine Confederation and then cried death to Masons and to others whom I did not hear. . . . He gave out badges and told them never to discard or sell them as long as they lived. [5]
> The following morning at daybreak Jacinto distributed to everyone the red badge as a sign to those who belonged to the true Religion. He said that they came to this town in order to free religion and to show people the horrors that would appear; but those who joined him would be safe from all danger.[6]

These were not maxims issued by the clergy but rallying cries of an action outside the limits of the church, as would be expected of a millenarian movement. Jacinto Pérez claimed to be an emissary of Solané and the promoter of his project. He was known to be a folk preacher in his own right, a mini-*curandero* as it were, who had a reputation in the Tandil countryside. He was heard to say that the end of the world was imminent and the last judgment near at hand, that Tata Dios had been sent by God to punish bad Christians and to give protection and prosperity to Argentines. If they wanted to be saved they had to kill gringos and Masons, the authors of great ills suffered by the natives of the country. These were God's commands, and when they were fulfilled a new city would be founded at the foot of Piedra Movediza, and the rock would move and fly the banner of Christ the King. Rumors were circulating that "there was going to be a revolution," that "on the 1 January there was going to be a catastrophe in Tandil and blood would flow," that "the common people were saying that there was going to be a great flood, and deaths would follow."[7] There was wilder talk that one hundred, even two hundred rebels were involved, there were other rebel groups, and even the Indians were coming. Indian invasions were not uncommon; there was in fact an Indian rising at Azul from the end of 1871, though this had no connection with the Tandil massacre.

Jacinto Pérez, then, played upon many of the gaucho's dreads and desires. By offering salvation and fortune in a new paradise, he appealed to both spiritual and material values, linking rural conditions with millenarian deliverance and inviting the people to join a campaign against foreigners or lose everything. This was a Christian version of the millennium: by their action they could escape calamity or they would perish in the flames. Pérez also insisted that this was the word of Solané and that he, Pérez, was merely the messenger. The shadow of the *curandero* loomed over the entire action.

If the movement had a messianic character, it came from Tata Dios, who seemed to embody the qualities of a demigod. He preached an apocalyptic message. The time of God's punishment was approaching for heathens and sinners, the gringos and the Masons; believers must be ready to carry out the punishments. Those who did not cooperate would see their wives and children perish and they themselves would drown in a sea of blood; those who acted now would enjoy prosperity in this life and happiness in the next.[8] The evidence of these exhortations was hearsay, but the environment in which they circulated was common knowledge. Solané was a messiah held in reserve by God and now unleashed to fulfil a mission. His sacred character had been confirmed by his extraordinary powers of prophecy, healing, and miracles. He had made journeys to places where he was invested with mandates. He was an archetypal figure of power and majesty which a movement needed if it was to convince. If his personality did not tower over Tandil, this was in line with the millenarian model. He was a messiah not in his personal qualities but because he fulfilled the messianic expectations of his people. In the event, Solané disavowed the action of those who invoked his name and disapproved of the crimes committed on 1 January, apparently willing to arouse yet reluctant to strike.

Solané bore some of the marks of a messiah, and the rising had millenarian traits. Yet doubts remain, or at least confine research within the bounds of hypothesis. In the first place, the events occurred in too short a time span, November–December 1871, to allow for the creation of a credible movement with a millenarian message. Second, what religious motivation could possibly inspire fifty country people without serious criminal records to commit crimes of this nature? Third, Solané himself lacks absolute credibility. His position and his disposition in the local community suggested that he accepted the prevailing power structure. His message, moreover, contained familiar ideas concerning foreigners and religion. Solané followed a known tradition in blaming foreigners for the problems of the country. Since independence, rulers, politicians, and ordinary people had pointed accusing fingers at foreign diplomats, merchants, and immigrants as authors of many of the ills which beset Argentina, and the favoritism shown to the British in particular was responsible for frequent complaints of landowners, farmers, and artisans over the erosion of rights and absence of protection. To say that foreigners were robbing Argentines of jobs and resources was not an exceptional statement. Foreigners were also held responsible for introducing yellow fever and other epidemics and for the many deaths from these scourges in the years immediately before events at Tandil. Yet common rumor was one thing, words from the mouth of Solané another. And to link foreigners with Freemasons, as he evidently did, added another dimension, for Freemasons were regarded as cultural aliens who would destroy the Christian faith and replace it by ancient paganism; moreover, Freemasons did not acknowledge any fatherland, being a cosmopolitan movement which would diminish rather than magnify national identity. Less than a messiah, Solané was more than a *curandero*. His followers, moreover, were exponents not only of millenarianism but also of popular Catholicism.

OLD RELIGION

Yellow fever was a fatal reproach. But foreigners were blamed, too, for contagion of another kind, that of false religion and alien values. This was the reason why the assassins' war cry linked foreigners and Masons and called for the death of both.

The Catholic Church in Argentina, though broadly supportive of independence from Spain, subsequently identified with conservative regimes and instinctively recoiled from liberalism.[9] Catholicism was also a component in the conflict between unitarists and federalists, the one espousing a secular, the other a religious view of Argentina. Catholics recalled the anticlerical policies of Rivadavia and his unitarist supporters, who declared freedom of worship, abolished the ecclesiastical *fuero* (immunity), and confiscated monastic property. Catholicism became closely associated with federalist and gaucho politics and often the ally of federalist caudillos. The clerical position was broadly in line with popular opinion in Argentina, though odious to liberal interest groups. After its experience at the hands of Rivadavia, the Argentine church was left a shadow of its former self and from that time regarded liberalism as its mortal enemy. Monsignor Mastei Ferretti, the future Pius IX, visited the country in 1824 and thought that what remained of the local clergy had become collaborators of Rivadavia and instruments of his liberal ideas. The structure of the church barely survived. Following Rivadavia, the church collaborated closely with Juan Manuel de Rosas, trading its freedom for protection and becoming in effect a department and a propagandist of the *rosista* state.[10] The religion of dictatorship assured popular support for church and state. But the church recovered no privilege and little property, and while the Jesuits were recalled, they were quickly repulsed.

The period 1830–60 was the low point in the history of Argentine Catholicism.[11] In these vast and underpopulated lands, bishoprics remained unfilled for decades, seminaries closed from apathy, priests were few and far between, and the religious orders waited in vain for new vocations. As late as 1864, the diocese of Buenos Aires contained only thirty-five secular priests, very few of them conscious of their calling. Disputes with Rome over appointments and jurisdiction severed normal relations for decades. The very weakness of the church tempered rampant clericalism and also left anticlericalism without justification. But this did not deter either side of the ideological divide. Most of the provincial constitutions designed between 1854 and 1860 recognized, to the disgust of liberals, the Catholic religion as the official religion of the state. The national Constitution of 1853, however, was ambiguous. The Catholic Church was established and funded as the religion of the state, which was obliged to "support" but not to "profess" the Catholic religion. The appointment of bishops and relations with Rome were controlled by the government, and freedom of belief and worship for other religions was guaranteed. The constitution, therefore, established a bias towards a "national" church, a situation which Rome abhorred but learned to live with.[12]

In place of religion the liberal elite espoused Freemasonry, and Masonic lodges became temples of the new Argentina, where politicians, businessmen, and professional people could associate under the direction of such luminaries as Mitre and Sarmiento. Offspring of the May Revolution, the Masonic lodges of Argentina had begun life as political cells rather than ideological covens and had translated mutual help and brotherly love into the promotion of independence from Spain. With the advent of Rosas, who tolerated no alternative allegiance, they had ceased to flourish, but the tradition was not extinct. On the fall of the dictator, and especially from 1860, the Masonic lodges enjoyed a new lease of life and became the means by which liberalism was transformed into a program of action under the direction of Freemasons, who could count on the direct support of their fellows. They could also count on the wrath of the clergy; while governor of San Juan, Sarmiento was denounced from the pulpit as a Mason and therefore a disciple of the devil because he diverted ecclesiastical revenues to public works and education.[13]

Masonry gave its adherents an institutional base to counter that of the Catholic Church and a secrecy probably more impenetrable than that of its rival. It was also a network of influence, no doubt exaggerated in popular imagination, which would help a liberal to advance in public life and without which provincial allies, such as those in Tandil, would have been isolated. Freemasonry was not so much a pressure group as a hidden establishment, protecting its own, promoting policy, and through its influence in the media constantly challenging Catholic beliefs and institutions. In crying "kill Masons" the assassins of Tandil targeted real, if unspecified, rivals and identified the enemies of religion with a particular social class and its foreign allies. The tragedy was that their victims, for the most part, knew nothing of Freemasonry and had never been inside a Masonic lodge.

Argentina's intellectual elite moderated the virulent anticlericalism of the Freemasons and expressed a more positive humanism, though one which posed a philosophical challenge to religionists. Speaking for the Generation of 1837, intellectuals such as Echeverría projected a program which would have bypassed the church. Basically they regarded religious belief as a thing of the past and an affront to reason. Their liberal and modernizing ideas saw Argentina as an essentially secular society and religion as little more than a moral code useful for civilizing the masses.[14]

Argentina was living disproof that Latin American liberalism was a tolerant creed. Alberdi admitted it: "To be free for Argentine liberals means to govern other people. Possession of government, there you have the whole of their liberalism. . . . Liberalism, in the sense of respecting the views of others when they are in disagreement with our own, is something which never occurs to an Argentine liberal."[15] Alberdi himself was a hard liberal. In spite of his nominal faith and overt deference to religion—he led a mission to Rome in 1857 which paved the way for diplomatic relations with the papacy—he wanted to marginalize the church. In particular he advocated its removal from education; the training of future generations of lawyers, statesmen, and businessmen should be left entirely to professional teachers who would give them the applied science and the English language which they needed.[16] He insisted on religious toleration. Immigrants had a role to play in educating Argentina, and they should be accommodated along with their religion:

Every altar and every belief deserve respect. The establishment of Catholicism to the exclusion of other religions reduces Spanish America to the solitude and silence of a convent. The dilemma is unavoidable. Spanish America is either exclusively Catholic and unpopulated, or it is populated, prosperous, and tolerant in religion.... The exclusion of different religions in South America means excluding the English, the Germans, the Swiss, and the North Americans, who are not Catholics, that is the very settlers this continent most needs. To bring them without their religion is to deprive them of that which makes them what they are.[17]

Alberdi, and with him the majority of the political elite, challenged the Argentine church on the fundamental issue of the day, to join or to disavow the process of national organization. Some Catholic leaders sought a place for religion in the task of nation making. In the words of Félix Frias, former enemy and exile of the Rosas dictatorship, religion was the only bond of unity and order among Argentines: "Let us plant the Cross in our soil. Doctors and artisans, businessmen and farmers, men in tails and men in *chiripá*, people of Buenos Aires and people of the provinces, let us all embrace each other as brothers and be as generous with our sense of charity as previously we were with our more cruel instincts, which for forty years have turned our country into a vast coliseum, where Argentine heads have been cut off by Argentine hands."[18]

But Catholicism tended to be exclusive. The church authorities would never voluntarily concede religious toleration and control of education. When in 1867 the liberal governor of Santa Fe, Nicasio Oroño, pushed through the provincial assembly a bill establishing civil marriage, the hierarchy was outraged and condemned it as "highly prejudicial to society, to public morals, and to the integrity and stability of the family."[19] The church was confident that in maintaining these principles it had a more popular base of support than Alberdi and the liberals. The intellectuals preached to the elite, while the clergy still preached to the people. By the 1860s they were preaching from a stronger institution and in a more insistent voice. The church became a beneficiary of the liberal state as well as its leading critic.

Mitre was primarily a secularist, but he respected religion and saw the church as a pillar of national unity. During his presidency (1862–68) the metropolitan diocese of Buenos Aires was created and secured its own archbishop, Mariano José de Escalada (1865–70); he was succeeded by Federico Aneiros (1873–94), who directed the church through its long conflict with the liberal state. New seminaries were established and old ones reactivated to train priests for the expanding population of town and country; by 1869 the seminary in Buenos Aires had forty-eight students. Seculars were joined by religious, and native priests by immigrant clergy.[20] Following the fall of Queen Isabel and the onset of the federal republic in Spain in 1868, some two hundred Spanish priests moved to Argentina, few of them highly trained or motivated, but additional recruits to an expanding church. The Jesuits returned and in 1868 founded the Colegio del Salvador in Buenos Aires, successful enough to be burned down in 1875 by an anticlerical mob led by an apostate Spanish priest. In the 1870s Don Bosco sent Salesians to Argentina. By 1880 there were eighty-four priests in the diocese of Buenos Aires. As the ranks of bishops and clergy increased and improved, a new impetus was given to the advancement of Catholic faith and morals through the pulpit, the school, and the Catholic press. Religion acquired a political edge as Catholic action took the gospel outside the church and the cloister; a vigorous clerical movement now surfaced, indigenous in its base but reinforced by inputs from Rome. The policy of Pius IX, the publication of the *Syllabus of Errors* (1864), and the impulse of renewed ultramontanism were grist to the mill of a church newly released from political constraints and seeking authority over conscience and country. In 1869–70 several Argentine bishops attended the First Vatican Council, where they witnessed and supported the definition of papal infallibility and from which they returned home ready to do battle with the enemies of religion. "Liberalism," declared *El Católico*, "is a distortion of liberty; it is the source and essence of Revolution and stands for the abolition of God."[21] The resurgence of the Catholic Church provoked in turn a new wave of anticlericalism, more violent than the reasoned arguments used by Alberdi.

In rural Buenos Aires people listened to the Solanés rather than the Alberdis. No doubt there was a long road between the beliefs of a prelate in Buenos Aires and those of a country *curandero*, and doctrine was distilled by distance. But popular religion was not new or autonomous; it had a history in the Catholic Church and a tradition in Argentina. Country people might be ignorant of doctrine, but they accepted religion when it was available; they had enough faith to attend Mass and the sacraments, minimally if not regularly, and only rarely the sacrament of marriage, to say prayers and to sing hymns. Solané represented not so much a specific millenarian cult as a known tradition of popular Catholicism, mixing religion and superstition in unknown quantities. His awareness of religion, deference to Jesus Christ, and devotion to Our Lady of Luján, a popular Virgin in Argentina, whose image he kept in his room, placed him in the mainstream of rural life and made his camp a substitute church. His folk medicine was linked to an element of faith healing, but this was common currency among *curanderos* and did not make him a messiah. The proliferation of *curanderos* and the survival of popular religion merging into magic and superstition filled a vacuum left by the Catholic Church and satisfied the spiritual needs of country people.

The church did not have a significant presence in the countryside, and its authority was not always enhanced by the behavior of the few clergy who actually lived outside major towns. Rural priests were reputed to pursue private interests and live immoral lives while they neglected the duties of instructing the people and administering the sacraments. So the priests of the pampas tended to be a scandal to the faithful and an object of ridicule to the liberals. Yet the church did not entirely abandon peons and their families and from the 1860s sought to improve the quantity and quality of the rural clergy. Each small town or settlement came to have its priest and its chapel, as much a cultural as a religious requirement. In Fraile Muerto an English observer described the priest as "an Italian, and not a very clerical character, but pleasant and good natured, and having been educated as a doctor, did all he could for the bodies of his parishioners, and I trust also for their souls. . . . During the cholera he exerted himself nobly for the people."[22] In the town of Tandil there was a church and a priest, usually a foreigner: Italians in the years 1854–61 and Spaniards after this, some of them refugees from religious persecution. After resistance from local officials, priests began to participate in municipal government, often with the support of the electorate.[23] The Protestant settler, Juan Fugl, used his authority in local government in 1869–70 to approach the Ministry of the Interior to obtain funds for a new Catholic Church in Tandil, a mission in which he was successful.[24] The concerns of urban religion, however, meant little to the gaucho.

Southwest of Tandil lay the frontier, and this was the terrain of missionary priests, who usually set a high standard of service and sacrifice in the cause of evangelization and also on occasion in the task of ransoming captives. The southern frontier of Argentina, starved of ecclesiastical resources, never reproduced the mission successes characteristic of Paraguay, Mexico, and California, and most of the pampa Indians remained enclosed within their own religious world, immune to Christian argument and example.[25] On the frontier "Christian" was a cultural term used to distinguish civilized whites from savage Indians. But in this multicultural society missionary priests ministered to anyone who came their way. In Indian territory Colonel Mansilla had a special friend, the Franciscan Fray Marcos Donatti, a priest "whose evangelical virtues were allied to the mildest of characters; he traveled the two frontiers under my command, saying Mass on improvised altars, baptizing, confessing, and preaching to a willing audience of poor women of poor soldiers."[26]

While the map of religion in the south was becoming more crowded and more complex, from Buenos Aires it looked as primitive as ever. The liberal press, never slow to attack the church, attributed responsibility for the massacre of 1872 to ecclesiastical power and religious superstition. "There [in the countryside] the clergy have taken control of all consciences. Unworthy priests of a religion which has so many venerable martyrs to its credit have propagated from the pulpit the grossest superstitions. . . . The country priest is almost always the absolute and infallible authority of the district. . . . It is impossible to discount the influence of this baneful propaganda and to avoid the conclusion that the monstrous deeds at Tandil are the accursed product of ignorance and superstition."[27] La Tribuna continued to drive home its message, accusing the church of unleashing a war against Masons and encouraging religious fanaticism: "The assassins of Tandil are not men with criminal convictions, nor people who kill for booty. They are Catholic believers who believed that they were following God's will and doing good in doing so much bad."[28]

Other newspapers took a similar line and attributed the crime of Solané to his Catholicism and to the preaching of the Catholic clergy at a time when the church was undergoing a public revival. In this interpretation the assassins became the militant arm of popular Catholicism. La República argued that the privileges granted to the church by the state in national and provincial constitutions were harmful to political life: "Politics have become saturated with fanaticism. Religion and politics have both fallen into fatal decline".[29] El Nacional also seized the opportunity to attack the church, the great enemy of freedom of conscience, possessor of excessive power and privilege. El Nacional thought it astonishing that "a serious newspaper" should seek to absolve the Argentine clergy of all responsibility for Tandil.[30] The newspaper in question was La Nación, which alone among the national press discarded the religious argument in favor of a sociological one:

If this were a matter of persecution of, or simply opposition to, religious beliefs, then it could be argued that the outburst was a consequence of adverse pressure. But who in our country has thought to molest anyone, much less the gauchos, for religious beliefs? No one.

Therefore the origin of the unrest must be sought elsewhere, namely in the deplorable conditions suffered by the gaucho of the countryside. The government sends him to the frontier for six months and keeps him there six years. When, or if, he returns, he finds that he has lost his job and his crops, his ranch has been looted, his farmhouse torched, and his wife and children are captives of the Indians, because the government which enslaves him for frontier service fails in fact to defend the frontier.[31]

La Nación was Mitre's paper, and Mitre himself was a Freemason. The salutary warning against facile judgments was not followed by everyone, even by those who were close to the scene of events. According to Juan Fugl, "The Catholic priests raged from their pulpits against the Masons, and this served to increase the hatred of foreigners, who had introduced into the country this very arm of the devil."[32] Fugl was a Danish Protestant, with his own viewpoint. It is true that a Masonic lodge had existed in Azul since 1867 and another was introduced into Tandil in 1872, after the massacre; these were easy targets for Catholic hostility. Yet the impression that the Argentine countryside was swarming with priests and that the church had a controlling grip on the population was exaggerated. Superstition rather than religion was the faith of the pampas. Gauchos were not easily recruited to any cause and were normally content to leave religion to women. According to an English observer, "The Gauchos make a perfect jest of everything connected with religion, and are scarcely ever seen inside a church, appearing to think that the women can do all that is necessary for them."[33] The antipathy may have been mutual. At the execution of Gutiérrez and Lasarte the priest attending was described by *La Nación's* reporter as harsh and unsympathetic, his words of admonition too gross to report, his whole attitude yet another scourge for the guilty, "like that of many priests in our countryside."[34]

The church was not so dominant nor rural people so docile as the press implied. Religion was present somewhere in the minds of the killers, but it would be difficult to establish a precise correlation between their actions and their beliefs. These men proceeded less by reason than by instinct. For some religion was a motive, for others a justification, for others a tribal cry. And it was not the only strand in traditional beliefs. Defiance of liberalism grew from a set of values which included political ideas; assertion of popular religion went hand in hand with claims for political space and defense of regional identity. The authority for these could be found in a more distant past, when Argentina kept liberals in exile and foreigners in their place.

Shadow of Rosas

The bandits of Tandil received emblems from their leaders. The red hatband and the scarlet ribbons were deeply symbolic and in the past had been signals of popular mobilization. The rebels shouted "Long live the Argentine Confederation!" thus invoking the former embodiment of federalism. Were the assassins, then, a throwback to *rosismo*, that amalgam of government and ideology imposed on Argentina by Juan Manuel de Rosas, governor of Buenos Aires in the years 1829–52? Rosas had left an impression, not necessarily accurate, of nationalism and populism, opposition to foreign invaders and death to their internal allies, protection of rural interests and support for gauchos, defense of provincial independence and war on liberal unitarists. Since the fall of the dictator, politicians had fought for constitutions and compromise, but in rural Buenos Aires echoes of the old regime could still be heard and *rosista* rhetoric was still invoked, defending religion and autonomy against secularists and centralists. Indeed, no one forgot Rosas, and in the primitive countryside he lived on. In one of his tales of travel and adventure in the Río de la Plata, Cunninghame Graham recalled a vivid scene in a *pulpería* in the southern pampas. A group of people were gathered in the bar, gauchos, singers and guitar players noisily drinking, boasting, and fighting, the women watching from the side. Suddenly an old gaucho, provoked by the talk of the younger men, raised his knife and shouted "Viva Rosas" to prove his defiance, savagery, and belief in an older order.[35] This was about 1876–77, twenty-five years after the fall of Rosas, five years after the massacre. It is safe to assume that Tandil witnessed many such scenes and that the assassins took part in similar encounters.

But what did *rosismo* mean after the fall of Rosas? The dictator had imposed red hatbands and badges as signs of political allegiance and loyalty to federalism. Did the southern pampas preserve a continuous tradition of his ideas? Were the battle cries of the bandits—"Religion and the Argentine Confederation!"—true reflections of *rosista* doctrine? And were they defenders of Argentine nationality against immigrants and foreigners? There are two possible answers to these questions. The first interprets the massacre at Tandil as an expression of gaucho allegiance to federalist politics and Christian values and places it in the framework of popular political traditions.[36] The second sees the resonance of *rosismo* in the events of 1872 as little more than the folk memory of an imagined past.

Martín Fierro is told by his friend Sargento Cruz that a gaucho has to endure injury and injustice "until there comes a real *criollo* to rule in this land."[37] Was this *criollo* a true Argentine, attentive to rural, provincial, and gaucho interests, as distinct from a liberal government serving *porteños*, foreigners, and immigrants? Was he a caudillo, a second Rosas? Hernández himself was not a *rosista*, but he supported another strong man, López Jordán, a caudillo with a provincial base and rural support against the politicians of Buenos Aires. The cry of the Tandil assassins for Figueroa and Machado could have been a cry for the ultimate support, petty caudillos to be sure, but real *criollos*, native Argentines. If so, the rebels were mistaken, for Figueroa and Machado were network officials, creatures of the politicians and servants of Buenos Aires.

Rosas himself, now in his twentieth year of exile in England, perceived the massacre of Tandil as an infamous act. Replying to a correspondent whose prejudices evidently mirrored his own, he denounced the killings as an attack on the rights of man in society, a sign of godlessness, and proof of the ill effects of modern education. Compulsory education was one of the favorite aversions of Rosas; he argued that it was prejudicial to the lower classes, for it diverted them from work, gave them ideas beyond their station, and prepared them for a life of crime. The poor peons of Tandil were unlikely to qualify for such reproaches, having never been deflected from their fate by education; even Solané was illiterate. The assassin band was living proof of cultural deprivation. Rosas continued in a more nationalist vein: "As for rights and duties, there is no doubt that the sons of the country are not receiving their due. And immigration as it is now allowed gives more rights and less duties to the immigrants than to the natives. If such injustice continues then we need not be surprised to see fatal results."[38]

Federalism, nominally the political creed of Rosas, was in fact destroyed by Rosas, who turned its two causes—resistance to the political and economic dominance of Buenos Aires—on their head and replaced them by his own dictatorship and an *estancia*-based power structure. By the 1870s, following their defeat by the liberals under Mitre and Sarmiento, the federalists became virtually extinct as a political force. Their influence lingered on as little more than a form of folklore and a nostalgia for the days when rural rebels could still raise the battle cry, "Religion or Death!"[39]

The massacre was the product of a confused mentality. The religious background of the assassins was popular Catholicism, revived by Solané and acclaimed by the local community. An undertone of millenarianism pervaded the movement and gave it an apocalyptic character which was fatal for its victims. The ideology of Rosas, real or imagined, filtered through twenty years of political change and entered the language if not the minds of the rebels. These ideas generated a great rage, as the killers saw liberals, officials, and proprietors, all their oppressors, incarnate in their immediate rivals, the immigrants. In this sense revenge was a kind of wild justice.

Above, *A Gaucho Song*, oil painting by Carlos Morel, 1840. Bonifacio del Carril, *El gaucho a través de la iconografía*, 199, courtesy of the Archivo General de la Nación, Buenos Aires.

Right, *The Pulpería of Miramar*, Province of Buenos Aires, by Tomás Di Tranto. AGN: inv. N° 295.744, caja 2.763, courtesy of the Archivo General de la Nación, Buenos Aires.

Above, *Country Store*, watercolor by
A. Durand, 1865. Bonifacio del Carril,
El gaucho a través de la iconografía, 190,
courtesy of the Archivo General de la
Nación, Buenos Aires.

LOS APOSTOLES DE TATA-DIOS

° Cruz Gutiérrez, 2.° Juan Villalba, 3.° Esteban Lasorte (a)
Casimiro Ramos, 4.° Antonio Ponce, 5.° Francisco Rodríguez (a) «Anatolio», 6.° Gregorio Larrea, 7.° Juan C. More-
no, 8.° Pedro Torres, 9.° Claudio Villarruel, 10.° Juan Fe-
rreyra, 11 Benito Lisaso, 12 Juan Arballo, 13 Santos Pereyra

(Fotografía de la época.)

Left, The leading assassins, contemporary
photograph. Courtesy of Fuerte Independencia, Museo y Biblioteca, Tandil.

Gauchos playing cards, oil painting by Juan L. Camaña, 1852. Bonifacio del Carril, *El gaucho a través de la iconografía,* 200, courtesy of the Archivo General de la Nación, Buenos Aires.

Interior of a Pulpería, lithograph by León Pallière, 1865. AGN, inv. N° 270.880, caja 2.589, courtesy of the Archivo General de la Nación, Buenos Aires.

The Last of England, by Ford Madox Brown. Published by permission of Birmingham Museums and Art Gallery.

6

Response and Recrimination

A Community in Shock

The trauma of the massacre was quickly followed by further shock when the people of Tandil learned that Solané, the alleged author of the crime, had himself been assassinated in a secure cell. In spite of the presence of some forty people in the courthouse jail, prisoners, officers of the court, local citizens, and a guard on the prime suspect, one or more attackers reached the outside of the cell at one o'clock in the morning of 5 January and shot Solané through the window; he died instantly of multiple wounds. The assailants were never found, and the authorities produced no evidence to indicate how, why, or by whom the crime was committed. Local opinion yielded various versions: (1) accomplices in the massacre shot the *curandero* to prevent his testifying and implicating others; (2) for a similar reason Figueroa was the assassin, or the paymaster, out of fear that Solané would reveal to the trial judge his relations with the justice of the peace; (3) the assassination was an act of vigilante justice; or (4) fearing the influence of Solané among powerful local officials, townspeople, probably foreigners, killed him to ensure his punishment. This last was the opinion favored by Fugl.[1] Whatever happened, the act of murder looked too easy to preclude the possibility of official connivance and the collaboration of the guards; someone was determined to destroy Solané's evidence. Thus, the crimes of Tandil continued to generate mystery and their investigators to compound confusion.

Failure of government and the hint of anarchy were becoming an embarrassment. As the leading official in Tandil, Figueroa was aware that the eyes of the public and the expectations of the government were focused on him. His response was to exude confidence and determination in dealing with the massacre and to pin responsibility for everything on one man, now the victim as well as the author of the crime. He reported to Buenos Aires that the assassination of Solané had been accomplished by an attack from outside the prison by assailants who had broken the window of the cell and fired on the prisoner, "causing his immediate death." Figueroa had no evidence as to the attackers but assured the provincial authorities that under his guidance local people were collaborating in enforcing the law and in restoring normal life to the area.[2] Whatever their effect on the government, Figueroa's protestations enjoyed little credibility in the Argentine press. Liberals denounced religious fanaticism, the hardship and excesses of frontier service for gauchos, and the tyranny of local government and its links with local potentates.

Figueroa's response was too bland. In fact, the popular reaction to the massacre was one of anxiety and outrage. People were bewildered by events and could not believe that the slaughter was the action of rational beings. Work stopped, businesses closed, townspeople speculated, settlers checked their guns. As citizens endeavored to come to terms with the killings, to reestablish their normal world and restore order out of chaos, their first thought was to defend themselves. In Tandil foreigners organized an armed force to patrol the town and protect houses and property; Basques, Spaniards, Danes, British, and French went about their business armed with ancient guns and swords. Then the community turned its attention to the authorities. On the evening of 1 January, shortly after news of the outrage began to circulate, townspeople met to demand action from Buenos Aires and punishment of the assassins. Expecting little from the justice of the peace, they made direct representation to the provincial government to intervene and save Tandil from the savages unleashed by Solané and his "anti-social ideas." The resultant document was signed by 463 citizens.

Foreigners began to seek the support of their ministers and consuls in Buenos Aires. The Italians of Tandil sent a petition of their own to the provincial governor seeking the protection of the state for their lives and property. The Danes requested their consul in Buenos Aires to intervene with the Argentine government and insist on urgent measures. They pointed out that Danes alone in Tandil numbered 150; of these 56 signed the petition. Within days the consuls of Denmark and Italy were demanding action from the provincial government to send judges to the south.

The British press, in Buenos Aires and in London, described the authors of the atrocities as "a band of ruthless assassins and villains, whose only banner was death to foreigners. The Government, we are happy to say, has acted with the greatest decision in the matter; but the local authorities in the South are so much to blame that we trust they will be brought up for trial to Buenos Ayres."[3] First reports were distinctly alarmist: "The bloodhounds are out in all directions"; "The conspiracy is spreading like wildfire"; "The sepoys of Tandil have risen to murder the foreigners. Their blood alone can slake the thirst of Gaucho fanaticism, and the lives of our countrymen are set on the cast every hour. . . . It eclipses the massacre of Glencoe and rivals the sepoy revolt in India of 1857."[4] *The Standard* of Buenos Aires thought that the English and the Germans, the "least numerous but still the most influential" foreigners, should take the initiative and in Buenos Aires raise a foreign regiment which would "exterminate the bad gauchos with the help of the respectable natives." And public rewards should be given for the heads of the assassins.[5]

The British chargé d'affaires, H. G. MacDonell, who for two years had been reporting on the danger to foreigners and their property in the River Plate republics, admitted he had seen nothing compared with the latest atrocity, which showed the ingrained addiction of the gaucho to "the vice of manslaughter, the disregard of human life, and the hatred of foreigners."[6] He enclosed a memorial from British settlers in Tandil and Azul setting out the facts: they were now living, they declared, "in terror of our lives" and demanded British pressure on the Argentine government for immediate trial and execution of the prisoners. The British consul, Frank Parish, reported to Earl Granville, minister for foreign affairs, what he described as the "most barbarous massacre yet recorded in the annals of crime of this country," including the killing of Mr. and Mrs. Gibson Smith, people of "a very respectable class," by a band of gaucho dupes and malefactors.[7] Parish launched a series of protests and accusations before the provincial government which was not well received and led to bitter recriminations between Britain and Argentina; foreigners were brusquely told that they had no right of access to government on internal affairs and should consult the local authorities.[8]

The government reacted to the massacre and the subsequent outcry with a program of damage control rather than a fundamental review of security. The local authorities were urged to increase vigilance, apply strict measures of law and order, and proceed promptly against the accused. Among the various guards posted in Tandil was one at the new branch of the Banco de la Provincia, whose opening coincided with the massacre and whose manager hastened to assure his head office that it was business as usual.[9] Military authorities acted to increase security in the surrounding countryside and to guard against any sign of rebellion. Exceptional security was ordered for the accused, and "the strictest vigilance" over their imprisonment.[10] Police agents were dispatched beyond Tandil and ordered to arrest accomplices in what was feared to be a province-wide movement. Justices of the peace throughout the south arrested, then released, suspected survivors of the Tandil band, but the real fugitives were never found or identified. *Curanderos* were scrutinized, alleged conspiracies detected, cults investigated, vagrants harassed, and Indian "risings" reported.[11] But the massacre remained a scar on the landscape, justice a distant prospect, and the local community as vulnerable as ever. The National Guard traditionally represented the interests of Argentine landowners; it formed in effect the military arm of the *estancia*, its guarantee of rural security. This was the priority of the authorities, too, and the bias was obvious to foreigners, who still saw themselves as marginalized and given scant protection. To many immigrants Tandil was synonymous with lawlessness; only weeks after the massacre a citizen reported that his farm had been burned down and his daughter raped in her own home, an incident all too familiar on the southern frontier.

The local oligarchy of office and land immediately came under scrutiny, and people seized the opportunity to settle old scores. Why, it was asked, had public security been so neglected? Why had the local authorities failed to act earlier, when the activities of Solané were public knowledge? These questions were also raised by the provincial governor, Castro, and by the government in Buenos Aires. Some foreigners pointed to the friendship between Ramón Gómez and Solané and the apparent leniency with which Justice Figueroa, brother-in-law of the Gómez family, had treated the large gathering at the clinic of Tata Dios. Others complained of the irascible and impulsive character of Figueroa, who had to admit that allegations were now focusing on him; his other brother-in-law, Colonel Benito Machado; and the parish priest as accomplices of the assassins.[12] Dr. Tomás Isla, the trial judge, had been instructed to make inquiry into the conduct of the local authorities and to produce a report and recommendations.[13] He reported on 16 February. In an anodyne document Isla defended officials against all allegations, concluding that there was no evidence to implicate Alcalde Ramón Gómez in the events of 1 January, as people alleged, nor was there any evidence of collusion between Gómez and Solané; in fact, Gómez was in the party that pursued the criminals.[14]

The people of the town were not satisfied with Isla's inquiry; resentment against Figueroa and criticism of his regime continued to agitate the community. Meetings were held, opinions collected. A committee appointed by the citizens of Tandil included Pedro Pereyra, Luis Arabehety, José Fuschini, Carlos Meyeren, Carlos Díaz, Ramón Santamarina, Nicanor Elejalde, and Enrique Thompson. They sought an interview with the governor of the province and obtained one on 15 February, expressing their concern not only over these particular events but over the general lack of security for their families and property. The governor assured them that everything was being done that needed to be done: the local police were being strengthened, and judgment was in the hands of the Supreme Court. The report of Judge Isla, however, was not reassuring to the committee, and they obtained an interview with the president of the Supreme Court, on whom they further pressed their views.[15] Meanwhile, Figueroa was fighting back. He prohibited public meetings, denounced the committee as agitators who questioned his authority, and reported them to the provincial authorities as "voices of subversion."[16] So began a war of words. The committee accused the justice of the peace of neglecting his duty and resorting to authoritarian ways; he was hostile to farmers and foreigners and a political fixer who schemed to exclude foreigners and other opponents from the electoral rolls. Meanwhile, the justice blamed the committee for disturbing the people and usurping authority, thus creating anarchy and disorder under the pretext of seeking punishment of the criminals.

Citizens continued to protest, natives as well as foreigners, and to direct their anger towards the justice of the peace. A strongly supported petition dated 5 May complained of his arbitrary and conflictive style of government and his hostility to foreign farmers and their agricultural interests. A request was made for his replacement. Specifically the citizens accused Figueroa of criticizing the municipality and preventing farmers, which meant foreigners, from participating in elections; moreover, his inertia during the crisis and tolerant attitude towards the assassinations proved his unfitness for office. They had the family network in their sights, denouncing Ciriaco Gómez, commander of the militia, as an ally and relation of Figueroa.[17] The pressure of town and province forced the justice to request leave of absence from office and to assign another ally, Moisés Jurado, as a temporary replacement. The provincial government soon replaced Jurado with Carlos A. Díaz, who was linked to opponents of Figueroa, and in the municipal elections of 1873 the Figueroa group lost further ground in what appeared to be another victory for the immigrants. The wealthiest immigrant in Tandil, entrepreneur and property owner Ramón Santamarina, now rose through municipal office to embark on a distinguished provincial and national career, proof that social rank could cut across national origins and open the way to political success. To achieve this, however, the immigrant had to join the elite rather than challenge it.

Were these events the beginning of political movement in Tandil, signs that the massacre had backfired? Did new social groups representing immigrant, farming, and urban sectors begin to emerge? Was there now a new balance of forces capable of breaking the power of Figueroa, Gómez, Machado, and Jurado and displacing the traditional alliance of *estancieros* and officials?[18] It is true that the action of 1 January failed in its presumed objective of terrorizing and expelling foreigners; by its own terms it gained nothing more than the settling of accounts with Chapar. The foreigners defeated the massacre by staying in post and fighting back, and the assassins were never reinvented as heroes or "social rebels" or honored by the community as fighters for justice. But if there was a shift in politics, it was not a fundamental change.

Politics in Tandil reflected national trends and centered on divisions between *mitristas* and *alsinistas*. Mitre stood for national unity under the leadership of Buenos Aires, Alsina for provincial rights, of which his Autonomist Party of Buenos Aires was an exponent. In 1874, Mitre lost the presidential election to Avellaneda, who fought on a provincial platform and subsequently governed with the support of Alsina. Against a background of economic depression and with some support from anxious landowners and merchants, Mitre rejected the electoral verdict and took to arms. The frontier was not immune to politics. Tandil, too, had its *mitristas* and *alsinistas*, and much of the postmassacre conflict in the region was factional and personal rather than a basic attempt to reverse the structures of power or to establish a new ideological position.

Upon news of the rebellion of Mitre against the election results in October 1874, Benito Machado, backed by his regiment Sol de Mayo and his old allies, the Indians of Catriel, dismissed the existing municipal officials in Tandil and joined the rebels. At this point the foreigners led by Fugl and others, "recalling the killings of Tata Dios," organized an armed unit in self-defense and endeavored to stabilize municipal government. They made it clear that their action was not intended to enforce a political position or seize municipal control, but purely to guarantee the security of the community against any repetition of 1872. When Mitre himself arrived, they negotiated an agreement with him to restore the municipal council; once this was done, they maintained their neutrality and remained aloof from politics during and after the brief rebellion.[19]

There is little evidence, therefore, of an advance of a "middle class" or any wholesale displacement of the local oligarchy in Tandil. Many of the old problems continued unabated or became worse. It would need a further period of liberal legislation, a higher growth of immigration, and greater expansion of agriculture to change the face of Tandil.

The Aftermath: Public Order in Tandil

Relations between immigrants and Argentines in Tandil worsened as a result of the massacre. While there was an angry response from foreigners, this in turn provoked a hostile reaction from native Argentines. The creole sector of the population either viewed the massacre as a natural reaction to foreign advance or dismissed it as an example of gaucho barbarism; there was little sense of shame or guilt. The municipal elections of November 1873 saw Tandil split uncompromisingly between Argentines and foreigners; there was no sympathy factor, and the foreigners won by only fifty votes in a poll of seven hundred. In this divided community each side sought the ear of local officials, who favored one or the other according to their own predilections. From the Figueroa camp Jurado reported: "The bloody events which took place in this district on 1 January have left a legacy of hatred between foreigners and native sons, causing a difficult situation for the local authorities. Our freedom of action is restricted by the pretensions of the foreigners, who are determined to be dominant and to become the ones who impose the law."[20]

While the authorities were suspect to foreigners, they were also distrusted by native Argentines. There was a tradition of solidarity in the pampas, where the popular sectors, the law-abiding and the outlaws, were all victims of the same injustices. The normal reaction of the gaucho population to police investigations was to retreat behind a screen of silence, and military conscripts were reluctant to hunt down gaucho outlaws. The events of 1872 did not change rural mentalities, as Juan L. Somoza, subinspector of the National Guard, soon discovered. Commissioned to reinforce the authorities of Tandil in early 1872, Somoza reported that the poor of the pampas tended to protect gaucho fugitives rather than denounce them, and that conscript soldiers resisted orders to capture bandits—a sign of solidarity, perhaps, but also of fear of reprisals. "Sir, I am not going to arrest them. Tomorrow they will escape and while I am away they will break into my farmhouse and cut the throats of my wife and children, as has happened to others."[21]

The provincial government was now nervous and watched Tandil anxiously for signs of further disorder, sometimes confusing political factionalism with more serious instability. "The Government has been informed," it wrote in September 1872, "that there exist in Tandil alarming signs of a threat to public order," and it gave instructions for additional measures to increase police activity and strengthen security. While Ciriaco Gómez, the National Guard commander, jumped to attention, the justice of the peace replied indignantly that all was quiet in

Tandil. There was no threat to public order, and these were rumors put out by a small number of disaffected people, "for everyone is totally occupied in going about their daily tasks, foreigners as well as nationals."[22] Díaz further explained: "These alarmist rumors emanate only from a small number of people, but they are people who have been in the habit of holding public appointments, or who are linked to these by ties of family, or who want to stir up trouble. . . . Frustrated by lack of public support for their ideas, they have only one objective, which is to gain prestige in public office."

The justice of the peace was complacent. Tandil was disturbed by more than local politics. Violent men lurked in its environs, and crime flourished in its countryside. On the night of 1 September 1872 a traveling Italian musician, Vicente Sebulo, had his throat cut by an assassin who was never traced. Justice Díaz reported the crime to the provincial authorities, his embarrassment cloaked in words of reassurance: "This is obviously an isolated crime. In spite of the method of killing, by no stretch of the imagination does it bear any relation to the unfortunate events of 1 January past."[23] On 2 September a group of peons from a covered wagon plying between Tandil and Las Flores was arrested on suspicion. The prime suspect was Camilo Domínguez, an eighteen-year-old, whose clothing was covered in blood; the others too were held for questioning.[24] In rural criminal procedure, however, suspects were more common than convicts.

The weaker the intelligence, the wider the net. The commissioner of police at Tandil began a policy of blanket arrests, sweeping up all the vagrants he could find and scouring the *pulperías* for drinkers and gamblers. It was a very traditional practice, simultaneously clearing the highways of criminals and filling the militia with conscripts, or so it was hoped. He planned to take in "all the rogues and vagabonds who can be found, in order to fill the quota of national guards due from this district for service on the southern frontier." This, of course, was one of the causes of rural unrest and one of the charges which reformers laid against the authorities in the aftermath of the Tandil massacre. The police chief argued that the character of the detainees justified conscripting them:

1. Blas Nieto, gambler, brawler, unemployed, rustler, and without known means of subsistence. A criminal, moreover, for in 1866 five prisoners conscripted for military service in the Army of Paraguay were snatched from their guards by Nieto and others, who opened fire on the detachment guarding them; yet he carries a military certificate of immunity issued by Commandant Dr. Moisés Jurado.

2. Felipe Bustamante, endowed with the same traits, and accomplice in the above crime.

3. Crescencio Coronel, gambler and vagrant.

4. Severo Berrios, hooligan and troublemaker, constantly drunk, has even taken up arms against the police here. Rated as incorrigible; sent to the Frontier by Commandant Ramón R. Gómez, but now back in this town and assistant of Commandant José C. Gómez.

5. Manuel Gorosito, gambler and without known means of subsistence.

6. Domingo Contreras, found without papers; engaged in horse-dealing with the Indians, occupation suspect.

7. Victor Delgado, deserter from Bahía Blanca, gambler by profession, freed by Commandant Jurado.

8. Teodoro Medina, deserter from Sauce. I handed him over to Commandant Ramón R. Gómez, who not only freed him but has granted him a certificate of military service as though he has actually done it. Low type, gambler, and constantly drunk.

9. Ezequiel Quintana, found without papers.

The commissioner of police complained that the local commandants were freeing these vagrants and giving them protection while other suspects were allowed to flee the district to escape the attentions of the police.[25] The inference was that the old regime in Tandil (the Figueroa-Gómez network) was still in operation; tolerance of delinquents went hand in hand with corrupt associations, to the detriment of law-abiding farmers, mostly foreigners. Justice of the Peace Díaz forwarded the information to the provincial government, but this was no reformist campaign. Police Commissioner Rivero was himself subsequently reported for neglect of duty and thought it wise to resign.

Beyond Tandil, in zones of greater lawlessness, settlers felt even less secure. In Bahía Blanca, targeted by both Indian raiders and gaucho outlaws, British settlers feared a repeat of the Tandil massacre. In November 1872 they wrote to the British minister in Buenos Aires stating that while Tandil had horrified the British, it had already been forgotten by many Argentines and glorified by others. They described Bahía Blanca as a settlement of former convicts which still retained its criminal character even though convict gangs were no longer being sent there. The population consisted of criminals and gauchos "of the worst possible description," several of whom were suspected of being involved in the events of New Year's Day. Bahía Blanca was an isolated place, and should the massacre of Tandil be reenacted, local officials would have little chance of capturing or punishing the culprits. Officials in fact were part of the problem. The justice of the peace in Bahía Blanca, one Estanislao Maque, was of a type that "if ignorance and prejudice were the standards of excellency, he might well be chosen as the only fit person to fill the situation." He was virtually illiterate, hated all foreigners, and blamed them for everything, including the weather. The situation was so flammable that it only needed the justice of the peace to spark the flames and the British residents would be in deep trouble. The British chargé had to inform the protestors that the Argentine government did not admit interference in such matters, and he advised them to communicate their misgivings directly to the provincial government and secure the removal of the justice of the peace in that way.[26]

The provincial government was alerted by events in Tandil and responded to them by increasing the security forces, or at least ordering their increase. In his message to the provincial legislature in 1873 the governor of Buenos Aires stated that the police service had been improved and security strengthened.[27] But foreign observers were not impressed, either in Tandil or in the other danger zone, Bahía Blanca. British officials in particular complained of two things, the absolute shortage of police and defects in the criminal justice system. The result, in Tandil and elsewhere, was notorious inertia in bringing escaped criminals before the courts. The combination of the Tandil massacre and the Indian raids caused the Emigration Commission in London to issue on 22 July 1872 another warning to prospective emigrants to Argentina, stating that "no adequate measures have been taken by the Government for the protection of the settlers or the punishment of the offenders."[28] Further Indian raids near Rosario invoked another warning on 9 October. On the basis of reports from Argentina, therefore, emigration policy was questioned and curtailed, and Anglo-Argentine relations suffered a further setback.

THE KILLING CONTINUES

The repercussions of Tandil unfolded against a background of implacable Indian hostility. Calfucurá launched a series of painful attacks on the southwest of Buenos Aires province in the first half of 1872, while Santa Fe bore the brunt of Indian raids in 1873. Meanwhile, underfunded government campaigns in support of security were further weakened by the need to face rebellions in Entre Ríos and disturbances accompanying the presidential elections of 1874. These had their implications for immigrants. British opinion identified Alsina (one of three candidates, with Mitre and Avellaneda) as the reactionary proponent of a return to the gaucho regime, "which is synonymous with plunder and murder and the dominion of might over right—the term 'gringos,' an opprobrious epithet applied to foreigners, being its watchword."[29] The elections themselves, according to British reports, were a recipe for disorder, not democracy: "Universal suffrage and vote by ballot are synonymous with armed intervention and abject terror," with troops on the streets, business paralyzed, transport interrupted, and church services postponed to make way for polling stations. Election day was said to have passed off quietly, with not more than a dozen killed and sixty or seventy wounded.[30]

British officials in Buenos Aires made no allowance for national susceptibilities. They applied the political and social standards of their own culture to those of Argentina without reference to stages of development or differences of history and environment. They maintained that government initiative and tougher policy could change conditions and improve security; unfortunately, the will to intervene did not exist. The Argentines replied that the British themselves were often their worst enemies. The consular service was well aware that not all British immigrants were pioneers or frontiersmen. William Ritchie was murdered in a brothel in Entre Ríos. "I have had, I am sorry to say, personal experience of the low and degrading habits acquired by young English gentlemen by residence in this country, and I am still more sorry to be obliged to add that such habits are generally considered here as characteristic of our countrymen." In this case, continued the consul, the waters were muddied by the fact that Ritchie was trying to extricate a fellow Briton from low company, and he was killed by a soldier of the Provincial Guard who had murdered foreigners before. The chances of the soldier's being brought to justice were remote.[31]

Nicolás Avellaneda was installed in the presidency in October 1874; the *mitristas*, refusing to accept defeat, raised the standard of rebellion and as quickly surrendered. But unemployed rebels were dangerous, and these added their own quota to the normal level of danger in the countryside. At Navarro in Buenos Aires province *mitrista* troops were probably responsible for the murder of the settler Lenihan, the rape of his wife, and the theft of their property.[32] The terror unleashed by the *mitrista* rebellion proved the last straw for many immigrants, and in its wake thousands of Europeans returned to the Old World.[33] Meanwhile, "ordinary" crime continued to target settlers and tax the patience of the Foreign Office. In January 1875, Samuel Waite was murdered at Laguna Larga in Córdoba province, attacked by five men while counting the proceeds of a sale of hides. Three suspects were arrested but released for want of evidence. Local opinion blamed his wife's family. The Foreign Office authorized a reward of five hundred Bolivian dollars for the arrest of the murderers, but the offer was considered inopportune by the Cordoban authorities.[34]

Life and property continued to be at risk in country districts, and there was no sign of improvement under the new presidency. An article, "Roads and the Police," in *The Standard* of Buenos Aires in February 1875 reported that during the last three weeks bands of robbers had been spreading terror in Chivilcoy, Cañuelas, and other districts in Buenos Aires province, and the governor did nothing to stem the tide. The excuse that Argentina was a new and developing country was not convincing; Australia and New Zealand were also new, but the life of the immigrant was more secure there. Even in Argentina life had been safer fifteen years before, when Buenos Aires was at war with the other provinces, than it was now. Crime had increased because the *partidos* were too large and justices of the peace were unpaid; police were practically nonexistent and prisons "absurdly insecure." The whole criminal justice system was "utterly disgraceful," and anyone convicted of a second murder should be executed "in spite of Bishops and Governors." The implications for immigration, concluded *The Standard*, were obvious.[35]

The cycle of crime and punishment—or, in the British view, lack of punishment—in these years was completed by rumor of another Tandil in the south, to the effect that the Alexandra colony, established by the London house of Thomson, Bonar and Co., had been wiped out by Indians. Several British settlers and thirty-seven Indians were supposedly killed. According to *The Standard* of 20 October 1875, three Britons had set out to look for stolen horses and had chased several Indians for an hour. These escaped, and on the return journey the Britons were ambushed by thirty Indians and slaughtered.[36]

The British ministers, however tactless their language, were expressing an anxiety widespread among Argentines as well as foreigners. The level of criminality and the performance of the law courts had exercised urban and rural elites since the time of Rosas and before. Social disorder in republican Argentina and the authorities' concern for public safety were constants throughout the period, despite changes in political leadership.[37] True, social control and punishment of criminals were pursued more actively under Rosas than under his liberal successors. But traditional clientage and barrio autonomy survived all regimes and closely affected the administration of justice. Under liberal governments many citizens, by making direct appeals to police chiefs or to other *patrones* within the barrio, using personal influence to bypass the bureaucratic process of criminal justice, sought instant justice against lower-class criminals who threatened their persons and property. This informal favoritism was not available to foreigners, and for British envoys in pursuit of justice the only recourse was to bring pressure to bear on government departments. The massacre at Tandil had been a gruesome demonstration that foreigners indeed suffered discrimination. The sequel was not reassuring.

Argentine governments took refuge in silence; they sought to avoid confrontation, but also to avoid responsibility. Presidents left massacres to ministers, ministers to provincial governors, and governors to local officials. When foreigners protested, they were passed down the line. But Sarmiento was too honest to ignore Argentina's lawlessness, and he took action where he could. In veiled language he even revealed his concern over events such as those at Tandil, which he regarded as a case of banditry; this in turn he attributed to delay in allocating national land and transforming the desert into farming communities: "Settlement of underpopulated territory is needed to counter banditry, which obstructs trade, destroys properties, takes lives, demoralizes the spirit, and paralyzes all social life. Banditry also obstructs immigration and keeps the countryside in a state of emptiness."[38] Immigration or banditry, another Sarmiento antithesis, a variation on the theme of civilization and barbarism. But the killers of Tandil demonstrated that there were people in Argentina who hated foreigners and resented immigrants, and they left a challenge to a government that looked the other way.

7

Massacre and Migrants: The British Reaction

TANDIL AND THE BRITISH

Death on the frontier was the fate of many migrants in the nineteenth century. The reputation of the Argentine frontier suffered in addition from the perceived inertia of the government. A decade of denunciation by foreign observers had produced no obvious improvement in security. British officials insisted that the Tandil massacre was simply the culmination of serial atrocities committed by gauchos and Indians, all of which had been logged and lamented by the legation—and ignored by the Argentine authorities. But the events of 1 January 1872 concentrated the mind and brought to the fore deeply held resentments. On the British side, reports of atrocities led to warnings to emigrants and disparagement of Argentina. The Argentines reacted furiously, defending their position and displaying their pride.

The British sense of outrage spilled over into official protests. The consul in Buenos Aires, Frank Parish, lodged a complaint with the provincial government over "the horrible massacre of Foreigners which has been perpetrated by some bands of Gauchos near Tandil.... Among the unfortunate victims were two British subjects, Mr. Gibson Smith and his young wife to whom he had been very recently married." Parish demanded more information on the origin and nature of the atrocity, as his countrymen were ever more anxious concerning security in distant parts of this province "and the constant exposure of life to which they are subject from the numbers of outlaws and criminals who roam with impunity throughout the country." He was confident that "any official instigation on my part would be unnecessary to induce Your Excellency's Government to adopt such measures as will ensure the speedy and condign punishment" of the criminals.[1]

These reproaches rankled in Buenos Aires, and Parish was kept waiting two months for a reply. Then he was curtly told that he had no standing in the matter nor any right to make official complaints to the provincial government; if he wanted more information about the massacre, he should consult the press. The British consul was incredulous. He had assumed that the delay was due to oversight, "and I was little prepared to hear from Your Excellency that it proceeded from an intentional disregard on the part of the Governor of any communication on the ground that I was not entitled to address his Government in such a case and that I might refer to the Public press for any information I might require on the subject." This was an extraordinary way of conducting business; the welfare of British subjects was certainly his concern, and in its pursuit he had right of access to the authorities. "Crimes on British citizens abroad create feelings of national interest and demand redress. It is in the interest of the Government of this Country, interested as it is in promoting Foreign immigration as a means of advancing the nation," to reassure foreigners of legitimate support. As for the press accounts of the massacre, they were inadequate; neither from these nor any other source had he been able to obtain a satisfactory account of the death of Mr. and Mrs. Gibson Smith, nor did he know what had become of their property.[2]

The Argentine reply treated Parish to a lengthy and ponderous constitutional lecture on national sovereignty and provincial rights but came to the same conclusion: the consul had no right to demand information, and in any case only the court could give that. The whole correspondence was then passed to the Argentine Foreign Ministry. Tandil was evidently a sore point with government officials. They were unwilling to discuss the details of the massacre and took refuge in constitutional proprieties. Yet Parish simply raised to diplomatic level what was common criticism in Argentina itself: the lack of serious investigation of the crime and the refusal of the authorities to provide, or even to seek, hard evidence of the motivation and nature of these horrendous events. Such obduracy was harmful to their own credibility as a government as well as to the welfare of foreign immigrants.

The argument moved further up the political ladder. The British chargé d'affaires, Hugh Guion MacDonell, a soldier turned diplomat with a long career of senior appointments ahead of him, lost no time in calling on Carlos Tejedor, the Argentine minister of foreign relations, to represent the fears of the British settlers, as expressed in written memorials, and the views of the British government. He demanded that an example be made of the Tandil criminals. He was undeterred by Argentine claims that his action amounted to interference in the internal affairs of a sovereign state. The essential fact was that barely a day had passed in the last six months when a Briton had not been killed by gauchos or Indians; the law had been defied with impunity by the former,

and the army, which was itself recruited from delinquents, was regarded with contempt by the latter. MacDonell was anxious not to
cross the line dividing legitimate concern from political intervention,
but he made it clear to Tejedor that he expected the Tandil murderers
to be given summary justice and the Indians to be driven back from
close proximity to the frontier. This was imperative to protect the lives
and property of the foreigners settled there, "which the Government
now knowingly and recklessly exposes."

In a defiant reply Tejedor made three points. First, he refused to accept
that the settlers had any greater rights than those of native Argentines,
and they had no right to address the government on matters of internal
administration. Second, foreigners must accept Argentine laws and pro-
cedures, which were very liberal towards foreigners and gave them protection equal to that of Argentines. Third, foreigners were not justified
in taking measures of self-defense against Indians but must rely on the
provincial government, and if they had complaints about the crimes of
Tandil, they should address them to the proper authorities.[3]

In Buenos Aires dignity took precedence over discretion. MacDonell
had understood that these exchanges were confidential and was indig-
nant when the Argentine government subsequently published them,
presumably to establish its nationalist credentials. He was even more
angry that foreigners were being denied the right to complain; President
Sarmiento's government would live to regret this "dangerous and blind
policy," for one-third of the population was foreign and the government's attitude would force immigrants to take the law into their own
hands.[4] Publication of the correspondence won few debating points for
Argentina. British opinion in Buenos Aires thought that Tejedor's reply
to MacDonell was "exceedingly insolent in tone," and the press claimed
that Tejedor ignored Article 2 of the Anglo-Argentine Treaty of 1825,
which stated that British subjects would enjoy "the most complete protection and security," and Article 14 of the Argentine constitution,
which guaranteed all inhabitants the right of petition. As for the wider
field of Anglo-Argentine relations, "What a blank the Republic would be
without English residents, English capital, English enterprise, English
industry and the good will of Englishmen both here and abroad."[5]

The *River Plate Times* dealt with each of Tejedor's points in turn.
First, it agreed that foreigners were subject to Argentine law. But the
local authorities were often in league with offenders, and central government did nothing. At Tandil, Tata Dios was said to be on close terms
with local officials and elite networks. At Bahía Blanca, after killing
Jordan, the Indians went into town to sell their spoils; fearing retalia-
tion from the foreign settlers, they asked for and received armed pro-

tection to return to their camp. Expeditions against Indians consisted of convicts disguised as "soldiers" who often fraternized with the enemy. Second, while Argentina had liberal and protective laws concerning foreigners, in practice these were ineffective. In many places the "so called troops are without arms or clothing and are almost as much a terror to the settlers as the savages whom they are supposed to keep at bay." Meanwhile, assassins such as those at Tandil are spared the death penalty by a paternal government, and the confidence of English settlers is further eroded. Finally, while it is true that foreigners should not take the law into their own hands but rely on the provincial authority for protection, authority does not do its duty. Are they to stand idly by while their property is stolen and destroyed? If the situation continues, immigration will cease, for the British government will warn emigrants what to expect. Surely Sarmiento cannot want this.[6]

Immigrant opinion was scathing in its criticism of official complacency. Settlers pointed to the great disparity between policy and practice. There is a great outcry about Tandil, one of them argued, but nothing will be done. Foreigners may settle on the frontier and see lives and possessions taken but may not fire on the Indians invading their land. The government thinks as much of an Indian as it does of a Christian; Tejedor gives protection to the Indians but not to the settlers; the law defers more to the criminal than to his victim. The military commander at Bahía Blanca compromised our security by going on a filibustering expedition against the Indians; we formed a committee to demand remedy for the Indian incursion which then ensued, but no action has been taken. Indeed, Tejedor has said that the frontier is no place for settlers (January 1870), yet only four months earlier the minister of the interior, Vélez Sarsfield, appointed a subcommittee for immigration to Bahía Blanca. Tejedor has got the facts wrong: he has said that foreigners only constitute 10 percent of the frontier population, but in Bahía Blanca they are 19 percent.[7]

British reporting from Argentina, official and otherwise, kept the massacre of Tandil before the eyes of the British public, and the details became known in political and social circles. The issue was raised in the House of Commons in August 1872. Mr. C. Dalrymple asked the under secretary of state for foreign affairs, following "the lamentable massacre of foreigners at Tandil, Buenos Aires," what steps Her Majesty's government had taken or intended to take to secure for the future the safety of British settlers in the Argentine Republic. He was assured that the Argentine government had been reminded of its duty to protect those whom it had induced to settle in the country; otherwise, "it must reconcile itself to the reproaches of those nations whose subjects suffer from its neglect of duty, and to the loss it will sustain by a cessation of the flow of immigration which has hitherto been directed to the country."[8] The reply revealed that the British government had little leverage over Argentina, short of cutting off trade and investment, and it had no wish to do that. At a political level British policy was firmly noninterventionist, and since 1846 gunboat diplomacy had not been an option in Anglo-Argentine relations.

COMPENSATION, FOR AND AGAINST

Some six weeks after the massacre, John Smith, brother of William Gibson Smith, wrote to the Foreign Office for further information on the murder of his brother and sister-in-law and to enquire whether the British consul had any duty to protect the property of deceased British subjects. He also asked if there was a case for requesting compensation from the Argentine government. In the course of his letter John Smith stated that judging from his brother's letters, he had between fifteen hundred and two thousand pounds sterling in moveable property—cattle, sheep, and shop goods.[9] The case was also pressed by John Hamilton, M.P., on behalf of Andrew Smith.[10]

The British government considered the problem. The law adviser to the Crown was consulted on possible compensation for the crimes committed at Tandil as well as in the Indian raid of December 1871 at Bahía Blanca.[11] The preliminary conclusion was that where property had been destroyed by Argentine subjects, and the local authorities were not providing adequate protection, there were grounds for claiming compensation from the Argentine government. But where the attackers were Indians, not gauchos, no such grounds existed. Foreign Secretary Granville thought that Tejedor's argument that settlers should approach local authorities with their complaints and use Argentine legal remedies was persuasive, if only property had been involved. Where the parties were dead, however, there could be no legal remedy. Granville instructed MacDonell to discover whether there had been negligence on the part of the local authorities in affording protection and if so to demand compensation. If no negligence was found, the British government could do nothing.[12]

The answer to the Smiths, therefore, should have been that a claim for compensation was justified, for the murderers were indeed under Argentine jurisdiction, and there was strong suspicion that the local authorities had been negligent, if not actively involved. But no compensation was considered, and the Foreign Office seems to have allowed the matter to lapse. Not so the Argentine government and its apologists, who continued to berate the Foreign Office for what they regarded as effrontery. An article in the semiofficial newspaper *La Tribuna* cited compensation claims as one of many British injustices against Argentina. Why, it was asked, should the government pay compensation? "There is no principle or practice which support Granville in this: he wants to treat us as a nation of fools and thinks that his name alone will fill us with dread and silence." We know that we need foreign capital and immigration for rapid progress, but there is something more important—our conviction of our rights. Even though England is involved, Granville's doctrine is an "abuse and a judicial and diplomatic monstrosity." If governments are responsible for the crimes committed on their territory, why has Granville suddenly decided to apply this principle to Argentina? He could have applied it equally well to the Paris Commune, the Polish killings, and the American Civil War. And will England pay diplomatic indemnity to diplomats of other countries whose subjects are murdered in London? Clearly not—it is ridiculous to think so. Crimes are attacks on law, and since the government represents the law they are also attacks on government. And this was true of the events at Tandil: all claims for indemnity in that case are "absurd, unfounded and unjust."[13]

In other cases pressure by British ministers produced results. The widow of a British settler robbed and murdered at Chivilcoy in October 1874 received thirty thousand dollars' indemnity for loss of property. An Irishman, MacCrea, was put in stocks by the military authorities for supposed involvement in *mitrista* subversion. On the intervention of the British minister he was released, compensated with one hundred pesos, and advised to pursue the matter through the courts. Mrs. Lenihan, widow and rape victim, was awarded twenty thousand dollars' compensation following the murder of her husband at Navarro.[14]

Compensation, however, was not a priority of the settlers themselves. MacDonell acknowledged for the purposes of compensation the distinction between depredations committed by gauchos and those by Indians, but pointed out that the settlers of Tandil and Bahía Blanca did not ask for compensation: they wanted the "moral support and assistance of their natural protectors." The Argentine government had to be told that Britain insisted on the right to be heard when its citizens suffered wrongs, as they had recently. The fact was, though he did not spell it out, that things had changed since the days of Mitre, an avowed Anglophile; the government of Sarmiento contained a number of ministers resentful of British hegemony. MacDonell was convinced that there was a "growing spirit of antagonism" in the attitude of the Argentine authorities towards foreigners and that the representatives of Her

Majesty's government were openly discounted; there was also a great jealousy of foreign enterprise, and "difficulties, obstacles, exclusions are daily placed in the way of British interests" despite the fact that the country was dependent on British capital. Meanwhile, gauchos continued to terrorize foreigners, especially Britons.[15]

Granville George Leveson-Gower, second Earl Granville, it might be supposed, knew little of Argentina beyond his reading of the dispatches from Buenos Aires; a stalwart of the Liberal party, he was more at home dealing with Europe or the colonies than with Latin American republics. But he knew enough to appreciate that it was not to Britain's advantage to pursue political, as distinct from economic, objectives in Argentina or to allow British policy to be defined by private interests. This was inherited wisdom. Granville's replies, no doubt read by Mac-Donell with increasing exasperation, were couched in words of benign remoteness and reproduced the reticence cultivated by the Foreign Office. He acknowledged that the settlers had been requesting protection rather than compensation, but here, too, the British government distinguished between the different kinds of injuries suffered by Britons, each type calling for a different degree of pressure on the Argentine government. Argentina incurred an obligation by inviting immigrants, and these should be treated like Argentine citizens and protected against Indians, as they have been in the past; but now there was not sufficient protection against the incursions of lawless people. This was "wholly incompatible with what might reasonably be expected from a civilized government," and if this state of affairs continued, Argentina would suffer the reproaches of other nations whose emigrants had settled there and would find that the flow of immigrants ceased. These were virtually the same words as those used in the House of Commons by Granville's under secretary of state.

The state of mutual incomprehension between the two countries emerged starkly in these exchanges, and again British demands provoked national susceptibilities. MacDonell was instructed to present Granville's dispatch to the Argentine foreign minister, Carlos Tejedor. An activist in the opposition to Rosas and among the exiles in Chile, Tejedor subsequently achieved distinction as editor of *El Nacional*, national deputy, law professor, and director of the Biblioteca Nacional. When Sarmiento appointed him minister of foreign relations in 1870, he was already deeply committed to the work of national organization and defense of the new state against foreign as well as internal interference. His reaction to MacDonell was normally negative and on this occasion distinctly hostile.[16] As Granville did not accept the position of the Argentine government, asked Tejedor, what was the point in presenting the dispatch? Foreigners already enjoyed greater privileges than native Argentines, and though equal before the law, they were generally more leniently treated. The law of Argentina was no more defectively administered than the law of England. Indeed, Argentina's record on crime, prisons, and public safety compared favorably with that of England. Immigrants came voluntarily to improve their lot, and they had no right to question the government's internal administration or to claim the assistance of British representatives. The frontier was the exclusive concern of the Argentine government: neither natives nor foreigners nor their representatives had any standing in the matter. If the British government wished to deter immigrants from coming to Argentina by depicting the country as a refuge of assassins and robbers, let it do so. Tejedor would not protest against such public statements, but would note this "unfriendly act" and repay it in kind at the first favorable opportunity. Meanwhile, the Argentine government would continue to encourage immigration.

MacDonell was equally uncompromising. He deplored the "narrow spirit of susceptibility" with which the Argentine government met the complaints of foreign representatives, especially those of the British; he claimed to see evidence of "a transparent feeling of unfriendliness, if not of animosity," manifested towards the British in official circles and throughout the country, though British immigrants had done much for Argentina. As far as Britain was concerned, it was no infringement of the "moral compacts binding civilised states" to urge on Argentina the need to protect settlers. The British government was only concerned to obtain for its citizens the kind of protection they enjoyed elsewhere in the world. MacDonell declined to argue about crime statistics except to point out that in the last eight years he had learned of one hundred murders and outrages committed against British subjects but only heard of one murderer punished for his crime, the rest being allowed to escape. As for the situation on the frontier, the British government had no wish to interfere in Argentina's defense policy, only to point out that British settlers had been attracted by promises of security for life and property, and these had not been honored. Argentina was running the risk of losing the sympathy and good will of the European nations, and this would affect both trade and immigration. If Argentina wanted good relations, the government "would do well" to find the means to protect foreign settlers; if not, the British government would not hesitate to dissuade Britons from coming, "however unpalatable such timely and needful dissuasion might prove to the Argentine government." Even Argentina's own National Chamber was voicing its anxiety over disorder on the frontier and had recently denounced the negligence of the authorities; surely foreigners were also entitled to appeal through their "natural protectors" against outrages committed against their persons and properties by both Indians and lawless natives.

This acrimonious dialogue between the two countries was continuous as well as wide-ranging. Britain was drawn into a further dispute, this time involving the diplomatic corps in general, when the Italian minister attempted to obtain compensation for losses sustained by Italian citizens in Uruguay. Foreign representatives witnessed yet another display of Argentine nationalism. In late May 1872, under the heading "La Europa y la América," an article linked to Héctor Varela, brother of former Foreign Minister Mariano Varela, appeared in *La Tribuna*, a newspaper founded by the Varelas after the fall of Rosas and now close to the national government. The article argued against the Italian claim, pointing out that lawyers disagreed on the responsibilities for losses sustained in war, but that most regarded them as acts of God, not subject to compensation. Reference was made to the British decision on losses sustained in the Franco-Prussian War, and it was demanded that weak nations should receive the same treatment as the strong. The writer then generalized from this case by claiming that the representatives sent by European states to America, with a few rare exceptions, did not carry out their functions in a way befitting the agents of great nations.

> They readily become irritated and espouse as their own the individual cause of their fellow countrymen, with all the exaggerations of that spirit of greed characteristic of an interested party, thus giving cause to their being frequently suspected of participating in the business. (This does not apply to the Italian Minister; his sense of honor is well known.) But it is a truth which should be proclaimed in plain words, that there is not a single American Republic which has not been a victim to the malevolence of some Consular or Diplomatic agents, it being always coincident that those agents who create the greatest difficulties are precisely those who arrive in the country with no other means but salary and who soon become landowners or capitalists. . . . If the matter be regarded in its proper light this may furnish us with the key to the different interpretations of International Law when the question arises of applying its principles to weaker nations.

MacDonell called the article "violent and disgraceful" and particularly objected to the allegation that the key to the claims of foreign subjects lay not in the "wholesale depredations and murders committed with impunity by the sons of the soil" but in the pecuniary profits shared by diplomatic and consular agents. Approached by the Italian minister, MacDonell and the representatives of Spain and France joined in a collective protest against the "gross and wanton" insult which they saw in the article. In his reply Foreign Minister Tejedor stated that the Argentine government shared the "injured feelings" of the diplomatic representatives and that it was always painful when the press—the true sign of the moral progress of the country—let itself and the country down. Even so, the government was also offended by the representatives' reaction to the article. They had taken what was intended to be a general point personally, and their decision to send him a collective note was a misjudgment. Tejedor defended the press. Although it sometimes made mistakes, it was the lifeblood of democracy; the government itself was under daily attack from the press, especially the foreign press, which criticized not only the government but also the country as a whole. The president rejected the unmerited charge made by the article and assured the diplomatic representatives of their good standing. MacDonell was apparently satisfied with this apology, grudging and tendentious though it was, reserving his verbal blows for future rounds.[17]

CIVIL DISTURBANCE

Disorder in Argentina was not confined to the frontier or to the action of delinquents. It also had its source in past conflicts between central government and provincial rights, the memory of which was still active in 1870. As the agents of national organization sought to impose themselves, the provinces reacted in a final convulsive defiance, partly an expression of innate impoverishment, partly the resistance of caudillos to national organization. In 1863 and again in 1866–68, Mitre had to suppress rebellions in the interior. In 1870 the province of Entre Ríos was in effect captured by Ricardo López Jordán, who killed his rivals and kept alive the cult of caudillism and rebellion against Buenos Aires until 1876.

These primitive disturbances were an irritant to modernizing presidents and a further embarrassment to Argentina in its relations with Britain. For Britain had subjects in the interior as well as in Buenos Aires, and its consuls were alert to their interests, especially to demands for compensation for damage suffered in Entre Ríos. This was already a contentious issue before the Tandil massacre added fuel to the heated exchanges between the two countries, and in the British view it confirmed the need formally to warn emigrants of the dangers in Argentina.

In June 1871, MacDonell pressed the Argentine government on behalf of British subjects who had sustained losses in the Entre Ríos rebellion. Foreign Minister Tejedor admitted responsibility for losses caused by government troops but refused to countenance claims for those inflicted by the rebels, citing in support a recent British decision that the French government was not responsible for damage to British property caused by the Germans in the Franco-Prussian War. Argentina, of course, was not at war, and civil disturbances were a different case, as the British were quick to point out. They argued that although foreign subjects were privileged in Argentina, those privileges were proportional to the advantages which the foreigner brought to that country, and without them the foreigner would not have come to Argentina in the first place. If the Argentine government succeeded in establishing the principle that henceforth foreigners must accept the same risks as nationals, intending emigrants should be warned that they came at their own risk and that no protection could be given them by the British government.

In the years since 1863 the Argentine government had been engaged in a long struggle with rebellious provinces at enormous cost to itself and great financial losses to private individuals. MacDonell reported that "the acts of plundered spoliation openly committed by the authorities both civil and military on these occasions are beyond belief, the government being neither able nor willing to check them." And if justice is sought at the law courts, "bribery and bribery alone can secure it."

Foreigners' privileges were resented in Argentina, and the risks were high. This was the British view. Foreigners were always the first to suffer during revolts from the exactions and requisitions of both the government and the rebels; at least the native belonged to one side or the other. Foreigners relied on the justice they hoped eventually to receive and in consequence worked more confidently and productively; their properties therefore offered greater temptation to marauders. Mac-Donell concluded that it would be unfair to deprive the foreigner of the "scant protection he now enjoys by assimilating him to the native."[18] The Argentine position was reaffirmed by Tejedor in a written statement. He again denied Argentine responsibility for losses caused by rebels in Entre Ríos and argued that if foreigners resided and worked in rebel territory they must expect to share the fate of the rebels. Tejedor cited international precedents in support of this contention. And President Sarmiento later announced that the government would not accept claims for losses sustained in civil war.[19]

The decision to refuse claims arising from the Entre Ríos rebellion was attacked in *The Standard* in two articles. The first, "International Law," argued that Tejedor was attempting to change the conditions on which emigrants came to Argentina; he ignored treaty obligations, and the government received taxes from the foreigner and therefore had a responsibility towards him. The second, "Foreign Claims," argued that the government should indemnify foreigners for losses in Entre Ríos since Argentina's future depended on foreign capital and foreign labor. It went on to cite the Anglo-Argentine Treaty, which exempted Britons from military conscription, forced loans, military exactions and requisitions and from paying any taxes greater than those paid by natives. It pointed out that the treaty did not distinguish between government or rebel exactions. The article warned that the precedent the government was setting would check immigration and cause foreign *estancieros* to leave, and it concluded that Tejedor's note was more ruinous to immigration than the adverse emigration notice issued in London.[20]

The final Argentine position on compensation was contained in a Green Book presented by Tejedor to Congress in May 1873. After citing various international precedents, the government rejected all diplomatic interventions regarding losses sustained by foreigners during the Entre Ríos rebellion, whether caused by national or rebel troops. The government insisted that these matters were for the courts and for them alone. Foreign governments could demand diplomatic discussion but not the reversal of court decisions.[21]

Anglo-Argentine relations in the years about 1870 were conducted in loud voices. Law and order, the risks to foreigners, the rights of immigrants, these particular issues excited the British and irritated the Argentines. But behind the arguments lay deeper emotions. What MacDonell was witnessing was a burgeoning of Argentine nationalism, in abeyance under Rosas, released during national organization, and now provoked by foreign pressure and insinuations concerning "civilization." He concluded, shrewdly enough, that Tejedor was not activated primarily by his reasoning but by the conviction held by many influential Argentines that however much Argentina had been dependent on foreigners for its development in the past, it now occupied a position in European financial and commercial markets which justified the shaking off of "that sort of moral tutelage which they [the Argentines] imagine to be exercised over them to the detriment of their independence."[22]

The British representatives in Argentina were conscious of Argentine hostility over Tandil and other matters. MacDonell discovered that the reply which Parish received from Malaver was very different from those received by other consuls; he assumed it was probably influenced by Tejedor's reaction to his own representations. He thought that it should be possible to intervene in a friendly fashion in a case like that of Tandil without upsetting the course of international relations.[23] British diplomacy, however, was special in Argentina and drew a particular animosity.

8

Immigration and Anglo-Argentine Relations

POLITICS AND PROFITS

Palmerston was convinced that countries like China, Portugal, and the republics of South America needed a dressing down every eight or ten years to keep them in order. "They care little for words, and they must not only see the stick but actually feel it on their shoulders."[1] The idiom of foreign policy had changed since Palmerston's days, and gunboat diplomacy was now a last resort. The policy of nonintervention in the internal affairs of Argentina, first enunciated by Canning but forgotten in the 1840s, was reaffirmed in the 1850s and firmly entrenched in the period 1862–75.[2]

British diplomacy responded positively to Argentina's national reorganization and its imperatives of free trade, investment, and modernization. Economic relations became the priority, and British policy was effectively managed not by diplomatic personalities but by businessmen dealing directly with the Argentine authorities and private interests. Political diplomacy was low-key, careful not to interfere or alienate government or groups. The period 1852–62 has thus come to be seen as a time of "transition from political to business diplomacy."[3] It was in these years that Britain exercised a moderating influence in Argentina and helped to prevent civil war between Buenos Aires and the rest of the republic; at the same time, it secured Argentine agreement for the complete repayment of the loan of 1824 and all its defaulted interest.

The advent of Mitre in 1862 confirmed these trends. The president himself led the way in encouraging British trade and investment, and prices, commodities, and interest rates became more significant than politics and protocol. British diplomacy remained aloof from the Paraguayan war, which was regarded as a diversion from the real interests of the Platine republics and an irritant rather than an obstacle to the expansion of Argentina's exports and imports. Conspiracy was a myth;

there were no secret deals, no international profits from Paraguay's prostration. While it is true that British loans contributed to the eventual victory of Argentina and Brazil, these loans were difficult to raise, for British businessmen were not interested in bankrolling wars in South America.[4] Trade and investment, on the other hand, responded positively to Mitre's free-market economy; banks, railway and tram companies, public utilities, these inaugurated the first phase of British capital investment from 1862 to 1875, before depression briefly brought the process to a halt.[5] The success of the system depended on collaboration between British investors and the Argentine state, the first providing funds for Argentine development, the second guaranteeing advances and profits.

Yet the primacy of profits could not remove the political element from Britain's relations with Argentina, and there was never a simple choice for policy makers. The first steps towards modernization also meant opening the gates to mass immigration at a time when Britain had people as well as capital to export. Although Britain contributed investment rather than immigration to Argentine development, British subjects did in fact settle in Argentina in the period 1862–75 in greater numbers than before. Argentina undertook to provide guarantees for both capital and colonists, but the latter obviously had a lower priority and in any case were more difficult to protect. British ministers in Buenos Aires, therefore, had problems on their hands besides trade and investment. It was part of a consul's duties to secure justice for British subjects whether they were businessmen or farmers and to direct their gaze to life on the frontier as well as in the port. When settlers were killed, consuls had to press for action, and if property was sequestered they had to demand compensation. British officials were thus drawn into conflict with the Argentine authorities at a time when the interests of business diplomacy required conciliation. A British chargé who spoke his mind could provoke the government and alienate the press. On the other hand, if he did not speak up for British subjects there would be questions in Parliament, complaints to the Foreign Office, and letters to *The Times*.

No doubt Argentine growth and British profits cushioned political tensions and kept outrage over massacres within bounds. But when depression struck, when the Argentine economy was hit by a fall in the international price of wool, as it was in the mid-1870s, the atmosphere could change. In 1862–72, British exports to Argentina were rising, and at an increasing rate, reaching a high peak in 1867–72, precisely the years in which concern for British settlers was mounting. In the succeeding decade British exports to Argentina began to fall, first in textiles and then in iron, steel, and coal. Soon the banks were in trouble.[6] Tension in the economic and financial sphere projected itself into political life, leading to calls for a reconsideration of British policy towards Argentina. In 1876 a direct threat was offered to one sector of British joint-stock investment when the Santa Fe government decreed the closure of the Rosario branch of the London and River Plate Bank, and in 1880 the outbreak of a brief civil war endangered the political stability of Argentina and its neighbors. These events raised a call for political intervention to protect British property interests.

The British government preferred to leave political and economic recovery in the hands of the Argentine authorities, backing Roca's campaign against the Indians and keeping calm during the civil war of 1880, the blockade of Buenos Aires, and the incidental threat to British capital and property. Britain took no action during this turmoil and refused to resort to gunboat diplomacy, thus helping to preserve political stability and restore economic growth to the River Plate.[7] Equally, experience had taught Britain to discourage enterprises such as immigration, which brought political disputes and allegations of intervention and thus threatened the free play of the market in Anglo-Argentine relations. In the meantime, however, many immigrants were in exposed positions, and their interests could not be ignored.

THE IMMIGRANTS

The age of migration was brought into being by population growth in Europe and improved transport to the Americas and Australasia.[8] A number of reasons persuaded people to emigrate: pressure on the land, the decline of rural industry, the effect of cheap American grain on farm incomes, and the tendency of dependent economies to tilt towards more developed ones. But developed economies, too, became migrating economies. Over the period 1851–1913 British emigration rates were among the highest in Europe, and about ten million, or 20 percent, of all European emigrants came from Britain.[9]

Of the emigrants from England and Wales, 35 percent came from London, the West Midlands, or Lancashire. The push-pull equation did not always apply; sometimes there was no push and little pull. The majority of British migrants came from an urban background and were not primarily the victims of decline in rural industry or the agricultural depression of the 1870s and 1880s. Nor were they drawn from the poor; they tended to be craftsmen and farmers, groups who were not forced out by poverty, unemployment, or other adversities and could in fact make a contribution to emigration costs.[10] This does not rule out economic factors. British emigration was responsive to short-run changes in economic opportunities at home and abroad, and by the 1880s emigrants were more likely to be laborers, though they, like other emigrants, were seeking better things rather than fleeing from absolute destitution. Emigration rates were related to the level of previous emigration and signified a chain of migration forged by a transfer of information back to England.[11] Networks of migrants offered safeguards: numbers generated more numbers through information, contact, and assistance.[12] Otherwise, in the absence of linkage and knowledge, emigrants would only go to places where conditions were exceptionally favorable and the risks manifestly minimal; such places were the United States, Canada, and Australia in the 1880s. For these reasons Latin America was not a serious attraction to British emigrants, and the poorest could not afford to migrate there.

The British government did not leave emigration entirely to market forces but intervened to provide a minimum of protection and support. In promoting, or at least facilitating, emigration the government hoped to relieve distress and to populate the colonies. Its methods were to give free or reduced passages as well as grants of land and implements to individual migrants; it also granted land in the colonies to speculators who made private arrangements to bring out settlers. These arrangements applied to the British empire. Emigrants to foreign countries such as Argentina had to be content with information, advice, and consular support. An Emigration Commission, one of whose functions was to warn emigrants of the risks involved in any given country, was established in London, staffed by civil servants and in liaison with the Foreign and the Colonial Offices.

The great wave of British emigration between 1851 and 1913 was directed almost entirely towards the empire and the United States. Even in Argentina, the Latin American country most favored by Britons and one where they could make their mark if they had capital in land and trade, their numbers were numerically insignificant, a bare 2 percent of total immigration in the nineteenth century. Perhaps they made an impact beyond their numbers; no doubt the British immigrants were strong consumers of British imports, and their purchasing power was superior to that of the working-class Italians and Spaniards. But they were never a mass market.

In the 1860s British immigrants and British capital continued to go primarily into sheep farming. They could buy and stock a sheep farm for £6,500 per square league—more for better locations and less, even £300 a league, in the remote interior. Some eleven hundred sheep farms were owned by British subjects and were worth about £2.5 million in

1875.[13] The British acquired land by investing their own resources. Some brought capital with them; others accumulated capital by the shares system or by working as an *estancia* administrator; yet others invested profits made in commercial enterprise in Argentina. In 1871 the British consul reported that of 10,533 British subjects known to be in Argentina, 5,971 were resident in the rural parts of Buenos Aires, the richest province, and engaged in pastoral enterprise, the most profitable part of the economy.[14] Sheep farming, though dynamic, could suffer setbacks in the European market when wool prices fell, but the most enterprising of the British then turned to wheat and cattle production and made fortunes from land later in the century.

These early British settlers were an economic elite. In the 1860s schemes were developed to increase their numbers. The Argentine government, the Central Argentine Land Company, various philanthropic people in Britain, and others with an eye to business were all anxious to promote colonization. Argentina was seen as a country suitable for the twin migration of people and capital, with the object of establishing colonies of farmers in the pampa region and earning profits for their promoters. Agricultural colonies were regarded as supportive for settlers and convenient for management. But they were expensive; migrants had to receive passage, pay, and capital advances until they were producing. So the Argentine government tended to leave such enterprises to private contractors, selling them large tracts of land at a moderate price on condition of introducing a given number of colonists. In the case of British colonizing companies, some recruited foreigners, while a few concentrated exclusively on British emigrants. In the view of the British legation in Buenos Aires, such colonists were "a cheap and inferior class of immigrant" who were bound to the colony for a limited term and with the possibility of possession if they fulfilled their contract. Many of them never did so. On arrival at the colony the immigrant had to fence in and break the allotted land, but being entirely under the control of the contractor or his agent, he became in fact an agricultural laborer. His earnings *just* defrayed the advances made to him at an onerous rate of interest and left nothing for profit. The colonist often gave up hope, defaulted on his advances, and so lost any claim to land. Meanwhile the contractor remained in possession of the land, now probably more valuable, and easily repeated the process with the next settlers.

Colonies of this kind were first established in Santa Fe province in the 1850s. But with the exception of San Carlos (1854) and Esperanza (1856), which survived at the cost of great hardship for their colonists, they were failures, victims of dishonest contractors, gullible immigrants, want of capital and resources, and the ever menacing Indians. The information given in the prospectus, even by British firms such as Thomson, Bonar and Co., was almost totally erroneous and invariably played down the Indian danger, advising, for example, the acquisition of a breech-loading rifle and revolver, "not that these arms are necessary, but to show the tame Indians that the colonists are armed, the moral effect being sufficient to protect the lives and properties of the latter."[15] Most of the early colonists recruited by the British companies were Swiss, Germans, and Italians. But the colony of Fraile Muerto established in 1863–64 near the Central Argentine Railway was an English enterprise in which the colonists themselves invested heavily. Farming proved difficult; a series of natural disasters and Indian raids combined with lack of capital and of profits caused many of the colonists to give up in despair. By the 1870s Fraile Muerto was struggling badly, and some colonists left for another settlement near Rosario. In 1875 there were still some one hundred English farmers in Fraile Muerto, proof that capital investment could make land profitable, but by then the great influx of Italians and other settlers meant that the colony was no longer really English.[16] The other British colony in Santa Fe, Alexandra colony, for which the London firm of Thomson, Bonar and Co. secured a concession from the provincial legislature in 1870, was more tenacious, in spite of the fate of Andrew Weguelin, son of the principal partner in the firm, who was killed by Indians. The colony was sited ninety miles beyond the "frontier," where land was cheap though insecure. But it survived and became profitable, reinforced by Italians and Swiss and in the form of *estancias* rather than farms. The colonies established by the Central Argentine Land Company in the 1870s contained some British settlers, but again the majority were Swiss and Italians.

Several British subjects settled in the 1860s in Sauce Grande, Bahía Blanca, on lands obtained from the Argentine government. On depositing a sum of eighty pounds sterling and undertaking the expense of erecting a house, sinking a well, and stocking land with at least one thousand sheep, each settler was allotted an area of frontier land free of rent for a term of eight years. By 1872, sixty British settlers were established in Bahía Blanca, variously owning, renting, or laboring on the land in promising economic circumstances—fertile soil and proximity to a port—but permanently exposed to Indian attack in a frontier zone virtually unprotected by the government. In other parts of the province British capital sustained British farmers against heavy odds.[17]

In 1863 interests representing the Welsh Emigration Society signed a contract with the Argentine government by the terms of which they undertook to establish colonies in Patagonia at the rate of three hundred to five hundred families annually for ten years. The government promised land, subsidies, tax exemptions, and protection. Fired by Welsh nationalism and dreaming of a location where they could satisfy their passion for Welsh language and culture as well as their economic needs, a group of 165 settlers arrived in the Lower Chubut Valley in 1865. They differed significantly from other British settlers. In the first place, they wanted a degree of political autonomy in return for opening up Patagonia and establishing an "Argentine" presence there; this was something the Argentine government was reluctant to grant. Second, they were determined to stay and make a success of their community, unlike most British colonists, who either abandoned their holdings or turned them into individual *estancias*. In the first years, before irrigation work was completed, farming, as distinct from sheep rearing, was impossible, and the Welsh settlers would probably have perished without the assistance of the Tehuelche Indians in the development of trade and hunting. This was another difference: whereas the Indians were the dire enemies of most British settlers, they were the saviors of the Welsh. By 1875 the settlement was ready to receive further waves of immigrants, and in the following decades the colony grew in numbers and in territory, developing wheat cultivation for export and pioneering sheep rearing in the Andes.[18]

In the early 1870s the emigration commissioners in London issued a series of notices warning intending emigrants to Argentina of the lack of security for life and property in that country. The notices do not appear to have had much effect in checking the overall flow of migration to Argentina, if only because the British share was never very great (Table 8–1). But they did generate bad feeling between the British and Argentine governments at a time when encouragement of immigration was a prime policy of the Sarmiento presidency.

The notices were not the only strain on Anglo-Argentine relations. The involvement of British consuls and representatives in pressing claims for compensation on behalf of compatriots who had suffered losses from Indian raids, civil disturbances, and lawlessness, and their attempts to intercede in legal cases, both criminal and civil, offended the Argentine sense of national sovereignty and further helped to generate bad feeling. And the tendency of foreigners to look to their diplomats for protection irritated many Argentines, who saw this as another affront to their nation. Sarmiento, who was always concerned to assimilate as well as to populate, was hostile to any action that helped to create foreign communities or prevented immigrants from acquiring Argentine identity and kept them aliens in their new homeland. He

Table 8-1. Immigration, Argentina, 1860–65

	Total	British	% British
1860	5,656		
1861	6,301		
1862	6,716	574	8.5
1863	10,408	883	8.6
1864	11,682	1,015	8.6
1865	11,767	1,583	13.4

SOURCE: Ford to Clarendon, 24 March 1866, Public Record Office, London, FO 6/262, pp. 59–64; Emigration Board to Foreign Office, 8 April 1869, Public Record Office, London, FO 6/287, pp. 39–40.

was also sensitive to any encroachment upon Argentine independence. He stopped the practice of British and French consuls' handling the reception of mail from England and France, he prevented the Italian legation from holding a census of Italians resident in Argentina, and he restricted the display of foreign flags. His concern focused more persistently on the Italians than on other communities, but integration in general was one of the policy preoccupations of his later years.[19] His views were echoed by *La Nación* in an article on foreign claims in 1871. The newspaper's argument was that foreign settlers came to live permanently in Argentina; they could not be allowed to form a society within a society "with all the privileges and exemptions from obligations" they expect. The law treated the property of foreigners in the same way as native property, and foreigners should receive indemnity only in accordance with the law. There was no place for diplomatic representations in this process.[20]

Thus, whatever the priority given to business diplomacy, political issues could not be ignored or conflict avoided.

THE RISKS

In early 1866 the Argentine minister in Paris, Mariano Balcarce, who was also accredited to London, wrote to Lord Clarendon that the enemies of Argentina were trying to undermine its moral credit by circulating reports of a revolution in Buenos Aires the previous December. The facts were quite different: Argentina was in a process of national organization, its trade and production were increasing, and conditions for immigration were exceptionally favorable.[21]

Asked to comment on Balcarce's letter, the British minister in Buenos Aires, Francis Clare Ford, son of the distinguished Hispanist Richard

Ford, reported that the material progress of the country had much increased in recent years, especially since President Mitre took over. The
export of hides had doubled since 1860, while that of wool had increased
by one-third since 1861. Immigration had increased from 5,656 in 1860
to 11,767 in 1865, and employment was available and well paid. But more
immigrants were needed; they were deterred by distance and ignorance
and by the continent's reputation for wars and revolutions. The reports
of a revolution in Buenos Aires the preceding December were circulated
by "unfriendly persons with a view to disparage the credit of a nation,"
probably by jobbers who had an interest in a loan then being negotiated
on the London money market. Balcarce might be right regarding the reorganization of the Argentine republic: the present ruler (Mitre) was
"enlightened, strong, good and beneficent." But in the longer term dangers existed; the issue of federalism versus unitarism was still hotly de-
bated, and no decision had yet been taken on the siting of the capital.[22]

The Emigration Commission in London relied on embassy reports
but exercised its own judgment in making recommendations. Up to
1869 it did not find any specific reason to interfere with emigration to
Argentina, other than the general insecurity of life there; the climate
was healthy, and the conduct of the Argentine government, as shown in
the treatment of the Welsh colony at Chubut, "has been in the highest
degree kind and liberal." The Argentine government had recently undertaken to grant 250 Patacones (about £50) a month to the Chubut settlement.[23]

Yet in the latter part of 1869 lawlessness in general and Indian raids
in particular increased the disquiet among foreign representatives. Indians attacked three colonies in Santa Fe province, causing havoc among
the Swiss, German, and Italian colonists but apparent indifference
among the local authorities. The California Colony in Santa Fe petitioned President Sarmiento (17 November 1869) for protection from the
Indians, who had become increasingly aggressive, while the local fort
manned by four Argentines and twelve paid Indians was totally inadequate. Indians in receipt of government rations had been seen driving
large numbers of probably stolen stock through the area, and the local
chieftain recently told one colonist that anyone who wanted to travel
from the colony would need a passport from him. The petition was
quickly followed by news from Santa Fe that two colonists had been
murdered, not by Indians but by provincial troops. The murders of
Roberts and Eivers (one British, the other a U.S. citizen) led the British
minister, MacDonell, a more abrasive personality than Ford, to remind
Foreign Minister Mariano Varela that because Argentina encouraged
immigrants, it should protect them. The national government always

argued that it could not interfere with provincial rights, though many of these "rights" were in the hands of unscrupulous and violent officials.[25]

Sarmiento was concerned. In January 1870, partly to reassure the foreign representatives in Argentina, he invited them and their gunboats to accompany him on a trip he was making to the provinces of Santa Fe and Entre Ríos to survey the railway between Rosario and Córdoba and inspect the agricultural colonies in Santa Fe.[25] He hoped that his guests would acquaint themselves "with conditions of the foreign colonies in these provinces and convince themselves of the deep interest which the Argentine government takes in their welfare and development."[26] He soon had occasion to vindicate his words. While he and his party were in Rosario, two Britons, Bold and Tait, were murdered on an *estancia* in Santa Fe. MacDonell at once instructed Consul Hutchinson to inform Sarmiento that if nothing was done to halt the "wholesale system of assassination now tolerated in the province," then the British government would be informed that it was hopeless to seek justice from the Argentine government, "whose authorities shelter assassins and sanction every description of crime." Sarmiento immediately offered five thousand hard dollars for the capture of the murderers, and his minister of war spoke energetically to Governor Cabal on the matter. Meanwhile, MacDonell was warning Varela that unless the murderers were properly dealt with, he would formally protest and urge the British government to discourage emigration to Argentina. Varela promised action and assured the British that Argentina's apparent want of energy was the result of constitutional limitations on the national government's power to interfere in provincial affairs. MacDonell did not believe this and continued to exert pressure, threatening official protests and further adverse reports to Britain unless the murderers of Bold and Tait were made "a summary example." Once the murderers were taken and sentenced to death, MacDonell used the same threats to force the national government to exert pressure on the Santa Fe legislature, which had the task of ratifying the sentences. These were eventually carried out later in the year.[27]

While the British legation voiced growing concern over security, the Royal Navy showed the flag when necessary. On the outbreak of an election riot in Rosario in 1870, Her Majesty's gunboat *Cracker* was ordered upriver to protect British lives and property. The riot was evidently caused by several hundred gaucho adherents of the two rival political clubs in Rosario, who swarmed into the streets on the day the votes were cast. The police opened fire, and although no Britons were killed, several had narrow escapes. Foreign consuls asked the minister of war, who had been sent by the national government to restore calm, for assurances that the government would do its utmost to maintain order. Unsatisfied with the answer given, Consul Hutchinson told the minister of war that "if the national government could not make its position as protector of the foreign element more decisive, it would be better to publish such a fact to the world at once."[28]

Law and order were not obviously improving. According to a report in *The Standard*, an Argentine family was butchered by nationals (probably marauding gauchos, but not identified as such) in Baradero, a repeat of the wholesale assassination of the Scott family in 1867, of which little notice was taken. The assassins had been arrested and sent for trial, but they had threatened the people of Baradero with reprisals "when they are freed." The public had no confidence in the judicial authorities. What future can there be for the country when murder and immorality prevail?[29]

MIGRANT WARS

Confrontation increased in 1870. In spite of Argentine efforts to reassure foreign representatives, the British government issued (22 February 1870) a warning notice to intending emigrants to Argentina. The immediate occasion was the murder in Santa Fe of two agricultural colonists, Roberts and Eivers, which caused a strong impression in London and led to direct action by the Emigration Commission:

> In consequence of despatches recently received from H.M. Minister at Buenos Aires, the Emigration Commissioners have been directed by the Secretary of State to point out to persons proposing to emigrate to the Argentine Republic that several British Emigrants and other foreigners . . . have recently been murdered . . . [and] that no effective steps have been taken by the Local Government either to bring the murderers to justice or to protect the survivors. . . . Emigrants must take notice that under these circumstances there appears to be no sufficient security for life in that country.[30]

There was one dissenting voice, and it came from within the Emigration Board. One of its members, T. W. C. Murdoch, opposed the publication of the notice on the grounds that Argentina's past record on immigration did not justify it. In a letter to the Foreign Office he referred to the dispatch of February 1869, in which Stuart reported that the Argentine government was trying to stimulate immigration from the United Kingdom, efforts that Stuart deprecated because of the lack of security in that country. Asked to be more explicit, Stuart explained that while there might not be sufficient grounds to interfere with emigration to Argentina, Her Majesty's government should not encourage it. Stuart considered the possibility of advising discouragement but rejected the idea, since many Britons had made a success of settling in Argentina. It was a fact, however, that several Britons had been murdered, and their murderers had not been punished, because of the lax administration of justice. Murdoch went on to argue that Her Majesty's government never intervened to encourage emigration to foreign countries but only to discourage it when necessary. This could be done through a notice, but at present sufficient cause had not been shown for taking what would be considered as an unfriendly act by the Argentine government, which had acted "with great liberality" towards British emigrants in the past. The number of Britons going to Argentina were few at present, not more than 412 in 1868 and 440 in 1869. The decision, he concluded, rested with the foreign secretary.[31]

The reaction of the Argentine authorities to the publication of the notice was fast and fierce. From Paris, Balcarce protested that the notice was unfair to Argentina and hostile in character; the president had offered a reward for the murderers of Bold and Tait, and they had been arrested.[32] The view from London was that murders and atrocities against British subjects and lack of action by the Argentine authorities justified the notice; it was not intended to be unfriendly to Argentina, but simply to give prospective immigrants fair warning and enable them to make their own decision. News of further outrages served only to confirm these views; no doubt the Argentine government sincerely wished to punish the guilty and was thwarted by provincial rights and local authorities. But equally the British emigrants had a right to be warned. According to the *Registro Estadístico* for 1865–66, 125 assassins had been jailed in Buenos Aires alone and sentenced to hard labor or to serve in the army, but not one had been executed, and escapes from jail were notorious. Britain expected the Argentine government to do better than this; action was needed to remedy the situation.[33]

The emigration notice also came under attack in the letters column of *The Times*. One correspondent, D. Lewis of the National College, Buenos Aires, called the notice "unfortunate, impolitic and unjust," a cause of unnecessary alarm. Foreigners were well received in Argentina, a country now making progress, where civil wars and revolutions were things of the past. National and provincial governments were "composed of liberal, honest and intelligent men"; Sarmiento was a great president and a friend of immigrants. True, there was crime, but reports of it were exaggerated, and over half the murders were committed by foreigners. If the English stopped frequenting *pulperías* and were less free in using their fists, they would not be killed.[34]

In Argentina the press gave vent to national indignation. In a report weak in logic and strong in outrage, *La Tribuna* denounced Stuart, now departed from Buenos Aires but identified as the calumniator whose reports caused the emigration commissioners to issue the notice. True, it admitted, there is crime in Buenos Aires and justice is slow. But where is it not? The greater the population, the more frequent the crime. There is more murder, comparatively speaking, in London than there is in Buenos Aires. And not all immigrants are worthy people; it is striking that where there are few foreign immigrants, there is less crime.[35]

La Nación attacked the notice as exaggerated and unjust and declared that its warning would not affect immigration. Immigrants are welcome in Argentina; they have just as good, if not better, rights than natives, and with a little work and determination they can make a fortune. Why do so few Britons here wish to return to England? The Argentine government is often urged to promote immigration artificially but has rightly refused to do so; it is better that immigrants come to stay and not for transient reasons. The notice paints us as barbarians and assassins and suggests that there is no authority, no social order, and no guarantees. This is not so. "There is no people more peaceful, more moral, more gentlemanly, more hospitable than that of Buenos Aires." It is true that previous safeguards are no longer sufficient in a time of growing population. But does this mean that we are idiots, murderers, and thieves? People realize that traditional security measures are inadequate and have protested, which shows that their sense of order and morality is deeply rooted. Nobody complained when Rosas's *mazorca* was cutting British throats; there was no emigration notice when López (in Paraguay) was shooting Britons or when California was in uproar.

The newspaper then appealed to British immigrants, calling on British colonists to speak out against these infamous exaggerations. How many disorders have there been in Britain in which authority has shown itself to be impotent? We will not mention the Rebeccaites or the Fenians. In Ireland agrarian crime is unchecked by the authorities, property is destroyed, and people are killed; nobody will testify, and the culprits go free. If that happened in Argentina, what would be said? And what warnings have been given to people in Ireland? Yet the Emigration Board, basing its warning on exceptional facts and disregarding the traditions of this country, seeks to stop immigration to Buenos Aires. There is a political motive in all this: most Britons who come here are Irish, and by stopping emigration from Ireland the British government is seeking to prevent the depopulation of that country. Foreign residents already have more rights than the natives; simply by being a foreigner you can have your case tried before the Supreme Court. Foreigners have more guarantees than the natives, but they want even more; they are trying to create a nation within a nation, a city within a city. They are not satisfied unless they bring the diplomatic corps into everything. We resist this tendency.[36]

The English-language newspaper, *The Standard*, could normally be expected to adopt a pro-British point of view, and on the immigration issue it made no exception. It reported that the emigration notice had caused a sensation in Buenos Aires. Argentines "doubtless feel annoyed" that their country is branded a hotbed of crime. They accuse the British minister of ingratitude. Some are offended by the notice. Others see it as evidence of a sincere interest in Argentina and as "a kindly effort on the part of the English government to awaken us all to a sense of the dangers which a too rapid growth of population inevitably entails." We have wretched prisons, and the state of criminal justice is deplorable. The wonder is that there is not more crime. The people of the River Plate are quiet, orderly, and peaceable, and with a proper system of law enforcement and the application of the death penalty, crime statistics would be favorable. During the last month the press has been saying precisely what Stuart has said, yet he is blamed. Immigration from southeastern Europe is increasing, and "in vain the obsolete Spanish form of justice struggles to hold its own." Argentines say that the jails are full of foreign criminals; this may be so, but it is not the point. Stuart said that nobody is punished—and who can deny it?[37]

The British action had evidently touched a number of sore points and aroused collective consciousness. Argentines rejected the idea that their country was not fit for foreigners, repudiated the charge that they were prolific in criminals and lenient on crime, and bristled at the slightest infringement of their independence. The debate in the press and in the country expressed a strong sense of national identity. Ironically, immigration and its consequences may be said to have added their quota to the growth of Argentine nationalism. No government minister or agency allowed the British action to pass unremarked. A letter from the Central Commission of Immigration to the interior minister, Vélez Sarsfield, protested against the "unjust and ill-considered" notice. If the British minister had simply commented that there is occasional indulgence in punishing crimes and that the means for apprehending criminals is sometimes insufficient, we could agree. But between these two charges and the assertion that there is no security for life "is the distance which separates the just from the unjust." There is comparatively less crime in Buenos Aires than in European towns of similar size, the reason being that it is easier to make a living here.[38]

The language of defiance masked another truth. Argentine spokesmen knew their country and its constitution. While they conceded nothing to British critics, they were aware that the weakness of central authority was fatal to effective social control. It was easy to attribute inaction to the existence of a federal constitution and the strength of provincial rights, but these were only part of the story. The Argentine government lacked essential agents of administration, law enforcement, and military power to carry its authority to distant frontiers and curb the enemies of migrants and settlers; experts such as Alvaro Barros admitted as much. Provincial government was closer to events, but not to a solution; there, too, defective institutions and inferior personnel limited the scope for action. Tandil was simply the most recent example of the inability of central government to influence the provincial, and of provincial government to constrain its local representatives. In the regions officials were part of a wider community of interests where patron-client relations and closely knit networks of land and office inspired local policy and determined local priorities. As they surveyed their new homeland, foreign settlers saw a number of power bases in their immediate vicinity—the *estancia*, the municipality, the justice of the peace, the National Guard—none of them instantly responsive to the benevolent words of President Sarmiento. An immigrant in Tandil deferred first to the local boss, then to the authority of provincial government, while the arguments between ministers and consuls in Buenos Aires passed over his head. As for security, he was on his own.

Argentines were conscious of these facts, but self-criticism is rarely on the agenda of diplomatic exchange. Ministers preferred to appeal to national indignation and to carry the attack to the British government; in the years about 1870 a series of migrant wars damaged relations between the British legation in Buenos Aires and the Argentine foreign ministry. In a lengthy interview on 11 April 1870 the interim foreign minister, Nicolás Avellaneda, informed MacDonell, Stuart's successor, that President Sarmiento and the whole government had been "deeply pained" by the Emigration Board notice, which he described as "unjust and undeservedly exaggerated" and as being deeply prejudicial against Argentina. The notice would have "the most serious consequences in creating a feeling of great irritation between Englishmen and Argentines." Although relations between Argentina and Britain had been cordial in the past, Stuart's unwarranted accusations against Argentina—where criminal statistics compared well with those of any European country—could not be overlooked. Avellaneda suggested that he would write to MacDonell along these lines and that MacDonell should reply that since he had taken charge of the mission he could attest to the fact that the Argentine government had done everything in its power towards checking crime and that Stuart's report on the insecurity of life was "ill founded and exaggerated."

MacDonell was astonished at this suggestion and made it clear that even if he disagreed with Stuart, which he did not, he could not contradict him without incurring a reprimand from his own foreign minister, Lord Clarendon. Stuart was only doing his duty, motivated not by any personal animosity towards Argentina but simply by the need to report the current situation. In acting on this the Emigration Commission was not attacking Argentina or inferring that the government willingly shielded criminals. But it was a notorious fact that crimes were committed with impunity in town and country, as the local press reported. MacDonell, however, did not spurn an opportunity to do a deal. If the Argentine government undertook to execute Bold's assassin, then in custody in Rosario, he offered to send a note stating that in the different cases he had brought before it the government had "fairly and boldly undertaken to vindicate the law."[39] Within weeks, however, MacDonell had the ground cut from under him when the British government began to backtrack.

Diplomats were a relatively small cog in the wheel of British policy. In London a number of influences, political, financial, and social, were normally brought to bear on any government, including the Gladstone administration of 1868–74. Emigration policy was no exception. Various financial groups and individuals in the city hoped to make profits out of emigration schemes. At the same time, Argentina had friends in Britain, and these, too, worked to change the notorious notice. In Buenos Aires, on 21 April, Foreign Minister Mariano Varela informed MacDonell that the British government was going to withdraw the notice. The diplomat politely expressed his doubts but soon learned that the information was correct—not, however, from his own government but from the Buenos Aires press. A note dated 6 April announcing the withdrawal of the notice was passed by R. G. Herbert of the Colonial Office to David Robertson, a businessman with extensive interests in Argentina and a prominent defender of the Argentine government in England. MacDonell was now familiar with the practice of the Argentine Foreign Ministry, and indeed of other ministries, of publishing confidential correspondence between governments in the Buenos Aires press, a crude form of open diplomacy. This note was similarly published, and a doubtless frustrated MacDonell admitted his error to Varela.[40]

Britain now tried a more positive approach to Argentina, anxious to lose no favor in the land of opportunity and to concede no advantage to international competitors. It was clear that emigration, especially from Italy, was growing, and significant, too, that orders for passenger vessels had been placed in British shipyards, a useful by-product of migration. It was also thought that land concessions to the railway companies could be used to promote settlement. Even the most myopic of observers could see that Argentina's great natural resources and future potential growth made it an attractive field for immigration as well as investment. But the argument always returned to the great proviso: success would depend on security for life and property. And in spite of all the exertions and all the protests, punishment of the guilty was still uncertain in Argentina and high expectations were placed at risk.

And so the discourse continued. The Argentine government pointed to President Sarmiento's vigorous efforts not only on behalf of immigration but also in support of law and order; he himself had offered and paid a large reward for the arrest of the Rosario killers of Bold and Tait. Varela reminded MacDonell—who had a different recollection—that only two or three Britons of the thousands who lived there had been victims of violence, and these lived in isolated places. The journey of the president to Rosario in January was precisely to study the interests of foreigners and to examine their situation. It was a pity that Mac-Donell did not accompany him; then, suggested Varela, he would have seen what the country has to offer and been in a position to place the alleged insecurity in a proper perspective.

In defining that perspective Varela, man of letters as well as of politics, raised the discussion to a higher level than British diplomats normally adopted and sought to make a valid comparison between a developed country and an underdeveloped one. Argentina, he argued, appreciates that security of life and property in England is good—apart from Ireland—but in America security is not so deeply rooted. Nevertheless, there are compensations. Traditional societies may have security, but they also have old land divisions, and people die from want. Argentina is a great country, enjoying a healthy climate and paying high wages. But in these vast lands the population is neither dense nor homogeneous, and society is not yet perfectly constituted. "It happens that among us there are more cases of personal violence and more difficulty in the application of justice." This does not mean, however, that the Argentine Republic fails to offer security for the life and property of its inhabitants. All Britons do well here, except "for some cases of incurable moral vice or physical incapacity." Not so in England, as the Poor Law shows. What wonder, then, that thousands or even millions of Englishmen, rather than die under an unimpeachable system of justice, should prefer to live in countries where, apart from some drawbacks which distance exaggerates, they are sure to be happy and even perhaps to bequeath a fortune to their families. President Sarmiento has given assurance that he will take every opportunity to awaken the public spirit in favor of the rapid prosecution of crime—in whose perpetration immigrants take part in proportion to their numbers, "thus paying here, as everywhere else, this tribute to human frailty."[41]

There were, of course, a number of gaps in Varela's argument. The suggestions that Argentina was a more open society than Britain and that its land policy was more egalitarian were highly debatable, and he made no reference to the nature of frontier society or hint that marginalization of the gaucho by land concentration was one of the causes of rural violence. The record is silent on MacDonell's side of the argument, as he did not write for the public press or stray from the pragmatic path of British diplomacy.

In his message to Congress in May 1870, Sarmiento announced that the British government had withdrawn the somewhat ill informed notice to emigrants because of "the warm protests of those who know the truth about Argentina." The president himself in previous messages to Congress had drawn attention to the insecurity of life and property and had called for reforms in the system of justice. In his message of 1870 he also appeared to endorse the British argument and to admit that insecurity of life and impunity of crime were such that they must give foreigners an unfavorable impression of Argentina, and he asked Congress to take steps to make more effective the criminal law of the country. MacDonell stayed away from the opening of Congress, anticipating an attack on Britain, and wrote to the foreign minister that he sincerely regretted the "rather inconsiderate" statements made by the president in censuring Her Majesty's government on such an occasion.[42] He denied that British policy was hostile to Argentina and maintained that Britain had to be concerned because of the presence of British subjects and capital in the republic. Friendly representations should not be interpreted as malevolence.

Once national suspectibilities were aroused, Argentines would not back down. Varela was determined to continue the argument and to challenge the "injustice" committed against the republic, though if the legation's translations are to be believed, the longer the discourse the more verbose it became. If the British government is so benevolent to Argentina, asked Varela, why issue the notice? But for the protest of our friends in England, the consequences of the notice may well have been prejudicial to this country. MacDonell has been impolitic in selecting events in Entre Ríos to support his contention. The government is now engaged in a war in Entre Ríos precisely to ensure that the crime committed against a high government servant (the assassination of Urquiza) should not go unpunished; the press and the political parties all support the government in this, even though not all of them approved of Urquiza. Their attitude responds

> to the sentiment and ideas of which the government which you represent makes a boast in the adoption of measures so excessively rigorous as those which that government are about to put into practice in Ireland, in order to assure security to life and property in that part of English territory, where it is not enjoyed as in the remainder of the United Kingdom. . . . A people which like the Argentine accepts a war with enthusiasm, raising for a banner the condemnation of crime, has a right to be considered as a people that aspires to cement its social order on the bases of morality and justice.

If the assassinations had been viewed with indifference by the Argentine government, then the notice may have been justified, but twelve thousand men are pursuing the criminal (López Jordán). There is as much justice in throwing discredit upon our country for the commission of that crime against Urquiza as there would have been in discrediting the United States of America because of the assassination of Lincoln. We do not think that events in Entre Ríos will have any effect on the British cabinet or that they will cause the cabinet to persist in the error of sustaining the notice.[43] MacDonell's response was to go back to the evidence, and in June he presented Varela with a list of murders involving British victims between 1865 and 1870.[44]

Beyond the political conflict over immigration, personal ill feeling also entered Anglo-Argentine relations in these years. When the Foreign Office had second thoughts about the notice it asked Stuart, the former chargé in Buenos Aires whose evidence had played a crucial role in the formation of policy, to comment on the subject. Stuart replied that he saw the emigration notice only after it had been issued and that he personally would not have published it without first threatening to do so in a strong dispatch to the Argentine government. He also indicated that there was an element of personal animosity in his relations with Argentine officials, particularly those of the Foreign Ministry, whose reactions to his representations on murders of British subjects were evidently not to his liking. "What irritated me was the apparent carelessness and want of responsibility of the Argentine Government in such matters. The Minister for Foreign Affairs used simply to smile and say he was sorry but that it was not within his power to interfere with the different provincial governments." Stuart had sought to impress on the federal government that since it had invited immigrants, it had a duty to protect them. Moreover, he would have liked the federal government to accept that foreign powers did have a right to call it to account unless proper activity and earnestness were shown in bringing murderers to justice.[45]

The British action, and the arguments used to defend it, touched a raw nerve among the ruling groups of Argentina. The controversy not only was a dispute over safety for immigrants but also became, for Argentina, a defense of national honor against foreign criticism and censure. The government continued to encourage immigration and to present Argentina as a country of opportunity. And even from Britain there was some response.

PROJECTORS AND PROFITEERS

Varela followed up his disputes with MacDonell by sending a circular to Argentine consular agents setting out the advantages for immigrants in the republic. But not all British emigrants were well advised or even qualified for life overseas. While the Perkins project to colonize lands owned by the Central Argentine Land Company with Swiss, French, and Spanish immigrants appeared promising, the colony projected by H. Henly looked unstable from the start. Some sixty emigrants invested £150 each and embarked for Argentina in early May 1870 to settle in the Fraile Muerto area near Rosario. Most of them were young, well-connected Englishmen, not the kind to succeed in Argentina, and the host government was insufficiently impressed to give them any assistance. "The River Plate," reported MacDonell, "requires a class of emigrants willing to toil under the greatest inconveniences and privations, not gentlemen of education with scanty capital, insufficient to last them until the time when they can reasonably expect to reap the fruits of the labour of those they employ. . . . In short, what is required in this country are labourers and not gentlemen with limited means."[46] By November the Henly colony was in trouble and broke up; the immigrants were unsuited for the life, loath to work, and largely ignorant of agriculture. Henly absconded, and the penniless colonists were cast adrift, a warning to unwary British emigrants against false expectations.[47]

Schemes of this kind were viewed with doubt and disapproval by British representatives on the spot. The murder of a Briton in Fraile Muerto renewed MacDonell's resentment of Argentine inertia. He had hoped, he reported, that the emigration notice and Her Majesty's government's representations would have persuaded the Argentine government to execute some of the dangerous villains now before the courts, an action which would have stemmed the increase of crime. But this was an illusion. Impunity of crime was mounting, abetted by interested parties in England, such as promoters of emigration companies and holders of Argentine stock "who, it is to be hoped, through ignorance of real conditions in Argentina" urged Her Majesty's government to withdraw the notice to emigrants. That notice did serve "to some small extent" to awaken the Argentine government to a sense of duty towards the settlers. The withdrawal of the notice, however, only convinced the government that the administration of justice was perfect and that emigrants were favored in Argentina. "I should tell you that I know of several persons, some officially connected here, others associated with commercial and political circles in England, who were chiefly responsible for HMG withdrawing the Notice." Since they are aware of the real conditions here, they must know that their representations were false.[48]

President Sarmiento was widely known as a supporter of immigration. In May 1870 he received a communication from the board of directors of the Emigrants and Colonists Aid Corporation (ECAC), which included the Duke of Manchester, Marquis of Devonshire, Earl of Denbigh, and other notables, declaring that they intended to promote English emigration abroad and would like to direct some emigrants to Argentina, to any place chosen by the president.[49] The scheme proposed that the Argentine government select the site for the colony and hand it over in trust. The Argentine government should also issue 6 percent bonds at 75 to cover the expenses, which were estimated at £175,000 for a colony of one thousand families. The bonds would be negotiated in London by the ECAC, which would receive out of the yearly repayments of the colonists 5 percent per annum on the amount of capital required for the colony, plus 5 percent in the first year for the negotiation of the bonds, plus annual commission on the loan. The remaining money would be remitted to the ECAC for interest and amortization payments on the bonds. When the bonds had been redeemed, the Argentine government could take over the colony and its administration. Each emigrant family (about four persons) would receive forty to sixty acres, together with the cost of maintenance for one year to cover passage, building, cattle, fencing, and other expenses, and the interest on this sum would be 10 percent per year.

Proposals of this kind were closely scrutinized by the Emigration Commission, and the report of T. W. C. Murdoch was ready in July. He concluded that the scheme would "not be unprofitable" for the ECAC. The Argentine government was to meet the expenses with 6 percent bonds issued at 75 when currently Argentine 6 percent bonds were quoted at 87–89. The ECAC was to receive 5 percent on the capital expended in founding the colony—£8,750—plus commission. Since the

ECAC contributed none of the finance, their remuneration "can scarcely be considered inadequate." With regard to the emigrant, his initial debt would be about £215, and interest at 10 percent would be £21 10s. a year. In fact, it would probably be more than this, with the result that after a few years the settler would have to quit his land. The scheme was almost certain to fail, and it contained nothing to remove the objections to Argentina as a place for British emigration. The whole project was "fraught with ruin" for the emigrant; "none but the most ignorant could probably be induced to accept such terms." Murdoch, who was certainly not anti-Argentine or antiemigration, strongly advised that the scheme should not be countenanced and that active steps be taken to discourage it.[50] Yet a Foreign Office official blocked this advice and stated that he did not want to interfere unless compelled to do so.

The ECAC sent an agent, J. Pfeil, to the River Plate to sound out the presidents of Argentina and Uruguay on the scheme. He reported that they both approved it in principle, though they would ask for some modifications, and in any case further consideration was delayed by the legislative recess in Uruguay and political events in Argentina. In fact the ECAC scheme never recovered from its obvious flaws. It was criticized for the heavy charges on the immigrants, which would make it impossible for them ever to escape from debt, and for the speculative character and excessive profits on the side of the ECAC, contradicting the supposed philanthropic object for which it was formed.[51]

Pfeil responded to these criticisms simply by denying them, but the Emigration Board stood its ground. Murdoch maintained that life in Argentina was insecure. The evidence? Fifty-six murders and sixteen murderous assaults on British subjects over the last five years. He regarded it as "simply incredible" that the immigrants would clear their debts easily, while the ECAC would make a large profit from floating the bond issue and administering the scheme. Her Majesty's government had already rejected, and rightly so, ECAC requests for land in Natal and Western Australia, not out of hostility but to protect the emigrant. Uruguay and Argentina had for some time past sanctioned a number of schemes for colonization, offering high premiums to speculators who would undertake to introduce immigrants. These schemes had sometimes involved English colonists, but the results were "far from encouraging." The Welsh colony in Patagonia had to be repeatedly helped by the Argentine government, which had come to its rescue "very liberally." Projects had also failed in Brazil. There was no reason to suppose that the ECAC would do any better.[52] The Emigration Commission finally won the argument.

Nevertheless, this did not prevent the emergence of other projects, many of them monitored by the British legation in Buenos Aires. In early 1871 a Mr. Montravel was in England seeking settlers for the Bahía Blanca region "under the usual conditions profitable to the promoters of such undertakings and detrimental to the unfortunate emigrant who confides in the empty promises of such schemes." At about the same time, the London house of Thomson and Bonar issued a prospectus inviting emigrants of limited means to purchase land freehold in the Alexandra colony at Santa Fe. Such schemes "resulted in exposing a number of helpless individuals to ruin, misery and privation, to say nothing of personal risk and danger, and this for no other purpose but that of benefitting the promoters themselves." The terms in this case were £2 10s. for four acres, minimum holding of one hundred acres, £8 to be paid before sailing and the balance over four years, with a 20 percent discount if paid in advance. Families were to be provided with seed, stock, and tools up to the value of £50, repayable over three years at 10 percent. In London, Murdoch of the Emigration Board also commented adversely on this scheme: "It is impossible to believe that a House of the standing of Thomson, Bonar and Co. Ltd. would knowingly publish a prospectus calculated to mislead emigrants," but their scheme differs little from others which have signally failed in the past.[53]

The ECAC and other schemes, flawed and failed though they were, are significant for their origins and objectives and for the light they throw on emigration ideas at the time. The reason why no mass migration developed from Britain to Argentina lay not in the details of profits and costs or the greed of promoters, but in the balance of advantage between Britain and Argentina. In view of the endemic insecurity in Argentina, the adverse factors in Europe would have to be strong to persuade emigrants to accept the risks. Economic and social conditions in Italy and Spain were such as to tip the balance of advantage in favor of emigration. This was not the case for British emigrants. In June 1871 the Emigration Board reported that at present no emigrants were leaving for Argentina through London, Liverpool, or Glasgow.[54] This was not the final statistic, but it indicated a trend.

FURTHER NOTICE

Even while Argentine excitement over the emigration notice of February 1870 was at its height and repudiation of British assertions became a routine, MacDonell was quietly collecting further evidence to support his charges. In mid-1870 yet another Indian raid was responsible for killing seven settlers and kidnapping many more; up to two thousand Indians and some eighty renegades were involved.[55] In July a Briton was murdered on an *estancia* near Fraile Muerto, probably by an old man well known in the neighborhood. MacDonell made representations to the foreign minister and at the same time reminded him of the Baradero murders. Despite such events, the national congress was considering the formal abolition of the death penalty. MacDonell declared that the root of crime was a result of the effective absence of capital punishment and the moral condition of the Argentine people, who would never attain a "proper level" as long as atrocities were treated with indifference and left unpunished or inadequately punished. "I regret to say that I have arrived at the sad conclusion that it is useless to demand and hopeless to expect ever to see the law properly vindicated in cases of murder."[56] In the British view clemency to criminals meant injustice to immigrants.

The emigration commissioners continued to monitor Argentina, and in February 1871 they issued a further warning. This time they were more specific and advised intending emigrants that Indian incursions in the Bahía Blanca region were endangering life and property. The pro-Argentine lobby reacted promptly. A letter writer to *The Times* took issue with the Emigration Board both on the subject of the Henly colony and on the Bahía Blanca invasions. The board had published its report on the failure of the colony in *The Times* of 13 January 1871, and the correspondent commented that those particular emigrants were obviously destined to fail in whatever part of the world they settled. As for Bahía Blanca, Indian invasions had been a common occurrence in recent years, as the settlers well knew; unfortunately they had been tempted to settle beyond the line of frontier forts, lured by the nominal price of land and by the privileges the government granted to first settlers. They therefore knew the risks, and if the cost turned out to be higher than expected, the Argentine government was not to blame. The government could not be expected to give them the security they could not extend to settlers on the open frontier of Buenos Aires, who also had a right to protection. The writer argued that Argentina was a good field for immigration: wages were high, employment was plentiful, and diligent immigrants could become independent within a few years. They would find that the climate was healthy, there was freedom of religion, exemption from military service, no obligation to take Argentine nationality in order to become a property owner, and the government was well disposed towards immigrants.[57]

The notice of February 1871 did not produce the angry exchanges which followed the first notice. Government and people in Argentina were distracted at the time by the yellow fever epidemic raging in Buenos Aires which closed public offices and paralyzed the public mind. But Mariano Balcarce duly protested, arguing that it prejudiced Argentina's credit in Europe. Argentina had a vast frontier which was very difficult to protect, especially where immigrants who wanted free land had settled in areas habituated by Indians. He concluded that the Bahía Blanca incidents were "regrettable and painful" but did not give grounds for the conclusions expressed in the notice.[58]

Yet the migrant war revived and continued. The opening of the Córdoba Exhibition in October 1871 gave MacDonell the opportunity to ambush unwary ministers and raise the subject of atrocities, particularly the murder of the Briton Andrew Weguelin. Justice Minister Avellaneda took the position that much as he regretted the incident, the government could not protect those who established themselves beyond the military cordon. Once again the British chargé explained that this could have serious consequences for emigration schemes and for the reputation of Argentina in Europe. Argentina's credibility was bound to suffer if nothing was done to protect the lives and property of emigrants, attracted to the country by the false assurances of emigration agents.

As Avellaneda backed away from this untimely encounter, MacDonell bore down on Foreign Minister Tejedor and informed him that the California colonists had offered to clear the frontier of Indians if the government would undertake to support them and their families for six months or a year. Tejedor replied that he was prepared to forward the colonists' petition to the president and also to provide information, but he would not accept criticism of the government's frontier policy or administration of the colonies; the British minister had no right to interfere in these matters. Tejedor expressed regret for Weguelin's death but added that it was the inevitable consequence of the imprudence of those who established themselves, from speculative motives, at the most extreme point of Argentine territory; this was the fault of the emigration schemes, not of the government. MacDonell, never at a loss for an argument, retorted that Thomson and Bonar had based their prospectus promoting the colony on information from Major Rickard, an Argentine inspector of mines; as one of their servants was involved, the Argentine government had an obligation in this matter. Tejedor brought the conversation to a close, insisting that the British government was free to warn emigrants against coming to Argentina, but it had no right to interfere in the internal administration of a sovereign state, especially one that had three thousand miles of frontier to protect.[59]

In a mood of disapproval and defiance, Britain and Argentina continued to harass each other in the course of 1872. The massacre of Tandil on 1 January was not a solitary occurrence; it was the culmination of a trend in the chronicle of violence, and the record was still not complete. Disillusion on the part of Britain had begun some years previously and was to continue for some time to come.[60] In April yet another emigration notice was issued, this time warning intending emigrants to Chubut that the colony was not receiving sufficient support from the Argentine authorities and that it might have to be moved. The Argentine government, perhaps considering discretion the better part of valor over Chubut, did not respond to the notice with its customary indignation.[61] But it reacted strongly enough to the legation's efforts on behalf of a British subject involved in a land dispute with the Argentine courts, defending Argentine law, repudiating British intervention, denying judicial privileges to foreigners, rejecting any British jurisdiction on Argentine soil, and, to the fury of MacDonell, publishing the whole correspondence in the Buenos Aires press. After these bruising exchanges, MacDonell suggested to Granville that he convey a quiet word to the Argentine minister to London "that a little more courtesy, discretion and deference and less misplaced susceptibility on the part of this government in the treatment of matters connected with British subjects and interests in this country, could only tend to consolidate those good relations, which have hitherto so happily existed between the governments of Her Majesty and this Republic."[62]

Argentine susceptibilities were not something that troubled the emigration commissioners in London. On 22 July 1872 they issued yet another warning to intending emigrants:

> By despatches recently received from H.M. Charge d'Affaires at Buenos Aires, it appears disturbances have broken out in the province of Corrientes which imperil the lives and property of the settlers. It further appears that some months ago attacks were made by Indians on the settlements of Bahia Blanca and Tandil; that at the latter place a number of settlers were murdered, and that recently the Indians had made a descent on one of the most populous centres of the province of Buenos Aires and have carried off more than 100,000 head of cattle. These outrages have caused great alarm, especially as no adequate measures have been taken by the Government for the protection of the settlers or the punishment of the offenders.[63]

Within a week there was a reply from the agent general for the Argentine Republic in London, Franco Torrome, who wrote to *The Times* protesting against the notice. Torrome described the notice as totally erroneous, its only object to divert the attention of intending emigrants from the great advantages which Argentina offers and to direct them towards other countries whose immigrant intake is declining. There are only a small number of Indians in the south and north of the country;

small colonies on the Gran Chaco frontier manage to keep the Indians at bay and prosper, and no one has ever been carried off from the Chubut colony. It is obvious that those killed in the latest incursions lived in remote places. No Indians would ever carry off a hundred thousand head of cattle; they rely on speed and generally take only horses. The assertion that Argentina is unable to suppress disturbances in Corrientes and that this harms the settlers is nonsense. The British government is unable to catch and punish all criminals, but this does not mean that it is weak. Safety of life and effects is as good in Argentina as it is in London. To be consistent the commissioners should warn off emigrants when bush rangers kill a sheep farmer in Australia or New Zealand or when violence occurs in Ireland. "In fact, with regard to the last named country a warning drawn up in terms equal in proportion to the facts would cause a stampede of all the farmers and others settled there."[64]

The notice invited criticism if only for its distortion of events at Tandil, though Argentine replies were hardly models of accuracy. Balcarce protested to Granville not only against the notice but also against various reports of MacDonell which the House of Commons had ordered to be published. Balcarce denied that the Argentine government failed to protect the frontier and repudiated the notion that there was antagonism between immigrants and native country folk. He alleged that the reports of the numbers of Britons killed had been exaggerated. There was no risk to life or property in Corrientes. The Tandil victims had been killed not by Indians but by country people led by a fanatic; their first victims had been Argentines, and in any event the criminals had been caught and sentenced. Argentina, he continues, has a vast frontier which is difficult to protect; it is hard to guarantee the safety of colonists who prefer to settle close to the desert, where isolated killings are impossible to prevent. The Argentine government has reacted vigorously to the Indian raids in Buenos Aires province and has sent two thousand men into the field; the cattle losses have been exaggerated. Congress will be asked to double the size of the army. MacDonell himself has given the Argentine government a note of thanks for its support of the Chubut colony. The Central Argentine Land Company has praised the government. Past British ministers have done the same, as have the representatives of other nations. MacDonell's reports and accusations are not correct.[65]

In late September 1872 the Emigration Commission drew up another notice warning intending emigrants that three hundred Pampa Indians had raided the Department of Rosario, by way of Buenos Aires province, killing all the men they encountered, carrying off thirty-two women and children, and plundering and destroying property. The number of lives lost was estimated at seventy, none of them British. Nevertheless, the incident conveyed a warning for all settlers: "The impunity with which these outrages are effected necessarily causes great alarm and distrust among settlers and paralyses the material progress of the country."[66] Before the notice was issued, however, Walcott of the Emigration Board wrote to the Foreign Office, thanking it for copies of MacDonell's dispatches on the continued insecurity of life in Argentina and noting that Tejedor had said that Her Majesty's government could continue to issue notices but that they would be regarded as unfriendly acts by the Argentine government. Walcott suggested that Her Majesty's government should continue to issue the notices if Argentine immigration agents attempted to neutralize their effect or if emigrants did settle in Argentina in any great numbers. He added that total immigration had fallen from forty thousand in 1870 to twenty-one thousand in 1871, and that 957 emigrants (448 cabin and 509 steerage passengers) had left Britain for Argentina between 1 January and 30 September 1872.[67]

The notice was published on 9 October and appeared in *The Times* two days later. On 15 October, Balcarce made his ritual protest, denying that the Argentine authorities had been negligent in protecting the frontier or that his country's progress had been paralyzed. Granville duly replied that the notice was only intended to warn prospective emigrants and that it had been based on information received from government agents in Argentina; if Balcarce disagreed with the notice, he was at liberty to publish the correspondence on the matter.[68]

The October notice stimulated a predictable response from Argentina's friends and agents in England, and a spate of letter writing to *The Times* quickly followed. Franco Torrome wrote to protest along the same lines as he had done the previous July. J. Bate, the late honorable secretary to the National Emigration Society, wrote to say that the recent Emigration Commission warnings showed that "one department of the Government is becoming alive to the grave Imperial responsibilities involved in an unchecked, indiscriminate emigration . . . of some of the best people of the United Kingdom" and recommended that the notices be displayed in every post office. Bate reserved his sharpest attack for emigration to South America, and it was this which provoked a number of responses. Mr. G. Woolcott defended the emigration scheme of the Central Argentine Land Company, and Mr. J. Olguin, an Argentine, insisted that his country was an attractive prospect for emigrants. But Bate continued to inveigh against emigration to South

America and argued that emigration, if it had to take place, should be directed towards British colonies. He also called for an investigation of those who sought to delude "our peasants."[69]

The notice of October 1872 was still drawing fire from Argentina's friends in England in the early months of 1873. In March, David Robertson wrote to Herbert at the Foreign Office attacking MacDonell's reporting and comparing it unfavorably with that of a previous British minister, F. C. Ford. Robertson asked why the British interfered with emigration when the German, Spanish, and Italian governments did not, and he alleged that emigration notices only made enemies. The October notice was "very impolitic" and "utterly indefensible." Mac-Donell was a mere "underling" who had quarreled with the authorities about emigration and whose reports had been entirely contradicted by those of "a well known very superior man, Mr. Ford."[70]

The publication of MacDonell's "Remarks on the River Plate Republics" only exacerbated the anger of the Argentines. President Sarmiento himself denounced this "semiofficial publication" as "a virulent defamation of our country . . . an odious caricature" which exaggerated the imperfections and ignored the advantages, not least for England.[71] Nevertheless, MacDonell's charges refused to go away. The Argentines themselves were conscious of lawlessness. In 1873 the governor of Buenos Aires stated in his message to the provincial legislature that the police service had been improved, but more police were needed, especially in rural areas; only this "can put a stop to the depredations and abuses which increase with astonishing rapidity."[72] In August in Santa Fe province Mr. Southam and his daughter were murdered, the daughter being first raped; both the bodies were mutilated. Southam had apparently been warned about living where he did but had declared he felt safe among "good republicans." It needed strenuous efforts by the British legation to secure the execution of one of the murderers.[73] While this campaign was proceeding, the legation received news of the murder of a British carter by troops at Chivilcoy.

From Buenos Aires a Mr. Fisher wrote to the emigration commissioners enclosing news cuttings detailing the murder of three Irishmen and three others by gauchos in June 1874. A petition from the Saint Patrick Society, members of which were fairly substantial Irish settlers and businessmen who in the previous year had disavowed MacDonell and rejected his strictures, now protested to the provincial governor of Buenos Aires against the current lawlessness, "a plague like cholera," and recommended a series of practical measures to deal with the situation.[74] English bankers asked for gunboat protection when *mitristas* raised a rebellion in Buenos Aires. The year 1874 was not a good year for law and order in Argentina.

Asked to comment on Fisher's lurid but accurate reports on lawlessness, Lionel Sackville-West, supposedly a more diplomatic observer, reported that the police were powerless to protect life and property and that judges were unwilling to punish criminals. As crime was committed with impunity, the Argentine authorities could not complain when they were criticized by foreign representatives. Justice was sometimes done, for example in the Southam case, but the national government was unable to impose prompt administration of justice because of the federal system, a constraint which was sometimes used as an excuse for inaction. Sackville-West did not favor the publication of a new emigration notice, but he suggested that the British government should consider making strong representations regarding the criminal justice system. The real remedy would only be found in a radical change in the system of government, and this would only be brought about by the influence of foreigners.

In his own version of the two cultures, Sackville-West concluded that English emigrants were not suited physically or morally to life in Argentina.[75] If this were true, then cultural differences were part of the problem. Were British settlers surrounded by an alien culture whose perception of violence and murder differed fundamentally from their own? In the wake of the Tandil massacre British thinking turned to consider the possibility.

9

A Conflict of Cultures: Argentina through British Eyes

Argentine statesmen, it is safe to say, knew more about Britain and its empire than British statesmen knew of Argentina. Among the Argentine admirers of Britain none was more committed than Bartolomé Mitre, who saw the British suppression of the Indian mutiny as a model for the Argentine war on the pampa Indians: "The people who lead the cause of freedom in the Old World, who have planted the fruitful seeds of democracy in North America, and whose example on more than one occasion has saved other peoples in their struggles, are well qualified to preside over the regeneration of a barbarous world, whatever the blemishes of the previous conquest and domination, notably more restrained in recent times."[1]

Few British ministers would be confident enough of their knowledge of Argentina to speak in similar terms, but further down the hierarchy Foreign Office officials maintained a reserve of information against the time when it might be needed, even if the first to consult it have often been modern historians researching in the Public Record Office. Tensions between Britain and Argentina in 1871–72 saw ministers in London reaching for their papers and replenishing their ideas. What class of country permits a massacre of immigrants? What kind of society produces a frontier like Tandil? Answers to these questions were inspired by British standards, values, and prejudices. They were also informed by detailed knowledge derived from direct observation, some of it contradictory, much of it credible.

In July 1871 the British minister in Buenos Aires, Hugh MacDonell, forwarded to Foreign Secretary Lord Granville a lengthy "Report on the Condition of the Industrial Classes and Immigration in the Argentine Republic" by Constantine Phipps, second secretary to the legation, son of a family long productive in politicians, ministers, and diplomats, and on the evidence of his report a serious observer of the Argentine scene.[2]

The British were strong on hygiene, and one of their first impressions of Argentina on stepping ashore was the insalubrious condition of Buenos Aires. The capital lacked adequate drainage and was scarred by open cesspits, with accompanying noxious fumes and diseases. Health hazards were in every street and building. The annual mortality rate, independent of epidemics, was forty-two per thousand as compared to eighteen to thirty-two per thousand in English industrial towns. The average lifespan, adjusted to take account of infant mortality, was thirty-one years in Buenos Aires compared to fifty in London.

Argentina had a world reputation for high wages, especially in the pastoral sector. The wages boom began in the 1860s, and wages remained high during the 1870s.[3] Phipps was impressed by the level of prices as well as wages. True, wages were higher in Argentina than in the United States or the British colonies, especially for the well-qualified and healthy mechanic who knew the language. Against this, lodgings and transport in Buenos Aires were extremely expensive. Bread, too, was dear because of fuel and labor costs and the profit expectations of bakers. Fuel was four times its cost in England. But consumer choice was widening. Food and drink patterns were changing under European influence: wine consumption, for example, was growing noticeably with the arrival of French immigrants.

Employment prospects for immigrants were good, but not invariably so. The wages of the lowest category of artisan or laborer was about 5 s. a day or £6 a month; necessary expenditure would consume about £4 13s. a month, with the balance for leisure and savings. The average worker, then, was better off than he would be in Europe. Italian immigrants worked harder and lived more frugally than the British and French, and being "excessively abstemious," they saved more. "Few if any English emigrants would persevere in such a frugal mode of living and such self denial while knowing that the means of enjoying comparative luxuries were at their disposal."

Phipps reported further details of the labor market. Skilled work is not automatically a better choice for the immigrant. Men can earn more by making themselves available as porters, or *changadores*, in the commercial sector of Buenos Aires than they can by being employed in their trade. Most artisan production is of an inferior standard, for output is judged by quantity, not quality; even building work is done on piece rates. European craftsmen soon fall in with local work habits and learn to exploit the labor shortage; workers are swift to take offense at employers, since there is no fear of unemployment. The English emigrant will find life in Buenos Aires uphill work unless he is a very high class mechanic; there are already too many compositors, shop assistants, and clerks. Manual labor is the best paid. Agricultural laborers earn thirty pounds a year plus food and lodging, and they can make extra cash at ditching. While prospects are variable, there is very little distress or poverty of the kind you find in England. Even though several industries are depressed at the moment, absolute misery is virtually unknown. No doubt many thousands have had to earn their living in more precarious conditions than hitherto, but they do not suffer real privation. It will be another summer before conditions improve. The Commission for Immigration in Buenos Aires has already announced this, but many Italians prefer to remain in town rather than go to the countryside or return home.

Immigration in Argentina, reported Phipps, is under the control of the Central Committee of Immigration, founded on 10 August 1869 on the basis of the old Immigration Society. The Central Committee encourages immigration and combats attempts to arrest its tide. The state pays for the landing of immigrants and supports them for the first eight days. Because of this, the government now has accurate statistics. Argentine diplomatic representatives abroad are at the service of the Central Committee. Sarmiento and his government are very keen to encourage immigration from northern Europe. The Central Committee has recommended that a state subsidy be paid for immigrants coming from northern Europe, but it is unlikely that it will be granted. The fare from there to the United States is £8 8s., and to Argentina, £12 4s. German migrants prefer the United States and then Brazil. Phipps did not elaborate, but the preference of northern Europe for the United States reflected a cultural bias rather than cheaper transport.

Phipps surveyed the recent history of immigration in Argentina. The first significant year was 1836, when Basque and Spanish settlers went to Uruguay, but this flow ceased in 1838 because of wars and civil disturbances. The movement began again in 1852 and took a step forward in 1863, possibly, thought Phipps, because of the prolongation of the Civil War in the United States, which deterred immigrants and accelerated a trend towards Argentina. But Argentine immigration was also subject to temporary setbacks (Table 9–1).

In the first six months of 1871, six thousand immigrants arrived, and a further fifteen thousand were thought to be arriving soon. This was the year of yellow fever. The epidemic killed twenty thousand to twenty-two thousand people, half of them Italians. Immigrants in the Asylum (the *Asilo de Inmigrantes*, or immigrant reception center) suffered particularly badly, as did the Italians, many of whom lived in *conventillos* (tenements). The Central Committee helped some migrants during the epidemic by paying their passage to Santa Fe and finding

Table 9-1. Immigration, Argentina, 1857–68

1857	4,951	1863	10,408
1858	4,658	1864	11,682
1859	4,735	1865	11,767
1860	5,656	1866	13,696
1861	6,301	1867	17,046
1862	6,716	1868	29,234

SOURCE: Constantine Phipps, "Report," in MacDonell to Granville, 15 July 1871, Public Record Office, London, FO 6/304, pp. 125–96.

them jobs there, but this was an emergency measure and not a new policy. And in spite of its health hazards, Buenos Aires remained the preferred destination. Phipps noted that of the one hundred thousand immigrants who arrived in the last three years, 60 percent have remained in Buenos Aires city, 30 percent have gone to the riverine towns, and only 10 percent to the countryside.

Migrants bring and create capital. They are calculated to increase national revenue, mainly through taxes received on imported goods; in 1869 this increase was fifty thousand pounds sterling, 19 percent of total government revenue. But immigration has not been as advantageous to the nation as some had hoped, and it has its critics: it is said that the propagandists of immigration have only succeeded in bringing the dregs of Italian cities to Buenos Aires, and Argentina is the loser.

English immigrants are much less numerous than those from southern Europe (Table 9–2), and their performance has been mixed. The English used to control the coasting trade and river pilotage, but they have now been pushed out by the Genoese. The English of this class prefer to drink away their hard-earned gains, and, unlike the Italians, they do not save to improve themselves or guard against the future.

Several British colonization schemes are afoot, but there is no free land for settlers. The land is conceded to companies, who sell to the immigrants only at a profit for their shareholders. Philanthropic enterprises are needed to help the deserving emigrant, but they do not exist, and the companies are prepared to sell to anybody. They lend the colonists money for their passage and property, and the colonists are in effect tied to the land for five years in a sort of debt peonage. There is no way to force the companies to honor their agreements; they make lavish promises regarding accommodation, tools, livestock, and other necessities and then do not fulfil them. The companies only seek dividends, and the colonists are a secondary consideration. The situation is very different in the United States, where the government sells land di-

Table 9-2. European Immigrants by Nationality, 1869

Italians	22,420
Spanish	2,280
French	7,980
Swiss	3,406
English	708
Germans	
Swedes	1,140
Total	37,934

SOURCE: Constantine Phipps, "Report," in MacDonell to Granville, 15 July 1871, Public Record Office, London, FO 6/304, pp. 125–96.

rect to the settler at five dollars an acre. It may be that better land laws are coming here, but difficulties between central and provincial governments make this unlikely.

The colonies of Santa Fe and Entre Ríos are mostly intended for Swiss and Italian immigrants, and so far they lack any facilities for education and public worship. Freight charges are high. The colonists are exploited by the present system: they labor on the land for five years, improve it, and then often have to leave. There are hazards of drought and sickness, and basically grain cultivation is not profitable unless it is done on a large scale.

English emigrants should be those who are prepared to do their own work in a "sober, abstemious and energetic" way, and they should have robust constitutions. They should not go into a colonization scheme immediately upon arrival, but take work as a laborer for a year or so to acquire experience and savings. Any capital they bring with them should be deposited at interest in a bank. Sheep farming and cattle rearing are not good fields in which to begin. English immigrants have failed because they expect a higher life-style and more comforts than do the southern Europeans; they also tend to relax when making good, while Italians, for example, work even harder.

One of the great drawbacks to settlement in Argentina is the impunity enjoyed by crime. As a matter of policy the government may wish to protect the settler, but in practice it does not have the will to do so. According to the official statistics for the province of Buenos Aires, two-thirds of all prisoners are discharged altogether, one-fifth

Table 9-3. Violent Crimes, Buenos Aires Province, 1866

	Under 1 yr. jail	1 yr+ jail	Penal Servitude	Army	Total
Murder	22	5	15	8	50
Wounding	19	25	3	9	56

SOURCE: Constantine Phipps, "Report," in MacDonell to Granville, 15 July 1871, Public Record Office, London, FO 6/304, pp. 125–96.

pay fines, one-twelfth are punished, and one-twelfth are sentenced to army service. None of the violent criminals of 1866 were executed, Phipps commented, and there was greater punishment for wounding than there was for murder (Table 9–3). The statistics for Buenos Aires province in 1867 showed that eleven murderers were condemned as opposed to fifty in 1866, and twenty-six woundings were punished as compared with fifty-six in 1866. The murderers of seventy to eighty Britons between 1864 and 1870 have gone unpunished, and in the case of the ten to twelve Britons murdered in 1870, only one assassin has been punished. Yet the British promoters of emigration accuse us of unfair exaggeration. The California colony and that in Bahía Blanca have both suffered from Indian attacks, and the army, recruited from the jails, is a further hazard, not a protection.

Phipps concluded that the industrious Briton can prosper in Argentina, but he would do just as well in a British colony, and there are no special advantages in settling in the River Plate countries.

HUGH MACDONELL: THE HARD LINE

The year 1872 raised immigration to a prime issue in Anglo-Argentine relations. As the British legation reported murder and mayhem, the Foreign Office read and warned, and the Argentine government defended its corner, so diplomatic niceties gave way to frank exchanges, and emigrants thought twice about embarking for Buenos Aires. The emigration paper became a favorite exercise, and descriptions of Argentina popular news items. From the front line Hugh Guion MacDonell sent his own dispatches, and in May 1872 he crowned these with a report entitled "Remarks on the River Plate Republics as a Field for British Emigration." Although MacDonell repeated many of the points made by Phipps, he was writing after the massacre at Tandil, and his clear and trenchant style is worth reporting in some detail. His military background—he had served in British Kaffraria with the Rifle Brigade—accounts perhaps for his refusal to place diplomacy before plain speaking, but he enjoyed the confidence of the Foreign Office and had major diplomatic posts ahead of him.

MacDonell considers the immigration policy of Argentina to be fundamentally flawed, not because it is unassisted but because it is tied to a faulty system of land tenure. The Argentine government sells large tracts of land to individuals or companies at moderate prices. The contractor then sells or cedes land to the immigrants on limited-term contracts, the land passing to the immigrant if the terms of the contract have been fulfilled. Advances are made by the contractor to pay for passages, settlement, and maintenance. The immigrant has to pay off this debt, and he may just be able to keep abreast of interest and amortization payments, provided things go well. But if he suffers some misfortune and breaks the terms of his contract, the immigrant is forced to leave the colony or to work out his debt and then leave. In this case the contractor keeps the land the immigrant has improved and is able to sell it at a higher price to others. This, more or less, has been the history of the Santa Fe colonies, and from it we have to conclude that either there is some radical defect in the Argentine system of colonization or else the class of immigrants is altogether unsuitable. So far the most successful colonies have been Swiss and German.

The other flaw in the agrarian structure is the gaucho. The British view of the gaucho, as expressed by MacDonell, reciprocated the loathing which the gaucho held for the foreigner. "The inhabitants of the camp, the Gaucho, illiterate, rude, greedy of money, addicted to gambling, implacable and revengeful, equally distrusts the foreigner and more openly displays his hostility; with such it is impossible to hold faith; they are the originators of all the disturbances that afflict the country and at times little better than paid assassins. . . . For a Gaucho who has murdered a 'Gringo,' or foreigner, there is, especially in the camp, usually complete immunity, shelter on the part of his countrymen and complete inactivity on that of the authorities."

There are about 18,000 British in Argentina, but immigration from Britain is declining. North European immigration in general has declined in the last twelve years. Italians constitute about one-half of all immigrants, and there is much prejudice against them. They tend to stay in urban centers and to become the most prosperous of all the immigrants. Each year 25,000 Italians arrive, and one-quarter return to Italy. Since 1862, 140,000–150,000 Italians have arrived, of whom no less than one-third have returned to Italy. At least the Anglo-Saxon settles here once he has arrived, though there are many trials to overcome. These are succinctly listed by MacDonell, who conveniently provides a framework for later research: "The chief obstacles to the success of the

British immigrant consist in the climate; the language, habits and customs of the natives; the tardy acquisition and hazardous tenure of land; the invasions of Indians; the unjust seizure of property both by rebel and government troops; the absence of the means of transit and communication, whether by roads, navigable rivers or railways; the defective administration of justice; and the jealousy with which he is regarded by the inhabitants of this country."

Cultural differences are one of the first shocks, and the English immigrant soon finds that there is no similarity of language, habits, or religion between his old world and the new. MacDonell's analysis of national cultures stands in sober contrast to the alternative view that Britons and Argentines were historic soul mates, their countries bound in a special relationship of shared interests.[5]

British officials, of course, were not social anthropologists. Their experience told them that Argentines, no less than other peoples, had a distinct cultural identity and that this could be observed and recorded, but they found this culture difficult to describe without declining into stereotypes. Their counterparts in Argentina were similarly handicapped. Reading between the lines of national discourse, it seems that Argentines respected the British for their history, economy, and institutions but were astonished by their ignorance of other countries and their lack of sympathy for other cultures. To be British was to be imperious. For their part the British betrayed a certain arrogance from time to time; while never describing the Argentines as inferior, they came near to using the term "uncivilized," and MacDonell believed that Argentines suffered from being a mixture of Spanish and Indian, thus combining "the vices of the two races." Among the defining characteristics which MacDonell identifies are the Spanish language, the Catholic religion, and attitudes towards crime. The language barrier was not easily crossed, at least by Anglo-Saxons, and this handicap would always mark the British off from Latin immigrants. So, too, would Catholicism. The immigrant would find religion either in a state of neglect or subject to "gross superstition." To cite religious difference, of course, ignored the Catholic Irish, who by MacDonell's own reckoning formed a large part of British immigrants. But religion was not automatically a cultural bond. MacDonell seems to have been insensitive to the lights and shades of religious practice and did not appreciate that the Irish were probably more uncompromising Catholics than the Argentines because of their puritanical upbringing and deference to priests. One of the greatest obstacles to assimilation, argued MacDonell, lies in the agrarian system prevailing in Argentina. Emigration agents and colonizing companies are not to be trusted, and they do nothing to prepare the immigrant for differences in material culture that await him. There are no liberal land laws, and property titles are sometimes difficult to establish. The immigrant will find that there is no economical and ready demarcation of land, no easy access to wood and water or to markets for the sale of products, and roads and bridges are notably lacking. The climate in general is healthy and the soil fertile, but plagues and droughts are not infrequent, and there have been three epidemics of cholera and yellow fever within five years. The immigrant will receive no exemption from taxation. Probably the safest way of acquiring capital at the beginning is share-cropping with sheep. But all rural activities are plagued by the lawlessness prevailing in the Argentine countryside.

Perhaps the greatest cultural difference between Britain and Argentina, as described by MacDonell, was the attitude towards law and order. Insecurity of life and property, he wrote, have been the greatest problems for immigrants and the most constant source of complaint on the part of their ministers and consuls. Her Majesty's government's warnings on inadequate protection have caused some anger in Argentina. The government has taken offense and claimed that criminal statistics here would compare favorably with those of any European nation. But the Argentine government has ignored the fact that "the accusation bore not specifically on the proportion of crime, but on the utter impunity with which the most notorious outrages and assassinations are being daily committed." The impunity of crime can be attributed to three basic causes: first, "the loose and improper administration of an already defective criminal code"; second, the "corruption and ignorance of the inferior judicial authorities, especially in the rural districts"; and third, the total absence of an effective, honest, and properly organized police and of prisons and penal settlements and all the instruments requisite to execute and avenge the law.

These conditions have long been tolerated, although the authorities deny it. "Yet crime has lately gained such monstrous proportions, and appears so deeply rooted, that the most appalling murders cease to excite attention, and are accepted, if not excused, as an unavoidable evil." Manslaughter is committed with impunity and will only be eradicated by the strict enforcement of capital punishment. Manslaughter is "so chronic a vice that, not only the 'Gaucho malo'—who is reared in the conviction that the life of a fellow creature is as insignificant as that of a sheep—but every criminal, foreign or native, becomes confirmed in his murderous propensities." These evils, hints MacDonell, point to a difference of moral values between the two societies.

English criminal statistics show one murder for every 178,000 inhabitants. In Argentina the figure is one for every 900 inhabitants. In England murderers rarely escape. In Argentina murderers are sentenced to army service or transported to Patagonia, from where they desert and return unobserved and unmolested. This is the case in Buenos Aires province; it must be worse in the interior, where governors and their entourages are gauchos by instinct if not in fact. National and provincial authorities are often divided against themselves, and the foreigner cannot count on the support of the national government if he is in conflict with provincial officials. At the same time, the "ever-recurring revolutions" in the provinces make for constant difficulties and insecurity; under the former government (that of Mitre) the emigrants had some chance of redress for property lost to rebel or government forces, but under this government (Sarmiento's) there is none.

The immigrant might escape the gaucho only to fall victim to the Indian. In the province of Buenos Aires between 1820 and 1870 the Indians stole and destroyed eleven million cattle worth twenty million silver dollars. The frontier was secure under Rosas, but since his fall Indian raids have caused great damage. The army, which nominally protects the frontier, has sixty-five hundred men, a third on active service. The composition of this body is "of the very worst character containing Gauchos, convicts, jailbirds and good-for-nothing or kidnapped foreigners; unpaid and undisciplined, such men are more likely to side with the Indian than protect the frontier." The annual cost of the frontier force plus subsidies to Indians is roughly one million pounds, but still the Indians invade. Only in the Chubut colony are relations with Indians good; the plight of the Welsh settlers was such that even the Indians took pity on them.

Previous English emigrants to Argentina came from rural areas. Most now come from manufacturing districts, breeding grounds of mischief in MacDonell's view: the "majority of present English immigrants of this class are an idle, intemperate and worthless lot," a discredit to themselves and England. Towns are presently overstocked with southern European workers, and the better English artisans should go to British colonies. Great fortunes were made here thirty or forty years ago because of the demand for labor, the progress of sheep farming, and the success of mercantile and industrial occupations in Buenos Aires. But the commerce of Buenos Aires is now peopled by Italians, Germans, and French. And the English estates in the interior of the province are not owned by the original immigrants but by their descendants. The old immigrants, who had "indomitable energy, determination and perseverance," were very different from the new. These often come without sound knowledge; they are underfinanced and sometimes unwilling to work hard. "The most undesirable class of immigrant is the young gentleman of very slender, if any, means; who by education and antecedents is neither fit to tend a flock of sheep, sweep a store, nor make himself generally useful. These come in a not insignificant number; useless and helpless, they sink lower and lower in the social scale."

This aversion to young gentlemen of slender means evidently evoked a strong response in a Foreign Office official, who penciled in the comment, "A horrid nuisance the whole world over." It was also shared by the British settler Richard Seymour: "We all suffered a good deal from what we called the army of loafers, i.e. a number of young men come out from England, under pretence of becoming sheep-farmers, who simply passed their time in going from one estancia to another, merely amusing themselves, and staying as long as their entertainers would keep them."[6] According to MacDonell, the best immigrants would be hardy, temperate men of some agricultural experience and some capital. The future of Argentina depends on attracting "superior foreign labour" of this kind, and the best course for the immigrant would be to invest his capital at 7 or 8 percent and work for a year to gain experience, rather than start immediately in an agricultural project. These negative views of Argentina were not shared by all British observers, but it was generally agreed that an immigrant had no prospects as a wage laborer and needed capital to make any progress.

MacDonell's report on immigrant conditions in Argentina secured a wide readership: it was printed in the *Parliamentary Papers* of 1872, accompanied by correspondence on the fate of British subjects in the republic. "It would be hard to find anything more calculated to discourage emigration to Argentina," commented Professor Ferns.[7] It amounted, in fact, to a public rebuke for Argentina, one which caused unsuppressed anger and frustration. Argentine ministers not only rejected British charges but also began to criticize MacDonell specifically and sought to isolate him from his colleagues. His reports were described as inaccurate and misleading. The idea that natives received greater protection than foreigners was rejected, and reports of rivalry between gauchos and immigrants were dismissed as exaggerated. MacDonell's murder statistics were questioned; he claimed that scarcely a day had passed in the last six months without a Briton being killed. Yet he only named six victims. What about the rest? The disorders in Corrientes were soon brought to an end. As for Tandil, the offenders were immediately pursued, and more than half of them were killed while attempting to escape; others were taken, tried, and condemned, and their chief had been killed. MacDonell's views were contrasted adversely with the friendly comments of past British ministers, especially those of Francis Clare Ford; it was hinted that his position, which was only temporary, would become very unpleasant, and he should be replaced.[8] Yet official comment on Tandil by Argentine ministers disguised as much as it revealed and was by no means an effective antidote to Mac-Donell or a source of enlightenment for the British government.

By early September 1872, MacDonell himself was convinced that he was about to come under serious attack from the Argentine government. The emigration notice had caused angry comment, Her Majesty's government was accused of attempting to injure the reputation of Argentina in Europe, and "ludicrous motives" were being ascribed to his reports on the subject of insecurity. MacDonell anticipated that the Argentine government would protest against the notice and complain of the inaccuracy and unfriendliness of his reports.[9]

The attack came in the semiofficial newspaper *La Tribuna* on 10 September 1872. An article entitled "Gobierno Inglés y la República Argentina" had harsh things to say about both Granville and MacDonell. They are worth citing at some length as an example of Argentine thinking about Britain in the age of migration and of a nationalist response to foreign pressure. The anonymous author begins by citing two dispatches from Granville to MacDonell; this was another example of open diplomacy on the part of the Argentines which so infuriated the British, though they themselves were not strangers to the practice. The dispatches instructed MacDonell to ascertain whether the Argentine government could be held responsible for the Tandil murders and if so, to press for compensation. The writer comments that the idea that governments are responsible for murders committed on foreigners has no precedent; all governments accept responsibility if the murders are committed by authority, but the government had nothing to do with the Tandil murders or the Indian raids. These were crimes, offenses against Argentine authority, and the Tandil assassins will pay the price with their own blood in two days' time. Their punishment shows that the Argentine government is not responsible for the acts of criminals and that we punish them severely. But their execution is not enough to satisfy England, and Granville speaks of Argentine money to pay for the lives the murderers have taken. But why should the Argentine government pay compensation?[10] Presumably aware that neither MacDonell nor British immigrants were in fact requesting compensation, the article changes tack and alleges that MacDonell's reporting of the Tandil massacre has increased the impact of these events on Granville and distorted his judgment.

MacDonell's reports from Buenos Aires, charges *La Tribuna*, are highly colored; he even talks of bringing pressure to bear on the Argentine Republic and excludes it from the category of civilized nations. Lord Granville is not here and is unacquainted with the truth; he does not know what the Argentine government has done in the past to chastise offenders. He proceeds on information from MacDonell, who has calumniated Argentina, and it is against MacDonell that our attacks must be directed. Judging from MacDonell's dispatches, published in the *Pall Mall Gazette* in July, he should be recalled at once. The Argentine government has no obligation to receive as the representative of a friendly nation "a man who is known to be hostile to it, who has calumniated it, has outraged it and who, consequently, can inspire no confidence." MacDonell is in this category and he should go. Until now diplomatic relations with England have been cordial; MacDonell is trying to destroy them. He has reported that there are no guarantees for foreign life and property and paints the country "as being in a deplorable condition of corruption, backwardness, and ignominy."

After citing a number of MacDonell's reports, the writer goes on to declare that MacDonell's conduct is such that he does not deserve any consideration from Argentina. The envoy blames Indian invasions on Argentine negligence and tries to make those invasions a diplomatic issue. "The love of calumny and of mischief, the ostentatious display of hatred and animosity towards this country, which Mr. MacDonell exhibits, lead him to say such things and to put forward the like absurdities." If government inertia gives rise to Indian invasions, Great Britain is even more culpable, for with greater power at its disposal, it permits tranquility to be continually disturbed in Ireland.

MacDonell has tried to intervene in judicial matters and has sought the punishment of criminals. He should have told the British government that without his intervention criminals have been arraigned and sentenced to death. In Rosario and Buenos Aires (to the shame of our penal legislation, which still preserves capital punishment) several guilty people, particularly the murderers of foreigners, have been executed in order to satisfy MacDonell. Yet he has not proceeded honorably and justly; rather, he sends exaggerated information to Europe about the country he hates. Recently he has been called upon by the English community to obtain the freedom of an Englishman charged with manslaughter. When the victim is English, MacDonell demands blood and death and makes a diplomatic issue of it, but when the criminal is English, he wants liberty and impunity. "These harebrained enemies of the country in which they are residing think the impositions and power of their government are to overcome Reason and Right, but they are mistaken. . . . We owe much, very much, to England, but it is not to the spirit of generosity of Englishmen, it is to their spirit of speculation and trade that we are indebted for whatever has been done for us." Capitalists who buy Argentine stock in the London Exchange are not philanthropists, they do not examine our needs but our responsibility, our guarantees and profits. The capitalists are enriched and we get our credit. MacDonell wants to destroy all this, but he will not succeed. Englishmen in Buenos Aires with contacts in London will tell their friends of MacDonell's calumnious assertions, and the truth will prevail. Sr. Tejedor will know how to deal with MacDonell and how to avenge the injury done to us. He will compel MacDonell, "who has shown himself so hostile, to withdraw from the country to which he is accredited."[11]

Lionel Sackville-West was appointed envoy extraordinary to Argentina in November 1872, and MacDonell left to take up a new appointment as secretary to the legation in Madrid.[12] Whether these changes were entirely the result of Argentine pressure it is impossible to say, since MacDonell's appointment to Buenos Aires had always been temporary. His situation in Argentina, however, had become increasingly difficult. Controversial events, combined with his own style of address, made his three years in Buenos Aires particularly turbulent, growing to a storm in the second half of 1872. The publication of his dispatches in the British press in July may have been the last straw for the Argentines and a factor in the decision to move him. Yet the departure of MacDonell in December 1872 did not immediately produce more cordial relations. The temporary chargé d'affaires who presented his credentials to Tejedor in January 1873 was asked whether his appointment meant that the British government no longer wanted a minister in Buenos Aires. Informed that Sackville-West would be arriving presently, Tejedor remained correct but "extremely cold."[13]

Even after his departure MacDonell continued to be a thorn in Argentine flesh. The publication of his "Remarks on the River Plate Republics" in late March 1873 brought forth a predictable flood of protest. Balcarce protested from Paris and questioned many of MacDonell's statements.[14] In London, land and colonization companies repudiated his views and defended their policies. Thomson, Bonar and Co. claimed that its Alexandra colony and others were prospering and that the Argentine government did in fact honor its duties to protect the colonies. The company understood that the Emigration Board wanted to direct emigration towards British colonies; in that case, the publication of MacDonell's remarks was not a justifiable means. They also denied that they made excessive or unfair profits from colonization.[15] In Buenos Aires MacDonell came under attack from British circles as well as from

Argentines. *The Standard* described a meeting of the Saint Patrick Society in which MacDonell was accused of "malicious spite" as well as other offenses.[16] Commenting on these attacks, the chargé, St. John, remarked that a year before, British residents had loudly denounced the "supineness and incapacity of the provincial authorities," on whom the responsibility of events which culminated in the Tandil massacre must rest: "But that wail of anguish was soon forgotten in this progressive country, at least by whose who live securely in cities and are amassing wealth by jobbing land speculations, the success of which depends mainly on an uninterrupted flow of immigration as well as on the amount of favour to be met with at the hands of the authorities, be they national, provincial or municipal."[17]

In May 1873 the president took the opportunity of his Message to Congress to criticize MacDonell. After remarking that immigration continued to increase despite efforts in Europe to divert its course, and that 14,468 immigrants had arrived in the first three months of 1873, Sarmiento attacked MacDonell, "an English functionary," for blackening Argentina's name at a time when English trade to the republic was booming. MacDonell told English residents in effect that they were unfortunate in acquiring great riches and in meeting with that consideration which was their due. "It is to be regretted that publicity should have been given to this pernicious pamphlet in which personal spleen takes the place of ability in the author and which makes the country an odious caricature by solely exaggerating imperfections," ignoring Argentina's great progress and advantages. But strong protests against his views in Europe and by English residents here have vindicated Argentina, "to which they are indebted for days of happiness and a better social position than they possessed in their own country." Finally, the Argentine government published a detailed rebuttal of MacDonell's "Remarks" in pamphlet form in Paris.[18]

LIONEL SACKVILLE-WEST: AN OLYMPIAN PERCEPTION

British ministers in Buenos Aires continued to report on Argentina exclusively as a country of investment and immigration. Local politics hardly interested them. They communicated a few details on presidential campaigns simply because some candidates looked less anti-British than others. In 1873 the candidates who appeared to be more favorable to foreigners were Avellaneda and Mitre, while Alsina was regarded as the candidate of rural conservatism, hostile to foreign interests.[19] The only reasons for European interest in the elections were trade and migration. This, at any rate, was the view of Lionel Sackville Sackville-

West, who took up his position as British minister in the second half of 1873 and remained in Buenos Aires until 1878, when he was posted to Madrid. Born to an illustrious English family, Sackville-West had entered the Diplomatic Service in 1847 and already had gained experience in France; he obtained steady, if unspectacular, promotion until his last appointment, to Washington, in 1881–88, from which he was recalled owing to his alleged intervention in a presidential election. He retired to Knole.

Sackville-West took a skeptical view of British immigration prospects in Argentina, though, unlike MacDonell, he blamed English character rather than Argentine conditions. However much any president facilitated and encouraged the entry of English labor, failure would be the usual result. This was not because the necessary conditions for success were lacking "but because the English emigrant can neither physically mor morally adapt himself to the circumstances in which he must inevitably find himself placed." Far better if he went elsewhere and left Argentina to the Germans, Basques, and northern Italians, who were better suited to the initial tribulations. The essential British interests—trade and capital—were not affected by the nationality of labor.[20] Sackville-West was aware that some of the British on whose behalf he had to intervene were hardly a credit to their nation. In Mendoza troops who had been dispatched to search the house of a British subject for arms were fired on by the suspect, and two were killed, and three Englishmen captured navigating a boat to the rebels of Entre Ríos were released only through the intervention of Sackville-West. He acknowledged that in view of the defects of the police force and the criminal justice system, British subjects should so behave that they avoided any contact with them.[21]

In September and October 1873, Sackville-West made an extensive tour of the provinces of Córdoba and San Luis in the company of Colonel Lucio V. Mansilla, formerly commander of the southern frontier and currently canvasing for Avellaneda, the official presidential candidate. The British envoy reported that both provinces were sparsely populated and subject to Indian raids. Foreign enterprise offered the only hope for the future, and native labor was useless unless managed by foreigners. An exhilarating climate and abundance of livestock and arable produce rendered life easy and pleasurable and produced a general disposition to avoid exertion, and without exertion no progress could be expected. These conditions gave rise to the gaucho of the pampas, "an obstacle in the way of all improvement," as President Sarmiento fully recognized. Sarmiento attempted to establish compulsory national education, and one could observe national colleges in San

Luis and elsewhere equal in every respect to those in the provinces of France. But it was unlikely that this education system would ever be generally adopted; the distances were too great, and provincial legislatures decided whether children went to school.

Mansilla talked long and hard to his English companion and evidently left an exact impression of his views concerning rural society. According to Sackville-West, Mansilla was truly attached to the gaucho and his way of life; he believed that the gaucho did not have to be pushed aside but could be improved by the progress brought by the immigrant. The Indian, too, could be a useful and faithful subject instead of an outcast exterminated for the welfare of the state.[22] Sackville-West listened carefully, but he was not wholly convinced; he thought that Mansilla's ideas were a modified version of the theory which led to "the supremacy of a man who was the greatest and most unscrupulous despot" known to Argentina, namely, Juan Manuel de Rosas. In these sparsely populated districts foreign colonists were few and far between; they rarely engaged in agriculture, though the soil was good, for economic conditions were not favorable for colonization at this time. The Railway Land Company made adequate provision for new settlements with Swiss and German colonists, while English colonists were not sought. In San Luis, Sackville-West encountered a few Britons engaged in gold mining, but most other foreigners were to be found in the trading sector.[23]

While Sackville-West was milder in his expression than MacDonell and probably a less abrasive companion, he recorded the same basic features which Englishmen normally regarded as obstacles to progress in Argentina. He noted that the constitution did not allow the national government to interfere in the provinces, even when the public interest was involved, and each province had its own legislature and judiciary. This also encouraged a convenient tactic: the national government used the constitution to avoid responsibility. Moreover, it would not allow diplomatic representatives to appeal beyond normal procedure and was extremely jealous of the activities of consular personnel in anything but commercial matters.[24]

Sackville-West's views on law and order in Argentina did not differ from those of MacDonell or of any other British envoy. He also added another factor. Universal suffrage and open voting plunged the country into disorder at every election and caused abject terror among the electorate. Granted the various hazards, Britons should remain aloof from Argentina. If anything, Sackville-West was more hostile to immigration from Britain than his predecessors had been. Early in 1875 he reported that steps taken by the German and Italian governments to

Table 9-4. Immigration, Argentina, 1868–74

1868	29,234	1872	41,002
1869	37,024	1873	79,712
1870	41,508	1874	68,277
1871	21,758		

SOURCE: Argentine Immigration Commission, Sackville-West to Derby, 13 June 1875, Public Record Office, London, FO 6/326, pp. 205–11.

Table 9-5. Foreigners Resident in Argentina, 1874

Italians	71,442	British	10,709
Spanish	34,080	S. Americans	42,112
French	32,383	N. Americans	1,551
German	10,857	Others	8,854

SOURCE: Argentine Immigration Commission, Sackville-West to Derby, 13 June 1875, Public Record Office, London, FO 6/326, pp. 205–11.

check emigration had caused a great impression in Argentina. There had been, in any event, a falling off in immigration, and if that trend continued, the labor market would be seriously affected. Italian immigration, the most important, was stationary because of the difficulties in making money. This could impair the productive powers of the country; that in itself would not necessarily damage Argentina, for Italians were thought to take more money out of the country than they produced.

Impediments to immigration included the insecurity of life and property and the defective administration of justice. Moreover, asserted Sackville-West, the type of immigrant who was ready to risk life and property and to submit to outrage in order to further his interests was not the type who tended to strengthen law and order or to improve social conditions. "On the contrary, it is a class which gradually becomes involved with the evils under which it is living and associates itself with the social deficiencies by which it is surrounded." There was thus a kind of downward mobility in moral standards, and immigrants were sucked into the morass. The Argentine government knew that something should be done but ignored the fact that the laws afforded practically no protection for the immigrant or his property. "Moves are afoot to enact more liberal land laws, but it is a fallacy to suppose that respectable immigrants will come to a country where laws to protect against outrages are inadequate. . . . Liberal land laws will only attract bad immigrants."[25]

British views on Argentina were entrenched. It was a violent country, hard on immigrants, lax on lawbreakers. European immigration in Argentina in the 1870s was not a constantly rising curve (Tables 9–4 and 9–5). Avellaneda's presidential message to Congress in May 1875 reported that immigration had declined in 1874, as it had in the United States. The main cause was conscription, war, and crisis in Europe, but Avellaneda believed that the trend could be reversed if Argentina adopted a policy of land grants and subsidized passages from northern Europe. The Argentine immigration commission blamed the current decline on measures taken by the European governments and on local difficulties such as the September revolt and the monetary crisis. They did not mention what British opinion regarded as the "real" cause, namely, the insecurity for life and property and the maladministration of justice. Instead, they proposed that forty thousand acres be divided between one hundred colonies of fifty families each.[26]

The British were not alone in condemning rural violence and government inertia in Argentina. This was a theme which José Hernández made his own in prose and poetry: "What is the point of having ports, railways, spinning mills, and exhibitions if the frontiers are undefended, the Indians plunder the helpless countryside, and its inhabitants are stripped of their freedom and rights to be left to the mercy of rebel caudillos and despotic bosses who, with official sanction, impose on them a military service which is at once unconstitutional and degrading?"[27]

Alvaro Barros, in his day military commander of the southern frontier, governor of Buenos Aires province, and active politician, scorned the heavy investment in modern infrastructure when the traditional obstacles to change were left in place: there was no internal security, no guarantee for rural property, no possibility of expanding pasture lands. Why? Because of "the constant threat imposed by the presence of Indians at the very heart of the nation." Barros could not contain his bitterness. "There lie our frontiers as they always were, forever open. There stands the dismal record of constant invasion and devastation. There stand the same forts, the same feeble horses, the same inadequate leadership, the same supplies, the same Indians, the same invasions and in their train the wounded men and captive women."[28]

The message of Barros was clear. Death in the pampas was the daily reality for men and women bold enough to settle there. British observers said no more than this. The difference was not that they were wrong but that they were foreigners.

10

Motive and Meaning:
The Massacre in Retrospect

The massacre of Tandil, brief in itself, was part of a longer history, product of a particular time, place, and people. It had its roots in two basic
conditions: frontier disorder and nativist discontent. From the years
about 1860, when the Argentine government was beginning to encourage immigrants and statesmen were preaching their virtues, conditions
on the ground were very different from Sarmiento's ideal. In the south
and west, Indian raids of increasing frequency and ferocity exposed Argentine defenses and made it impossible for settlers to plan a secure future. Tandil was no longer at the leading edge of the southern frontier,
but the values and traditions of that violent society seeped backwards
and affected the lives of law-abiding citizens.

Within the frontier immigrants could expect hostility from both ex-
tremes of rural society, from traditional landowners resentful of competition and from gaucho outcasts seeking vengeance on their newest
neighbors. Settlers would say that they feared the knife rather than the
spear. If the Indian was a fleeting enemy appearing from nowhere, the
gaucho was a more imminent danger and one responsible for the daily
criminality on the frontier. As rural Argentina enacted the last days of
a dying culture, European immigrants took their first steps into the unknown.

The expansion of the colonial frontier in South America was traditionally seen as the advance of Spanish power, the conquest of the
desert, and the creation of new settlements. More modern studies preferred to emphasize the invaded rather than the invader, to consider the
Indians as actors, observers, and victims of the frontier. But Indians
could influence as well as obstruct. Where they were sedentary and
docile they might provide labor and resources, and civilian institutions
could flourish. Where they were hostile and mobile, as in Argentina, the
fort and the garrison prevailed. Research preferences now seek to ac-

commodate all these approaches, and historians study frontiers as "geographic zones of interaction between two or more distinctive cultures."[1]

In the United States, according to a classic theory, the struggle for land and survival in a free frontier played a key role in the formation of American character and institutions. The theory does not travel easily to Latin America. In Argentina the frontier was a no-man's land where white settlers competed with Indians and gauchos for space and resources; here the distribution of wealth was uneven, society immobile, the state more interventionist, and institutional life far from democratic. The Argentine frontier duplicated some of the negative features of the Anglo-American West. Natives were excluded by force or by choice, and on both frontiers they remained resistant to conquest and conversion. But there the comparison ends. The Anglo-American frontier was driven forward by greater economic and demographic advantages than those enjoyed by Argentine frontiersmen, and the rewards were usually higher. The pampas contained no hidden treasure and experienced no gold rush. The Indians of the south, moreover, were formidable enemies. Apparently dispersed and nomadic, in fact they were part of a network of trade and resources which united east and west of Araucania and could augment Argentina's Indians with reinforcements from Chile.

The eighteenth century saw the increasing "Araucanization" of the pampas and adjacent regions, a process which drew from the colonial authorities first a military response and then, in the last decades of empire, a more political strategy in which trade and gifts played a major role. Behind both approaches lay military sanctions. But rural society did not take readily to militia service and devised various forms of resistance ranging from individual insubordination to mass desertions. Regular forces were hardly more reliable, and the life of the common soldier and his women was one of unrelieved deprivation and indiscipline.[2] Thus was born the violence of the frontier: Indian raids, gaucho independence, and forced conscription. The militarization of frontier society, the settlement of new land, and the activities of cross-frontier prototypes such as fugitives and captives continued through independence and into the republic. The frontier carried dangers for whites as well as for Indians, especially for *estancia* peons, apparently the favored targets and prizes of the raiders. As for fugitives, this was a two-way process, and Indians sought refuge in white society, where primitive forms of existence were hardly different from their own. In any event the pioneers and defenders of the frontier did not enjoy its fruits, and the ideal of reformers, that the pampas would become a land of opportunity for landless migrants, was never realized. The first squatters, the peasants who made the frontier productive, had no property rights, and by the early nineteenth century they were being marginalized by new invaders, existing *estancieros* in most cases, who quickly established titles, created estates, and ensured that the frontier of Buenos Aires remained a white frontier, not a mestizo frontier. The new model of settlement was the large estate, cost-effective, functional, and protected by government legislation.

When later migrants arrived in the 1860s, they found the best and safest land already occupied by powerful *estancieros* and were forced outwards into territory disputed by the Indians. By 1870 competition for land and cattle between traditional enemies still endured, though the future lay with the landowners, while the Indians and gauchos, bound together at least in a common fate, were gradually pushed out. But they did not go without a fight, and in their fierce response they harmed immigrants as well as Argentines. Settlers from Britain, Denmark, France, Italy, and the Basque country were caught unaware, victims of Indian raids and gaucho defiance.

While lawlessness in Argentina erupted from below, from Indians denied and gauchos repelled, the state, too, played its part in fomenting the growing violence of the 1860s. The ebb and flow of fighting and the constant repetition of identical crimes were signs that the government was not in control of its own territory or in charge of its own officials. The delay in resolving the conflict between center and periphery perpetuated the militarization of rural life, in the interests not of order but of conflict. Once national reorganization began, from 1862, the campaigns against rebel caudillos were fought with a ferocity equal to any action of the *montoneros*, and Sarmiento's methods recalled the state terrorism practiced by Rosas. The tactics of extermination fed the lust of killing in Argentina and gave it a certain legitimacy. Meanwhile, statesmen still failed to determine their priorities correctly and preferred to seek gain and glory abroad while at home rural violence and frontier disorder remained unchecked; many provincial revolts could be traced directly to resentment at the military and economic consequences of Mitre's foreign policy. The forced conscription of gauchos for frontier service, even more relentless while the regular army withdrew to other fronts, was itself a form of violence and further barbarized the countryside.

The spirit of an age is not contained in a single event. But the event itself has a history; it is born of the past and serves to create the present. The massacre at Tandil epitomized many of the problems of mid-nineteenth-century Argentina. National organization, in spite of its positive achievements in state building, failed in two vital tests of a modern state, the control of distant officials and the provision of security for its citizens. Civil and military administration at the periphery was not closely monitored or disengaged from local interests; settlers were left without protection from ill-disposed officials and violent neighbors. This was a result not only of provincial constitutions or adverse conditions but also of flaws of policy. The weakness of the southern frontier was perpetuated by Mitre's decision to join the Triple Alliance with Brazil and Uruguay in order to wage war on Paraguay (1865–70).[3] Military personnel were diverted, foreign loans were wasted, and eighteen thousand troops were killed in an opportunistic bid to dominate a neighboring state and advance Argentina's position in the north instead of incorporating its own southern frontier more effectively into the nation. Settlers petitioned the government in vain, convinced that this was the critical flaw in immigration policy. As Richard Seymour observed, President Mitre had other preoccupations: "The long and unhappily protracted war with Paraguay has for some time past drained the Argentine Republic of all their soldiers, and the Government has been powerless to protect us." He had greater confidence in the newly elected Sarmiento and expected him to rescue settlers from their "helpless condition."[4] It was a false belief. Peace in the pampas was just as illusory in 1870 as it had been in 1860.

The Argentine government alleged that the British protested too much and exaggerated the dangers of life in the plains. But Indians on the horizon were not phantoms, and rural killers were not inventions of the British legation. The government then blamed those settlers who farmed beyond the frontier for their own misfortunes and thus laid itself open to the criticism that it was more interested in *estancieros* than in immigrants and to the worse charge that it used immigrants as frontier guards. The traditional *estancias*, with their armed peons and state militias, had the resources to defend themselves against Indian raiders, while foreign farmers finding their way in a strange country were easy targets. Immigrants were tempted to settle further out than was safe because of the empty spaces and the cheapness of land, advantages officially promoted. Their holdings became not an extension of the frontier but a buffer between Indians and haciendas. There was no sense of belonging among this generation of settlers.

The massacre of Tandil, its prelude and its postscript, formed a significant chapter in the history of Argentine nationalism. Argentina was slow to develop a sense of national identity. Most people in the River Plate found their identity in local communities; the province was the substance, Argentina the shadow. Colonial experience had been one of remote control by a distant government. The wars of independence were fought not only against Spain but also against Buenos Aires, the new metropolis; as the flimsy viceregal structure collapsed and each province became a ministate, so the new rulers lost any chance of creating a single state or extending the concept of nation to the mass of the people. The dictator Rosas claimed to speak for a confederation, and he punished provincial caudillos who stepped out of line, but he made no attempt to create, or even to debate, a constitution for Argentina or to foster any sense of loyalty to the nation. As for the opposition, its leaders recoiled in horror from the *rosista* state and were more interested in liberal reform than in nation building. After the fall of the dictator the leaders of national reorganization had to struggle for the soul of Argentina as well as for its constitution, and loyalty to regional interests was still alive in the 1860s. In the creation of a new state out of the wreckage of caudillism, institutions with a national dimension—federal justice, the army, the National Bank, the press—were an important ingredient. So, too, were the immigrants.

The massacre of Tandil assailed the mind, but the shock was felt more by foreigners than by natives. Beyond the assassin band, in the wider community of Tandil, there were signs of hostility between native Argentines and foreign immigrants well before the massacre, and these did not disappear even after its horrors were fully known; indeed, it was reported that natives felt less strongly than foreigners about the events of that gruesome day.[5] Foreigners came together in open solidarity. And if the history of terrorism is a guide, it is likely that the terrorists of Tandil had circles of silent support in the wider community. Further afield, compassion soon faded. Some *hacendados* placed attacks on property higher in the scale of criminality than assaults on the person. In a session of the Rural Society in September 1873, its president, Eduardo Olivera, described rustling as a more important problem than the massacre of Tandil.[6] The tragedy offers a glimpse into the minds of many native Argentines in these fateful years, when hatred of foreigners became a distinct feature of the political landscape.

Sarmiento, the prophet of immigration, the statesman who believed that people from Europe would make Argentina a great political and economic power, also feared that migrants would create ghettoes of foreigners instead of integrated communities, and he saw modern education as an essential agent of a common culture. In fact, immigration, as a form of external shock, stimulated a nationalist reaction, an experience not exclusive to Argentina. Anger erupted at two levels, popular and elite. There was resentment in Argentina against the influx of foreigners who took away land and work that should belong to native Argentines. This was an instinctive reaction to foreign farmers, traders, and creditors, who seemed to be arriving in a flood, not a trickle, and were seen by Argentina's own dispossessed as usurpers and usurers.

The foreigners, or some of them, were also branded as heretics, and the idiom of the massacre was apocalyptic. The rebels of Tandil were not unique in using religious metaphors; Latin American insurgents often adorned their secular discourse with conventional pieties.[7] In some cases the sacred and the profane coalesced to produce an authentic messianic cult; later in the nineteenth century religious enthusiasm and social anxiety found expression in two religious movements in the northeast of Brazil—Canudos and Joaseiro—each of which looked to a messianic leader for deliverance from affliction into a heavenly city. In northern Mexico in 1891 the rebels of Tomochic proclaimed a strong millenarian message as they resisted government forces and struggled to build their utopia.

The assassins of Tandil occupied a position somewhere between secular rebels and religious enthusiasts. Their rhetoric seemed to echo the book of Revelation, though the ideology and the environment of the movement were less millenarian than Catholic. This did not mean, as liberals accused, that the Church was an agent of xenophobia; many of the clergy of the renewed Church were themselves foreigners and had growing links with Rome. But folk Catholicism tended to give simple messages, and its adherents tended to look to religion for instant salvation. The assassins saw themselves as fighting foreigners and liberals. This was a popular cause, not a conspiracy with landowners. No doubt the hostility of local *estancieros* and officials towards foreign settlers was an advantage to the killers. But the basic war cry was "Kill a foreigner or die in the deluge!" A heresy or a blasphemy? Either way, the massacre was a mystery.

Sarmiento himself warned that Argentine parents would live to see the social decline of their children as ambitious foreigners used their superior talents to prosper and to rule. And in the countryside, while foreigners were able to acquire land, employment, and exemption from frontier service, the native gauchos and peons were harassed and rejected as remnants of the past. The nativist resentment of the foreigner was a basic motivation in the massacre of Tandil, and no one was more nativist than the gaucho, as was eventually recognized. Vilified in literature, marginalized from rural society, defeated by the combined forces of the state, the hacienda, and the immigrant, the gaucho vanished, to be later rediscovered as an embodiment of native virtues. Nostalgia is a powerful deceiver. When, at the beginning of the twentieth century, foreign hordes threatened to submerge Argentine tradition and to turn immigration into an invasion, politicians and intellectuals, liberal as well as conservative, began a new search for that elusive quality, *argentinidad*; then the gaucho was reinvented and became, ironically, the national archetype, the authentic representative of a nativist Argentina.[8] Traditionalists came to see Sarmiento's thesis of two cultures, civilization and barbarism, as a vile antithesis which denied the role of the gaucho and the values of rural Argentina.

While in the years about 1870 natives fought immigrants for rural space, resentment among the elites was directed at another target: those foreigners, especially the British, who appointed themselves the protectors of immigrants and demanded government action to provide a safer infrastructure for the newcomers. A war of words broke out between the Argentine government and media on the one hand and foreign officials and their allies on the other in which some of the characteristic features of Argentine nationalism are revealed: pride in national achievements, jealousy of national resources, and rejection of outside intervention.

Resentment of foreign criticism came at a time when Argentine statesmen and political elites were particularly sensitive about their national institutions. National organization was a source of pride as well as a sign of progress. Argentina's rulers had a lofty perception of what they were doing and expected their country to receive greater recognition in the world. Yet they were also conscious of Argentina's place at the rear of history. This combination of confidence and doubt helps to account for the tense relations with British authorities, who while overtly respecting the new Argentina made disparaging remarks about its culture. Argentine statesmen were particularly proud of their constitution and their legal system. When British representatives criticized these, they were criticizing basic components of national development, and Argentines bristled.

The British ministers in Buenos Aires were not an inferior breed consigned to a backwater for failed officials. They were professional diplomats, experienced observers and reporters, most of whom had solid careers behind and ahead of them. They knew Argentine policy and law, understood the temper of the age, and respected Mitre and Sarmiento. They reported events thoroughly from Buenos Aires and ensured that the Foreign Office was rarely less than well informed on Argentina; as for their political masters, government ministers absorbed as much as they needed. The British public, on the other hand, was mostly ignorant of Argentina. In the age of Disraeli and Gladstone, parliamentary reform and colonial wars, public attention was not normally focused on South America. Nevertheless, diplomats abroad could not ignore domestic opinion. They had to investigate and agitate on behalf of British subjects; otherwise there could be trouble back home and people would ask what the Foreign Office was doing. News of Tandil soon reached the British press, the House of Commons, and the desks of ministers. Yet Tandil was not a solitary reproach; it was part of a long record of British criticism and the signal of more to come.

In spite of their good intentions, the British ministers in Buenos Aires could not avoid misunderstandings. There were two levels of government in Argentina, federal and local; two points of observation, Buenos Aires and the provinces. British ministers addressed the central government and conducted a discussion, or a dispute, with educated politicians who behaved correctly. But the reality for immigrants was a life in the wilderness under the jurisdiction of local officials who were often ignorant and corrupt and usually indifferent. At this level British complaints were bitter and were taken seriously by the legation if not by the Argentine ministries. British officials belonged to a different culture, one of public service, impatience with disorder, and extreme severity towards criminals. They wrote at a time when law enforcement was improving in Britain but apparently remained starved of resources in Argentina, even in Buenos Aires, where the police were deficient in numbers and badly directed. In particular, there were different concepts of criminal justice and different standards of sentencing between Britain and Argentina. The British seem to have been unaware that there was a tradition of relatively lenient punishment in the Argentine courts which survived even the Rosas regime.[9] Although British officials and observers were careful not to state explicitly that Argentina was a barbarous country, the implication was there, as can be seen in Granville's reference to the expectations held of "civilized government" and MacDonell's insinuation along the same lines. According to this view, if you have barbarians in your midst you need to impose more punishment, not less. The British did not allow for different cultural levels or for arrested development; they expected Argentina to behave as an advanced European country instead of a developing American one.

Yet in the final analysis, the British position was one of protest, not action; even the emigration notices were a form of words and led only to a war of words. The massacre at Tandil was a monstrous act, but one which grew in the telling and created more recriminations than were justified. This at least was the view of the Argentine government. The Foreign Office did not agree but lacked any leverage to force Argentina to conform to norms acceptable to British opinion. The only weapons were trade and investment, and Britain was not prepared to jeopardize these. There were two parallel relationships, the political and the economic. While heated exchanges over security, immigration, and compensation worsened relations between the two countries, British investment, trade, and shipping all continued to prosper and to dominate the economic life of Argentina. Does this mean that the clash over Tandil and the treatment of immigrants were not serious or were less important than British trade with Argentina? If this were true it was because the British government kept its head about the killings and was always determined not to allow political differences to harm trade, or private disputes to force its hand, in the belief that it was better to deter immigrants than investors. The contest was inconclusive; neither side was a winner.

Nevertheless, Tandil and adjacent disputes were left in the mind and became part of a historic resentment in Argentina against imperial Britain. In a curious inversion, the event which began as an Argentine crime was transformed into a British transgression. The roots of mistrust went back to the British invasions of 1806–1807, when military expeditions arrived in the Río de la Plata not as liberators but as conquerors and when local patriotism first expressed itself in armed action to repel a powerful enemy. Forty years later Britain struck again. The Anglo-French blockade of Buenos Aires and armed intervention in the River Plate in 1845–46 secured little for Britain and took nothing from Argentina, but again it scarred the memory and became a milestone of national independence to generations of Argentines. Death in the pampas and British charges of official neglect in the years 1865–75 were thus part of a history; they stirred latent grievances and added a further layer to Argentine resentment of Britain. These historic disputes were precursors of others, the Baring crisis of 1889–90, the Roca-Runciman Treaty of 1933, the nationalization of the British railways in 1947, and the Falklands war of 1982. In the long term, spasmodic conflict is the story of Britain's relations with Argentina, and both countries have suffered from the curse of history.

Yet for over a century Britain and Argentina were bound by trade and investment—by the British demand for agricultural imports and Argentina's need for capital investment. National organization was financed, to some extent, by British capital, and British investors bankrolled Mitre's foreign policy. The loan of 1865, employed to finance the Paraguayan war rather than economic development, was followed by further massive loans in 1868; these earned the London banks great profits and the British the gratitude of Mitre.[10] From then on British capital in Argentina rose from £5.3 million in 1865 to £23 million in 1875 and to £45.6 million in 1885 and was applied to the infrastructure of state building, port development, transport, and railways, thus helping to improve the market for British trade and lower the costs of Argentine exports. European interest in the Latin American market and the expansion of trade with the subcontinent were determined to a large extent by the presence of immigrants from the home country.[11] As Sarmiento observed, each of the immigrant communities became an important element in developing trade with the homeland—the Italians in importing pasta, wines, and cheeses; the Spaniards in importing olive oil, fish, and cottons.[12] This was true also of the British, but in North America, not in Argentina.

British emigration to Argentina declined in the years after 1872. The depression of the Argentine economy in and after 1875 was a deterrent to all immigrants, but especially to the British, interrupting the trickle that survived previous obstacles. Total foreign immigration figures in Argentina began to recover in the early 1880s, but not until 1884 did they exceed the 76,322 who had arrived in 1873. Total British immigration in Argentina over 1857–90 was not more than about 30,000, reaching a peak of nearly 6,000 in 1889 (mainly Irish) but falling sharply to 1,100 in 1890. The British proportion of the whole remained 3 percent, and the percentage of Britons to the total population of Buenos Aires fell from 3.5 percent in 1860 to 0.93 percent in 1914.[13] Immigration and colonization projects boomed briefly in 1889–90, but experience soon taught that exclusively British colonization did not work in Argentina, and British business flourished without it. British land companies and private owners made comfortable profits in the pampas in the last decades of the nineteenth century, but many of the investors were resident in the United Kingdom, and among the British public Argentina was a minority interest.[14]

Immigrant clusters attract further immigrants. From the start there were never enough British immigrants in Argentina to generate a continuous flow; there was no compatriot factor, no existing support group, as was the case with Italians and Spaniards. Mass emigration needs a chain of certainty between the source and the destination; to take ship at Liverpool for the River Plate required a degree of confidence that did not exist among the British. The standard of living in Britain (though not in Ireland) was better than that in Italy and other European countries of origin; housing and food in Argentina were worse for the English, whereas Europeans had much less to lose. Language and climatic differences could perhaps be overcome, but the ignorance of agriculture among many of the English immigrants, urban in origin for the most part, was a more basic problem. And capital was never sufficient; the funds provided by individual colonists, by companies, and by the Argentine government did not amount to an investment capable of sustaining struggling immigrants, whose prospects of acquiring land, as distinct from providing labor, were by no means propitious. All these factors help to explain why the British did not join the mass migration from Europe to Argentina.

Insecurity on the frontier and the warnings of the Emigration Commission in London reinforced the reluctance of British emigrants to commit themselves to Argentina. From the early 1860s a number of British settlers had found that their search for El Dorado led only to a dead end. Word got back and convinced potential migrants that the problem with Argentina was not simply a matter of land and language but of life and death. The massacre at Tandil diminished the image of a nation in the making; it gave warning that killers were still active in the southern pampas and that the danger to immigrants came not only from Indian invaders but also from enemies within the Argentine state, whose authority was not yet complete.

Notes

INTRODUCTION

1. *The Times*, London, 13 Feb. 1872, p. 5.
2. Richard W. Slatta, *Gauchos and the Vanishing Frontier*, p. 172.
3. Hugo Nario, *Tata Dios: El Mesías de la última montonera*, and *Los crímenes del Tandil, 1872*.

CHAPTER I

1. *Los Debates*, 14 Feb. 1858, in Tulio Halperín Donghi, *Proyecto y construcción de una nación (Argentina, 1846–1880)*, 169; on judicial and army reforms see Academia Nacional de la Historia, *Historia Argentina Contemporánea 1862–1930*, vol. 2, part 1, pp. 30–34; part 2, pp. 272–92; on national organization, see Oscar Oszlak, *La formación del estado argentino*, 37–86.
2. F. J. McLynn, "The Argentine Presidential Election of 1868," *Journal of Latin American Studies* 11, no. 2 (1979): 303–23.
3. The early history of Tandil can be traced in José María Suárez García, *Historia de la Parroquia de Tandil*; R. Gorraiz Beloqui, *Tandil a través de un siglo*; Osvaldo Luis Fontana, *Tandil en la historia*.
4. H. Armaignac, *Viajes por las pampas argentinas: Cacerías en el Quequén Grande y otras andanzas, 1869–1874*, 108–11; M. G. Mulhall and E. T. Mulhall, *Handbook of the River Plate*, 87–88.
5. Alvaro Barros, *Indios, fronteras y seguridad interior*, ed. Pedro Daniel Weinberg, 74; *La Prensa*, as reported by H. G. MacDonell, "Remarks on the River Plate Republics as a Field for British Emigration," 14 March 1872, *Parliamentary Papers*, 1872, vol. 70, p. 41.
6. Leonardo León Solis, *Maloqueros y conchavadores en Araucanía y las Pampas, 1700–1800*, 50–63, 200–206; Raúl Mandrini, ed., *Los Araucanos de las pampas en el siglo XIX*, and the same author's "Las transformaciones de la economía indígena bonaerense (ca. 1600–1820)," in *Huellas en la tierra: Indios, agricultores y hacendados en la pampa bonaerense*, ed. Raúl Mandrini and Andrea Reguera, 45–74.
7. Lucio V. Mansilla, *Una excursión a los indios ranqueles*, ed. Julio Caillet-Bois, 76.

8. Ibid., 80.

9. Ibid., 176, 180–87, 392–93; Mandrini, *Los Araucanos de las pampas*, 33; Richard Arthur Seymour, *Pioneering in the Pampas; or, The First Four Years of a Settler's Experience in the La Plata Camps*, 53.

10. Armaignac, *Viajes por las pampas argentinas*, 118–30; Mandrini, *Los Araucanos de las pampas*, 25–32.

11. Sir Woodbine Parish, *Buenos Ayres and the Provinces of the Rio de la Plata*, 190–95.

12. Mansilla, *Una excursión a los indios ranqueles*, 55. The hierarchy of Indian leadership may be graded as *cacique, caciquillo, capitanejo*.

13. Seymour, *Pioneering in the Pampas*, 175; Barros, *Indios, fronteras y seguridad interior*, 88.

14. John Lynch, *Argentine Dictator: Juan Manuel de Rosas 1829–1852*, 53–55.

15. Kristine L. Jones, "Indian-Creole Negotiations in the Southern Frontier," in *Revolution and Restoration: The Rearrangement of Power in Argentina, 1776–1860*, ed. Mark D. Szuchman and Jonathan C. Brown, 103–23.

16. Barros, *Indios, fronteras y seguridad interior*, 78–81; Juan Fugl, *Memorias de Juan Fugl: Vida de un pionero danés durante 30 años en Tandil, Argentina, 1844–1875*, trans. Alice Larsen de Rabal, 230.

17. Mitre, *Los Debates*, 22 Oct. 1857, in Halperín, *Proyecto y construcción de una nación*, 337.

18. F. J. McLynn, "Consequences for Argentina of the War of the Triple Alliance, 1865–1870," *The Americas* 41, no. 1 (1984): 81–98.

19. Juan Carlos Walther, *La conquista del desierto*, 300, 313.

20. Ibid., 272–73.

21. Gould to Stanley, 9 Jan., 20 Feb., 1868, PRO, FO 6/273, pp. 6–9, 123–24.

22. Mansilla, *Una excursión a los indios ranqueles*, 393.

23. Gould to Stanley, 21 April 1868, PRO, FO 6/273, pp. 310–12; Leonardo León Solis, "Alianzas militares entre los indios araucanos y los grupos indios de las pampas: La rebelión araucana de 1867–1872 en Argentina y Chile," *Nueva Historia* 1, no. 1 (1981): 3–49.

24. MacDonell to Clarendon, 21 Oct. 1869, PRO, FO 6/284, pp. 118–20.

25. MacDonell to Clarendon, 24 June 1870, PRO, FO 6/291, p. 304; 12 July 1870, FO 6/292, pp. 43–45. Walther, *La conquista del desierto*, 330.

26. MacDonell to Granville, 4 Dec. 1870, PRO, FO 6/292, pp. 264–72. Walther, *La conquista del desierto*, 331–32.

27. On Sarmiento's Indian policy, and particularly the influence of North American methods, see Kristine L. Jones, "Civilization and Barbarism and Sarmiento's Indian Policy," in *Sarmiento and His Argentina*, ed. Joseph T. Criscenti, 35–43.

28. Domingo F. Sarmiento, "Investigaciones sobre el sistema colonial de los españoles," *Obras de D. F. Sarmiento* 2:214.

29. Mansilla, *Una excursión a los indios ranqueles*.

30. Ibid., 224–25.

31. Ibid., 393.

32. Gould to Stanley, 11 June 1868, PRO, FO 6/274, p. 174; Walther, *La conquista del desierto*, 331.

33. MacDonell to Granville, 2 May 1871, PRO, FO 6/302, p. 286.

34. MacDonell to Granville, 14 Mar. 1872, PRO, FO 6/309, pp. 210–11; Walther, *La conquista del desierto*, 333–38; Sarmiento, *Obras* 51:188–91.

35. MacDonell to Granville, 10 June 1872, PRO, FO 6/309, p. 328; Rinaldo Alberto Poggi, "Derrota pero no vencido: Calfucurá depués de San Carlos," *Nuestra Historia* 21 (1978): 134–57.

36. Consul Joel to Granville, 10 July 1872, PRO, FO 6/318, pp. 86–87; Joel to MacDonell, 27 Sept. 1872, FO 6/309, pp. 460–62; Joel to MacDonell, 26 Oct. 1872, FO 6/318, p. 217.

37. Sarmiento, "Mensaje de Apertura del Congress," May 1874, *Obras* 51:404.

38. Barros, *Indios, fronteras y seguridad interior*, 82, 112–16, 359.

39. Ricardo E. Rodríguez Molas, *Historia social del gaucho*; Lynch, *Argentine Dictator*, 101–16; Slatta, *Gauchos and the Vanishing Frontier*, 7–16, 30–56; and Richard W. Slatta, *Cowboys of the Americas*, 31–35, 105–106.

40. Jonathan C. Brown, *A Socioeconomic History of Argentina, 1776–1860*, 158–59.

41. Mansilla, *Una excursión a los indios ranqueles*, 293–94.

42. Domingo Faustino Sarmiento, *Facundo*, 44–45, 53–63, 65.

43. Mansilla, *Una excursión a los indios ranqueles*, 57.

44. Seymour, *Pioneering in the Pampas*, 45–46.

45. Rodríguez Molas, *Historia social del gaucho*, 261–85; Slatta, *Gauchos and the Vanishing Frontier*, 180–92; Hebe Clementi, "National Identity and the Frontier," in *Where Cultures Meet: Frontiers in Latin American History*, ed. David J. Weber and Jane M. Rausch, 147–50. For good visual effect, see Bonifacio del Carril, *El gaucho a través de la iconografía*.

46. The chronicler Gerónimo de Vivar, *Crónica y relación copiosa y verdadera de los Reinos de Chile (1558)*, ed. Leopoldo Saez-Godoy (Berlin, 1979), 182–84, describes lassos made of *liana*, a tough willow fiber, used by the Araucanians to capture invading Spaniards.

47. See Mark D. Szuchman, *Order, Family, and Community in Buenos Aires, 1810–1860*, 81–82, for the urban family.

48. Wilfred Latham, *The States of the River Plate*, 35–36, 249–50, 326–27.

49. *El Nacional*, 25 Sept. 1856, in Sarmiento, *Obras* 23:320; Benito Díaz, *Juzgados de paz de campaña de la provincia de Buenos Aires (1821–1854)*, 204–18.

50. Armaignac, *Viajes por las pampas argentinas*, 172–73; Mansilla, *Una excursión a los indios ranqueles*, 219.

51. Halperín, *Proyecto y construcción de una nación*, 361–63.

52. Tulio Halperín Donghi, *José Hernández y sus mundos*, 224–77, 279.

53. Barros, *Indios, fronteras y seguridad interior*, 278.

54. Walther, *La conquista del desierto*, 303–304.

55. José Hernández, *El Río de la Plata*, 4 Sept. 1869, in Halperín, *Proyecto y contrucción de una nación*, 355.

56. Vice-Consul Gordon, Córdoba, to Stuart, 25 June 1869, PRO, FO 6/283, pp. 320–39.

57. José Hernández, *El Gaucho Martín Fierro*, bilingual ed., trans. Walter Owen, 42.

58. Quoted by Walther, *La conquista del desierto*, 310.

59. Fugl, *Memorias*, 230–31, 238.

60. Díaz, *Juzgados de paz*, 23–24, 70–73, 133–40; Latham, *The States of the River Plate*, 333; Hernández, *El Río de la Plata*, 16 Nov. 1869, in Halperín, *Proyecto y construcción de una nación*, 361–63.

61. McCrie to Consul Joel, 9 Dec. 1871, PRO, FO 6/305, p. 239.

62. Ford to Clarendon, 12 July 1866, PRO, FO 6/263, p. 58; Gould to Stanley, 15 Jan. 1868, PRO, FO 6/273, p. 47.

63. Seymour, *Pioneering in the Pampas*, 10.

64. Barros, *Indios, fronteras y seguridad interior*, 74.

65. Seymour, *Pioneering in the Pampas*, 34.

66. Tejedor to MacDonell, 11 Jan. 1871, MacDonell to Granville, 15 Feb. 1871, PRO, FO 6/302, pp. 59–64.

67. "A Voice from Bahia Blanca," by Settler, *The Standard*, Buenos Aires, 6 Mar. 1872.

68. See the reports of G. B. Stanley to Foreign Secretary in 1866–67, PRO, FO 6/263, p. 267.

69. G. B. Mathew to Russell, 21 Nov. 1866, PRO, FO 6/266, pp. 274–76.

70. See above, p. 17.

71. D. G. Johnstone to Clarendon, 21 June 1869, PRO, FO 6/300, pp. 10–11.

72. Seymour, *Pioneering in the Pampas*, 54–55.

73. Ibid., 136–39.

74. Ibid., 148–52.

75. Mathew to Stanley, 10 Nov. 1866, PRO, FO 6/266, p. 282; Mathew to Stanley, 26 Mar. 1867, FO 6/267, p. 61; Seymour, *Pioneering in the Pampas*, 71–72, 75.

76. Seymour, *Pioneering in the Pampas*, 109–10.

77. *The Standard*, Buenos Aires, 13 Jan. 1869. See also PRO, FO 6/300, p. 4.

78. MacDonell to Clarendon, 12 April 1870, PRO, FO 6/300, pp. 142–44.

79. Copy of Notice in PRO, FO 6/294, p. 251.

80. MacDonell to Clarendon, 12 Feb., 9 April, 22 June, 1 Sept. 1870, PRO, FO 6/300, pp. 106–108, 136, 194–95, 199.

81. Parish to Clarendon, 11 May 1870, PRO, FO 6/294, pp. 82–86.

82. Reported in Stuart to Eliot, 25 May 1870, PRO, FO 6/300, pp. 185–90.

83. MacDonell to Clarendon, 8 June 1870, PRO, FO 6/293, pp. 190–92.

84. "The Bench and the Dock," *The Standard*, Buenos Aires, 24 June 1870; MacDonell to Clarendon, 24 June 1870, PRO, FO 6/291, p. 306; 23 July 1870, FO 6/292, pp. 61–71.

85. MacDonell to Clarendon, 27 July 1870, PRO, FO 6/292, pp. 77–85, 87–89.

86. MacDonell to Granville, 4 Dec. 1870, PRO, FO 6/292, pp. 264–72; MacDonell to Tejedor, 16 Jan. 1871, *Parliamentary Papers*, 1872, vol. 70, pp. 93–94.

87. MacDonell to Granville, 8 Feb. 1871, PRO, FO 6/302, pp. 29–30; MacDonell to Granville, 12 May 1871, *Parliamentary Papers*, 1872, vol. 70, p. 96.

88. MacDonell to Granville, 22 Oct. 1871, *Parliamentary Papers*, 1872, vol. 70, pp. 97–98; Michael G. Mulhall, *The English in South America*, 443.

89. MacDonell to Granville, 22 Oct. 1871, PRO, FO 6/303, pp. 127–37; British settlers in Bahía Blanca to MacDonell, Dec. 1871, FO 6/309, pp. 21–23; *River Plate Times*, 7 Mar. 1872.

90. Tejedor to MacDonell, 22 Jan. 1872, PRO, FO 6/309, pp. 48–52.

CHAPTER 2

1. Hilda Sábato, *Agrarian Capitalism and the World Market: Buenos Aires in the Pastoral Age, 1840–1890*, 23–39.

2. Ernesto J. A. Maeder, *Evolución demográfica argentina de 1810 a 1869*, 22–26, 33–34; Szuchman, *Order, Family, and Community*, 188–89; Sábato, *Agrarian Capitalism*, 73–74.

3. Lynch, *Argentine Dictator*, 56–76.

4. Jonathan C. Brown, "Revival of the Rural Economy and Society in Buenos Aires," in *Revolution and Restoration*, ed. Szuchman and Brown, 246; see also Juan Carlos Garavaglia and Jorge D. Gelman, "Rural History of the Río de la Plata, 1600–1850: Results of a Historiographical Renaissance," *Latin American Research Review* 30, no. 3 (1995): 75–105.

5. Brown, "Revival of the Rural Economy," 247.

6. Slatta, *Gauchos and the Vanishing Frontier*, 57–68.

7. *El Nacional*, 25 Sept. 1856, in Sarmiento, *Obras* 23:320; Brown, "Revival of the Rural Economy," 251–53.

8. Sábato, *Agrarian Capitalism*, 25–30.

9. James R. Scobie, *Revolution on the Pampas: The Social History of Argentine Wheat, 1860–1910*, 27–43; Brown, "Revival of the Rural Economy," 253–54.

10. Mitre, *Los Debates*, 6–7 June 1857, in Halperín, *Proyecto y construcción de una nación*, 318–21.

11. Brown, "Revival of the Rural Economy," 255.

12. Fugl, *Memorias*, 186.

13. Sábato, *Agrarian Capitalism*, 78–81.

14. Carlos A. Mayo, *Estancia y sociedad en la pampa, 1740–1820*, 101–16.

15. Ricardo D. Salvatore, "Reclutamiento militar, disciplinamiento y proletarización en la era de Rosas," *Boletín del Instituto de Historia Argentina y Americana "Dr. E. Ravignani,"* 3d series, vol. 5, no. 1 (1992): 25–47.

16. Brown, "Revival of the Rural Economy," 258–64.

17. Sábato, *Agrarian Capitalism*, 23–27.

18. H. S. Ferns, *Britain and Argentina in the Nineteenth Century*, 335–73.

19. Mitre, Speech on the inauguration of the Southern Railway, 7 March 1861, in Halperín, *Proyecto y construcción de una nación*, 304; Colin M. Lewis, *British Railways in Argentina, 1859–1914: A Case Study of Foreign Investment*, 25–31, 197.

20. Jeremy Adelman, *Frontier Development: Land, Labour, and Capital on the Wheatlands of Argentina and Canada, 1890–1914*, 63–70.

21. Sábato, *Agrarian Capitalism*, 27–29, 292.

22. José Carlos Chiaramonte, *Nacionalismo y liberalismo económicos en la Argentina, 1860–1880*, 48–68.

23. Mulhall and Mulhall, *Handbook of the River Plate*, 367.

24. Manuel Bejarano, "Inmigración y estructuras tradicionales en Buenos Aires (1854–1930)," in *Los fragmentos del poder*, ed. Torcuato S. Di Tella and Tulio Halperín Donghi, 75–149; Sábato, *Agrarian Capitalism*, 50–52.

25. Fugl, *Memorias*, 190–200.

26. Ibid., 244–45.

27. Manuel Brunel to Mariano Saavedra, 2 Jan. 1872, Banco de la Provincia de Buenos Aires, Archivo y Museo Históricos, Correspondencia, 1, fols., 2–5, reference kindly facilitated by Professor Samuel Amaral.

28. Eduardo José Míguez, "Política, participación y poder: Los inmigrantes en las tierras nuevas de la Provincia de Buenos Aires en la segunda mitad del siglo XIX," *Estudios Migratorios Latinoamericanos*, nos. 6–7 (1987): 337–79.

29. Fugl, *Memorias*, 195.

30. Ibid., 204.

31. Ibid., 305–16.

32. Ibid., 431–32.

33. Rodríguez Molas, *Historia social del gaucho*, 163–67; Sábato, *Agrarian Capitalism*, 85–89.

34. "Mas agitaciones en la campaña," *La Nación*, 16 Jan. 1872.

35. Nario, *Los crímenes del Tandil, 1872*, 10–11.

36. Sábato, *Agrarian Capitalism*, 88–89.

37. Slatta, *Gauchos and the Vanishing Frontier*, 125.

38. "Apelación y alegato del doctor Martín Aguirre," in Antonio G. Del Valle, *Recordando el pasado: Campañas por la civilización*, 2:572–90; Nario, *Los crímenes del Tandil*, 76–83.

39. Fugl, *Memorias*, 372.

40. Ibid., 374, 409.

41. Nario, *Tata Dios*, 11, 60; Nario, *Los crímenes del Tandil*, 10–11.

42. Nario, *Tata Dios*, 211.

43. Juan José Santos, "Una revuelta rural en la frontera sur bonaerense: Tandil 1872," unpublished paper kindly facilitated by the author.

44. Slatta, *Gauchos and the Vanishing Frontier*, 171–72.

CHAPTER 3

1. For a discussion of the answer to this question, see José Carlos Chiaramonte, "El federalismo argentino en la primera mitad del siglo XIX," in *Federalismos latinoamericanos: México, Brasil, Argentina*, ed. Marcello Carmagnani, 81–132.

2. Esteban Echeverría, *Dogma Socialista*, 112, 126–27.

3. W. H. Hudson, *Tales of the Pampa*, 347.

4. First a nation is imagined, and "once imagined, modelled, adapted and transformed" (Benedict Anderson, *Imagined Communities: Reflections on the Origin and Spread of Nationalism*, 2d ed., 81, 141).

5. Juan Bautista Alberdi, *Las "Bases" de Alberdi*, ed. Jorge M. Mayer, 248.

6. Mansilla, *Una excursión a los indios ranqueles*, 133, 185, 196.

7. Nicolas Shumway, *The Invention of Argentina*, 292–93.

8. Mansilla, *Una excursión a los indios ranqueles*, 157.

9. Quoted by Sergio Bagú, *El plan económico del grupo Rivadaviano, 1811–1827* (Rosario, 1966), 128–31.

10. *Los Debates*, 1 April 1852, in Halperín, *Proyecto y construcción de una nación*, 167.

11. *El Nacional*, 25 Sept. 1856, in Sarmiento, *Obras* 23:318–21.

12. Quoted by Slatta, *Gauchos and the Vanishing Frontier*, 166.

13. Sarmiento, "Mensaje al abrir el congreso de 1869," 1 May 1869, *Obras* 50:163–64.

14. For an analysis of the "ambiguity" of the liberal-conservative ideology in the post-Rosas period, see Tulio Halperín Donghi, "¿Para qué la inmigración? Ideologías y política inmigratoria en la Argentina (1810–1914)," *El espejo de la historia: Problemas argentinos y perspectivas latinoamericanas*, 203–204, and the same author et al., "Sarmiento's Place," in *Sarmiento, Author of a Nation*, 19–30. On Sarmiento's preoccupations concerning immigration, see Samuel L. Baily, "Sarmiento and Immigration: Changing Views on the Role of Immigration in the Development of Argentina," in *Sarmiento and His Argentina*, ed. Criscenti, 131–42.

15. Sarmiento, "Educación Popular," *Obras* 11:35–36.

16. Sarmiento, "Mensaje de Apertura del Congreso," 1874, *Obras* 51:392.

17. Quoted in Shumway, *The Invention of Argentina*, 4.

18. Alberdi, *Las "Bases,"* 240–41, 250, 252.

19. Shumway, *The Invention of Argentina*, 146–56. For an analysis of Argentina's immigration policy during the period 1880–1914, see Carl E. Solberg, *Immigration and Nationalism: Argentina and Chile, 1890–1914*, 8–32.

20. Hernández, articles in *El Río de la Plata*, 1869, reproduced in José Panettieri, *Inmigración en la Argentina*, 122–24, and Halperín, *Proyecto y construcción de una nación*, 295–33.

21. Juan Carlos Korol and Hilda Sábato, *Como fue la inmigración irlandesa en Argentina*, 81–112.

22. H. G. MacDonell, "Remarks on the River Plate Republics as a Field for British Emigration," 14 March 1872, *Parliamentary Papers*, 1872, vol. 70, pp. 1–85.

23. Slatta, *Gauchos and the Vanishing Frontier*, 162.

24. Ibid., 163.

25. Enrique Amadasi et al., *Estructura y dinámica de la población, evolución económica y empleo en el partido de Tandil*, 55; Table 3–2; Eduardo José Míguez, "La frontera de Buenos Aires en el siglo XIX: Población y mercado de trabajo," in Raúl Mandrini and Andrea Reguera, *Huellas en la tierra: Indios, agricultores y hacendados en la pampa bonaerense*, 191–208.

26. Slatta, *Gauchos and the Vanishing Frontier*, 162.

27. Nario, *Tata Dios*, 54–56.

28. For the earlier history of the *pulperías*, see Carlos Mayo, ed., *Pulperos y pulperías de Buenos Aires, 1740–1830*, 25–42, 77–112, 139–50.

29. British settlers in Tandil and Azul to MacDonell, 7 Jan. 1872, *Parliamentary Papers*, 1872, vol. 70, p. 109; John Smith (William's brother) to Foreign Secretary, 19 Feb. 1872, PRO, FO 6/312, fols. 75–76.

30. Fugl, *Memorias*, 98, 104–105, 186.

31. Nario, *Tata Dios*, 56–58.

32. Donald S. Castro, *The Development and Politics of Argentine Immigration Policy, 1852–1914*, 102–106; Panettieri, *Inmigración en la Argentina*, 106–10; Academia Nacional de la Historia, *Historia Argentina Contemporánea, 1862–1930*, vol. 2, part 1, p. 51; Scobie, *Revolution on the Pampas*, 114–22.

33. Seymour, *Pioneering in the Pampas*, 179.

34. Thomas J. Curran, *Xenophobia and Immigration, 1820–1930*, 28–43, 58–74.

35. Maldwyn Allen Jones, *American Immigration*, 126, 127–38, 216–40.

36. Hernández, *El Gaucho Martín Fierro*, 57.

37. Halperín, *Proyecto y construcción de una nación*, 405–407.

38. Lynch, *Argentine Dictator*, 261–62.

39. Rodríguez Molas, *Historia social del gaucho*, 248–50.

40. For evidence of this incident, see Colonel Wenceslao Paunero to Governor Pastor Obligado, San Nicolás, 9 February 1854, Archivo General de la Nación, Buenos Aires, Sala X.27.3.1. I am indebted to María Alejandra Irigoin for kindly supplying this reference.

41. Ibid.

42. Slatta, *Gauchos and the Vanishing Frontier*, 169.

43. "The Plague of 1871," PRO, FO 6/306, pp. 404–18.

44. Rivas to Minister of War, Azul, 20 April 1872, quoted by Walther, *La conquista del desierto*, 338–40.

45. MacDonell to Granville, 30 June 1872, PRO, FO 6/309, pp. 397–402.

46. See above, pp. 30–37.

47. Halperín, "¿Para qué la inmigración?" 208–209.

48. Eduardo José Míguez, "Política, participación y poder: Los inmigrantes en las tierras nuevas de la Provincia de Buenos Aires en la segunda mitad del siglo XIX," *Estudios Migratorios Latinoamericanos* 6–7 (1987): 337–79, especially 360.

49. Ibid., 371.

50. Fugl, *Memorias*, 145–46.

51. Jones, *American Immigration*, 78.

52. *The Standard*, Buenos Aires, 9 Jan. 1872.

53. Parish to Granville, 13 Jan. 1872, PRO, FO 6/311, pp. 68–72; *Parliamentary Papers*, 1872, vol. 70, pp. 111–12.

CHAPTER 4

1. Manuel Brunel to Mariano Saavedra, Tandil, 2 Jan. 1872, Banco de la Provincia de Buenos Aires, Archivo y Museo Históricos, Correspondencia, 1, fols. 2–5. Curanderos and their female counterparts practiced folk, herbal, and superstitious remedies and were usually held in high esteem by the gauchos; see Armaignac, *Viajes por las pampas argentinas*, 94.

2. "Sumario," quoted by Nario, *Tata Dios*, 69; *The Standard*, 9 Jan. 1872.

3. *La Verdad*, Buenos Aires, 9 Jan. 1872; *The Times* of London, 22 Feb. 1872, drawing on the *River Plate Times*, gives a detailed account of Solané and his activities.

4. Statement by Ramón Rufo Gómez, in Nario, *Los crímenes del Tandil*, 35–36.

5. Figueroa to Malaver, 2 Jan. 1872, Archivo Histórico de la Provincia de Buenos Aires, Ministerio de Gobierno (hereafter cited as AHPBA, Min. de Gob.), leg. 2, exped. 108, fol. 11.

6. Statement by Ramón Rufo Gómez, in Nario, *Los crímenes del Tandil*, 36–37; statement by Eufrasio Gómez, in ibid., 38.

7. Ibid., 54.

8. *La Verdad*, 9 Jan. 1872.

9. Nario, *Tata Dios*, 81.

10. Ibid., 89–98.

11. Figueroa to Malaver, 2 Jan. 1872, AHPBA, Min. de Gob., leg. 2, exped. 108, fol. 11. Also reproduced in *La Verdad*, 9 Jan. 1872; Nario, *Los crímenes del Tandil*, 18. For a profile of Tandil, see Armaignac, *Viajes por las pampas argentinas*, 108.

12. Statement of British settlers, Tandil, 7 Jan. 1872, PRO, FO 6/309, pp. 25–27; *Parliamentary Papers*, 1872, vol. 70, p. 109. See also *The Times*, 13 Feb. 1872, p. 5; Nario, *Tata Dios*, 107.

13. Nario, *Tata Dios*, 108–109.

14. José Ciriaco Gómez to Figueroa, 2 Jan. 1872, AHPBA, Min. de Gob., leg. 2, exped. 108, fol. 11; also reproduced in *La Verdad*, 9 Jan. 1872. Chapalcotú is variously spelled Chapaleofu, Chapadleufu in the sources.

15. Somoza to Malaver, 14 Jan. 1872, AHPBA, Min. de Gob., leg. 2, exped. 108, fol. 49.

16. Statement of Apolinario García, 9 Jan. 1872, AHPBA, Min. de Gob., leg. 2, exped. 108, fols. 27–28. García was present at the scene, having arrived for treatment by Solané.

17. Figueroa to Malaver, 2 Jan. 1872, AHPBA, Min. de Gob., leg. 2, exped. 108, fol. 11.

18. Fugl, *Memorias*, 415–16.

19. AHPBA, Min. de Gob., leg. 16, exped. 874, fols. 1–2.

20. Court to provincial governor, 18 June 1872, AHPBA, Min. de Gob., leg. 14, exped. 772, fol. 1. Those arraigned numbered more than the captive remnants of the assassin band.

21. See above, p. 51.

22. *La Nación*, Buenos Aires, 14 Sept. 1872, in Nario, *Los crímenes del Tandil*, 88.

23. Nario, *Los crímenes del Tandil*, 63, 69–76.

24. José Ciriaco Gómez to Figueroa, 2 Jan. 1872, AHPBA, Min. de Gob., leg. 2, exped. 108, fol. 11.

25. Mr. Harrow to MacDonell, Loma Clara, Tandil Azul, 27 April 1872, PRO, FO 6/309, p. 296.

26. Fugl, *Memorias*, 409.

27. Emilio Castro, provincial governor, and Antonio E. Malaver, provincial minister of interior, to Martín de Gainza, minister of war and navy, 4 Jan. 1871 [sic] 1872, AHPBA, Min. de Gob., leg. 2, exped. 108, fols. 1–3.

28. Malaver to Somoza, 4 Jan. 1972, ibid., fols. 4–7.

29. Statement of Juan Henestrosa, statement of Lisandro de la Cuesta, AHPBA, Min. de Gob., leg. 2, exped. 104, fols. 182–86, 194–96; Nario, *Los crímenes del Tandil*, 34, 39–40.

30. Figueroa to Malaver, 2 Jan. 1872, AHPBA, Min. de Gob., leg. 2, exped. 108, fol. 11; see also Nario, *Los crímenes del Tandil*, 21–22.

31. Roger D. McGrath, *Gunfighters, Highwaymen and Vigilantes: Violence on the Frontier*, 85, 100–101, 199, 255–56.

32. Joel Jacobsen, *Such Men as Billy the Kid: The Lincoln County War Reconsidered*, 87–91; Robert S. Utley, *High Noon in Lincoln: Violence on the Western Frontier*.

33. John Charles Chasteen, "Violence for Show: Knife Dueling on a Nineteenth-Century Cattle Frontier," in *The Problem of Order in Changing Societies: Essays on Crime and Policing in Argentina and Uruguay*, ed. Lyman L. Johnson, 47–64, provides analogous evidence from the borderlands of Uruguay and Brazil.

34. W. H. Hudson, *Far Away and Long Ago*, 107.

35. Quoted in José S. Campobassi, *Sarmiento y su época*, 1:548.

36. Mansilla, *Una excursión a los indios ranqueles*, 206.

37. Hernández, *El Gaucho Martín Fierro*, 68.

38. Statement of Gutiérrez, in Nario, *Los crímenes del Tandil*, 23–24.

39. *La Nación*, 14 Sept. 1872.

40. Statement of Lasarte, in Nario, *Los crímenes del Tandil*, 24–25.

41. *La Nación*, 14 Sept. 1872.

42. Statement of Torres, in Nario, *Los crímenes del Tandil*, 25–26.

43. Slatta, *Gauchos and the Vanishing Frontier*, 171–72.

44. *La Tribuna*, 5 Jan. 1872.

45. *La Tribuna*, 7 Jan. 1872.

46. Richard Maxwell Brown, *Strain of Violence: Historical Studies of American Violence and Vigilantism*, 95–97. Brown refers to "socially constructive" committees of vigilance (118). See also McGrath, *Gunfighters, Highwaymen, and Vigilantes*, 225–46.

47. Jacobsen, *Such Men as Billy the Kid*, 107–108.

48. Brown, *Strain of Violence*, 146–67.

49. McCrie to Consul Joel, 9 Dec. 1871, PRO, FO 6/305, p. 239; MacDonell to Granville, 13 Jan. 1872, FO 6/309, pp. 9–14; Tejedor to MacDonell, 22 Jan. 1872, FO 6/309, pp. 48–52.

50. Richard W. Slatta, ed. *Bandidos: The Varieties of Latin American Banditry*, 33–47, 49, 65, 191–98.

51. Hugo Nario, *Mesías y bandoleros pampeanos*, 91–95, 120–22.

52. Brown, *Strain of Violence*, 21–22.

53. MacDonell to Granville, 8 Feb. 1871, PRO, FO 6/302, pp. 29–30.

54. Figueroa to Malaver, 2 Jan. 1872, in Nario, *Los crímenes del Tandil*, 19.

55. *The Standard*, 9 Jan. 1872.

56. Nario, *Los crímenes del Tandil*, 29.

57. Ibid., 31.

58. *La Verdad*, Buenos Aires, 9 Jan. 1872; Nario, *Mesías y bandoleros pampeanos*, 42–43.

59. Figueroa to Malaver, 7 Jan. 1872, AHPBA, Min. de Gob., leg. 2, exped. 108, fols. 45–46.

60. MacDonell to Granville, 13 Jan. 1872, *Parliamentary Papers*, 1872, vol. 70, pp. 105–106.

Chapter 5

1. Juan Carlos Torre, "Los crímenes de Tata Dios, el mesías gaucho," *Todo es Historia* 4 (August 1967): 40–45.

2. J. F. C. Harrison, *The Second Coming: Popular Millenarianism, 1780–1850*, 3–10, 11–12; Damian Thompson, *The End of Time: Faith and Fear in the Shadow of the Millennium*, 20–28, 57–60. See also Norman Cohn, *The Pursuit of the Millennium: Revolutionary Millenarians and Mystical Anarchists of the Middle Ages*.

3. Harrison, *The Second Coming*, 214–23.

4. John Leddy Phelan, *The Millennial Kingdom of the Franciscans in the New World*, 2d ed. (Berkeley and Los Angeles, 1970), 45–48; W. Hanisch, "Manuel Lacunza S.I. y el milenarismo," *Archivum Historicum Societatis Jesu* 40 (1971): 496–511; Paul J. Vanderwood, "'None but the Justice of God': Tomochic, 1891–1892," in *Patterns of Contention in Mexican History*, ed. Jaime E. Rodríguez, 227–41.

5. Statement by Cruz Gutiérrez in Nario, *Los crímenes del Tandil*, 56; see also Nario, *Tata Dios*, 124.

6. Statement by Juan Villalba in Nario, *Los crímenes del Tandil*, 58–59.

7. Statements by various witnesses in Nario, *Mesías y bandoleros pampeanos*, 33–35; *Los crímenes del Tandil*, 62–63; and *Tata Dios*, 91–92.

8. Fugl, *Memorias*, 409–13.

9. Austen Ivereigh, *Catholicism and Politics in Argentina 1810–1960*, 44–49.

10. Lynch, *Argentine Dictator*, 183–86.

11. Guillermo Furlong, S.J., "El catolicismo argentino entre 1860 y 1930,"

Academia Nacional de la Historia, *Historia Argentina Contemporánea 1862–1930*, vol. 2, part 1, pp. 251–54.

12. John Lynch, "The Catholic Church in Latin America, 1830–1930," in *The Cambridge History of Latin America*, ed. Leslie Bethell, 4:566–67.

13. Ariel Eugenio De la Fuente, "Caudillo and Gaucho Politics in the Argentine State-Formation Process: La Rioja, 1853–1870" (Ph.D. diss., State University of New York at Stony Brook, 1995; UMI, Ann Arbor, Mich., 1996), 472–74.

14. Tulio Halperín Donghi, ed., *El pensamiento de Echeverría* (Buenos Aires, 1951); Ivereigh, *Catholicism and Politics in Argentina*, 50–54.

15. Quoted by Furlong, "El catolicismo argentino," 261.

16. Alberdi, *Las "Bases,"* 234–35.

17. Ibid., 258–59.

18. Félix Frias, 12 Oct. 1853, in Halperín, *Proyecto y construcción de una nación*, 43.

19. Quoted by Furlong, "El catolicismo argentino," 261.

20. Ibid., 254–59.

21. Quoted in Héctor Recalde, *La iglesia y la cuestión social, 1871–1910*, 35.

22. Seymour, *Pioneering in the Pampas*, 80–81.

23. Míguez, "Política, participación y poder," 359.

24. Fugl, *Memorias*, 431–32.

25. Slatta, *Cowboys of the Americas*, 226–27.

26. Mansilla, *Una excursión a los indios ranqueles*, 11.

27. "La superstición religiosa, los crímenes del Tandil," *La Tribuna*, 7 Jan. 1872.

28. "Los asesinatos del Tandil," *La Tribuna*, 9 Jan. 1872.

29. "La superstición religiosa: Los crímenes del Tandil," *La República*, 10 Jan. 1872.

30. "Efectos del fanaticismo," *El Nacional*, 11 Jan. 1872.

31. "Mas agitaciones en la campaña," *La Nación*, 16 Jan. 1872.

32. Fugl, *Memorias*, 409.

33. Seymour, *Pioneering in the Pampas*, 81. See also Slatta, *Cowboys of the Americas*, for the lack of religion, as distinct from superstition, among cowboys and gauchos.

34. *La Nación*, 14 Sept. 1872.

35. R. B. Cunninghame Graham, "La Pulpería," in *Thirteen Stories*, 172–75.

36. De la Fuente, *Caudillo and Gaucho Politics*, 480–83.

37. Hernández, *El Gaucho Martín Fierro*, 93.

38. Rosas to Josefina Gómez, 12 May 1872, in Juan Manuel de Rosas, *Cartas del exilio, 1853–1875*, ed., José Raed, 170–72.

39. David Rock, *Authoritarian Argentina: The Nationalist Movement, Its History and Its Impact*, 27–28.

CHAPTER 6

1. Fugl, *Memorias*, 415–16.

2. Figueroa to Malaver, 6 Jan. 1872, AHPBA, Min. de Gob., leg. 2, exped. 108, fol. 25.

3. *The Times*, London, 12 Feb. 1872, p. 7, reporting from *The Standard*, Buenos Aires, 9 Jan. 1872.

4. *The Times*, 13 Feb. 1872, quoting *The Standard*.

5. *The Standard*, 9 Jan. 1872.

6. MacDonell to Granville, 13 Jan. 1872, PRO, FO 6/309, pp. 7, 25-27; *Parliamentary Papers*, 1872, vol. 70, pp. 105-106.

7. Parish to Granville, 13 Jan. 1872, PRO, FO 6/311, pp. 68-72.

8. Parish to Malaver, 11 Jan. 1872, *Parliamentary Papers*, 1872, vol. 70, pp. 112-13, and rest of correspondence, pp. 117-18.

9. Brunel to Saavedra, 2 Jan. 1872, Banco de la Provincia de Buenos Aires, Archivo y Museo Históricos, Correspondencia, 1, fols. 2-5.

10. Provincial government to Justice of the Peace, 31 Aug. 1872, AHPBA, Min. de Gob., leg. 12, exped. 695, fol. 1.

11. Slatta, *Gauchos and the Vanishing Frontier*, 173-74.

12. Nario, *Tata Dios*, 173-74.

13. Malaver to President of Supreme Court, 11 Jan. 1872, AHPBA, Min. de Gob. leg. 2, exped. 108, fols. 39-42.

14. Gorraiz Beloqui, *Tandil a través de un siglo*, 114-15.

15. Report to the "Pueblo de Tandil," 18 Feb. 1872, AHPBA, Min. de Gob., leg. 3, exped. 209, fol.2.

16. Ibid., fols. 2-4.

17. Figueroa to Min. de Gob., 21 May 1872, AHPBA, leg. 7, exped. 430, fol. 15v-21v; Nario, *Tata Dios*, 193-201.

18. An argument used by Nario, *Tata Dios*, 185-87, 211-12.

19. Fugl, *Memorias*, 440-51.

20. Moisés Jurado to Min. de Gob., 11 May 1872, AHPBA, leg. 8, exped. 489, fol. 17. On the elections of 1873, see Nario, *Tata Dios*, 186-87.

21. Quoted by Nario, *Mesías y bandoleros pampeanos*, 52.

22. Carlos A. Díaz to Federico Pinedo, Min. de Gob., 28 Sept. 1872, AHPBA, leg. 14, exped. 812, fol. 2.

23. Díaz to Pinedo, 3 Sept. 1872, AHPBA, Min. de Gob., leg. 18, exped. 1010, fols. 1-2.

24. Díaz to Pinedo, 21 Sept. 1872, ibid., fol. 4.

25. Joaquín Rivero to Díaz, 7 Oct. 1872, AHPBA, Min. de Gob., leg. 18, exped. 1010, fols. 7-9.

26. A. McLachlan, Flexmen, A. Thomson to British minister in Buenos Aires, 9 Nov. 1872, MacDonell to these, 9 Dec. 1872, PRO, FO 118/145.

27. St. John to Granville, 30 June 1873, PRO, FO 6/315, pp. 59-70.

28. Notice dated 22 July 1872; for the original draft, see Murdoch to Herbert, 27 June 1872, PRO, FO 6/318, pp. 83-85.

29. St. John to Granville, 8 May 1873, PRO, FO 6/314, pp. 120-24.

30. Sackville West to Granville, 4 Feb. 1874, PRO, FO 6/320, p. 13.

31. Consul Wells to West, 14 April 1874, PRO, FO 6/320, pp. 117-21.

32. Consul Cowper to Derby, 26 Jan. 1875, PRO, FO 6/330, pp. 63-64.

33. Consul Cowper to Derby, 1 May 1875, PRO, FO 6/330, p. 85.

34. Derby to West, 25 Feb. 1875, PRO, FO 6/325, p. 8; West to Derby, 30 April 1875, PRO, FO 6/326, p. 167.

35. West to Derby, 8 Feb. 1875, PRO, FO 6/326, pp. 20-22.

36. St. John to Derby, 15 Oct., 20 Oct. 1875, PRO, FO 6/328, pp. 27, 45.

37. Szuchman, *Order, Family, and Community in Buenos Aires 1810-1860*, 52-64.

38. Sarmiento, "Mensaje de Apertura del Congreso," May 1872, *Obras* 51:213.

CHAPTER 7

1. Parish to Malaver, 11 Jan. 1872, AHPBA, Min. de Gob., leg. 4, exped. 232, fols. 3–4; Parish to Granville, 13 Jan. 1872, PRO, FO 6/311, pp. 74–75, encl.

2. Parish to Malaver, 14 March 1872, AHPBA, Min. de Gob., leg. 4, exped. 232, fols. 9–12; MacDonell to Granville, 15 March 1872, PRO, FO 6/309, pp. 222–29, encl.

3. Tejedor to MacDonell, 22 Jan. 1872, PRO, FO 6/309, pp. 48–52.

4. MacDonell to Granville, 9 March 1872, PRO, FO 6/309, pp. 196–201.

5. *The Standard*, Buenos Aires, 5 March 1872.

6. *River Plate Times*, Montevideo, 7 March 1872.

7. "A Voice from Bahia Blanca," by Settler, *The Standard*, 6 March 1872, p. 20.

8. House of Commons, 5 Aug. 1872, *Hansard Parliamentary Debates*, 3d ser., vol. 213 (London, 1872), 455.

9. John Smith to Secretary of State for Foreign Affairs, 19 Feb. 1872, PRO, FO 6/312, pp. 75–76.

10. Hamilton to Granville, 2 March 1872, PRO, FO 6/312, p. 80.

11. See above, p. 36.

12. Granville to MacDonell, 26 March 1872, PRO, FO 6/308, pp. 17–19.

13. *La Tribuna*, 10 September 1872, in MacDonell to Granville, 14 September 1872, PRO, FO 6/309, pp. 452–53.

14. Sackville West to Derby, 25 Feb. 1875, 4 Sept. 1875, PRO, FO 6/326, pp. 27–28, 141; 25 Nov. 1875, FO 6/328, p. 151.

15. MacDonell to Granville, 14 May 1872, PRO, FO 6/309, pp. 290–96.

16. MacDonell to Granville, 30 July 1872, PRO, FO 6/318, pp. 90–99.

17. MacDonell to Granville, 1 June 1872, PRO, FO 6/309, pp. 300–13.

18. MacDonell to Granville, 14 June 1871, PRO, FO 6/302, pp. 337–48.

19. MacDonell to Granville, 17 June 1871, PRO, FO 6/302, pp. 387–94; 4 July 1871, FO 6/303, p. 1.

20. MacDonell to Granville, 15 July 1871, PRO, FO 6/303, pp. 26–30.

21. St. John to Granville, 30 May 1873, PRO, FO 6/318, pp. 194–212.

22. MacDonell to Granville, 30 July 1872, PRO, FO 6/318, p. 99.

23. MacDonell to Granville, 15 March 1972, PRO, FO 6/309, pp. 216–17, 222–29.

CHAPTER 8

1. Quoted by David McLean, *War, Diplomacy and Informal Empire: Britain and the Republic of La Plata, 1836–1853*, 189–90.

2. D. C. M. Platt, *Finance, Trade, and Politics in British Foreign Policy, 1815–1914*, 318–19.

3. Ferns, *Britain and Argentina in the Nineteenth Century*, 290, 323.

4. Rory Miller, *Britain and Latin America in the Nineteenth and Twentieth Centuries*, 64, 124–25.

5. Ferns, *Britain and Argentina in the Nineteenth Century*, 327–36; see also the same author's "Argentina: Part of an Informal Empire," in *The Land That England Lost: Argentina and Britain, a Special Relationship*, ed. Alistair Hennessy and John King, 53–4.

6. Ferns, *Britain and Argentina in the Nineteenth Century*, 375–77.

7. Ibid., 386–95.

8. J. D. Gould, "European Inter-Continental Emigration, 1815–1914: Patterns and Causes," *Journal of European Economic History* 8, no. 3 (1979): 593–679.

9. Dudley Baines, *Migration in a Mature Economy: Emigration and Internal Migration in England and Wales, 1861–1901*, 10, 45.

10. Ibid., 88.

11. Ibid., 171–77, 280–82.

12. Charles Tilly, "Transplanted Networks," in *Immigration Reconsidered: History, Sociology, and Politics*, ed. Virginia Yans-McLaughlin, 79–95.

13. Mulhall, *The English in South America*, 529.

14. Ferns, *Britain and Argentina in the Nineteenth Century*, 367.

15. MacDonell, "Remarks on the River Plate Republics as a Field for British Emigration," *Parliamentary Papers*, 1872, vol. 70, pp. 9–17.

16. D. C. M. Platt, "British Agricultural Colonization in Latin America," *Inter-American Economic Affairs* 18 (1964): 3–38; Eduardo José Míguez, *Las tierras de los ingleses en la Argentina (1870–1914)*, 28–29.

17. MacDonell, "Remarks on the River Plate Republics as a Field for British Emigration," *Parliamentary Papers*, 1872, vol. 70, pp. 22–23; Míguez, *Las tierras de los ingleses*, 32–38, 103–105.

18. Glyn Williams, "Neither Welsh nor Argentine: The Welsh in Patagonia," in *The Land that England Lost*, ed. Hennessy and King, 109–22, and the same author's *The Desert and the Dream: A Study of Welsh Colonization in Chubut, 1865–1915*.

19. Campobassi, *Sarmiento y su época* 2:177; Baily, "Sarmiento and Immigration," in Criscenti, *Sarmiento and His Argentina*, 131–42.

20. *La Nación*, Buenos Aires, 4 June 1871.

21. Balcarce to Clarendon, 4 Jan. 1866, PRO, FO 6/265, pp. 1–2.

22. Ford to Clarendon, 24 March 1866, PRO, FO 6/262, pp. 59–64. Son of the author of *Handbook for Travellers in Spain*, Sir Francis Clare Ford (1828–99) entered the diplomatic service in 1851 and reached the post of secretary of legation, Buenos Aires, in 1865. Following similar appointments at Copenhagen and Washington, he was promoted envoy extraordinary and minister plenipotentiary to Argentina in 1878 and subsequently to Brazil, ambassador at Madrid 1887, at Constantinople in 1892, and at Rome in 1893–98; see *Dictionary of National Biography (DNB)*, vol. 22, Supplement.

23. Emigration Commission to Foreign Office, 8 April 1869, PRO, FO 6/287, pp. 39–40; Stuart to Clarendon, 12 April 1869, FO 6/282, p. 266.

24. MacDonell to Clarendon, 21 Oct. 1869, PRO, FO 6/284, pp. 118–20, 11 Dec. 1869, FO 6/300, pp. 94–104. Mariano Varela (1834–1902), son of Florencio Varela, a distinguished opponent of Rosas, was a journalist and politician who founded *La Tribuna* in 1853; he was appointed minister of foreign affairs by Sarmiento.

25. Campobassi, *Sarmiento y su época*, 2:145.

26. MacDonell to Clarendon, 12 Jan. 1870, PRO, FO 6/291, p. 19.

27. MacDonell to Clarendon, 12 Feb., 9 April, 22 June, 1 Sept., 1870, PRO, FO 6/300, pp. 106–108, 136, 194–95, 199.

28. MacDonell to Clarendon, 22 March, 6 April 1870, PRO, FO 6/291, pp. 97, 120–24.

29. "The Bench and the Dock," *The Standard*, Buenos Aires, 24 June 1870; MacDonell to Clarendon, 24 June 1870, PRO, FO 6/291, p. 306.

30. A copy of the notice may be found in PRO, FO 6/294, p. 251. Evidence that it was these particular murders which precipitated the warning may be found in a Foreign Office memorandum by Eliot dated 23 May 1870, FO 6/300, pp. 177–83.

31. Murdoch to Rogers, 27 Jan. 1870, PRO, FO 6/294, pp. 220–22.

32. Balcarce to Clarendon, Paris, 12 March, 27 March 1870, PRO, FO 6/293, pp. 440–41, 449. In fact, it was not these murders which precipitated the notice; see note 30, this chapter, above.

33. Clarendon to Balcarce, 19 March, 8 April 1870, PRO, FO 6/293, pp. 446–47, 454–55.

34. Letter to *The Times*, 14 April 1870.

35. "El Ex-Ministro Inglés en la República," *La Tribuna*, 10 April 1870.

36. *La Nación*, 10 April 1870.

37. "Security for Life," *The Standard*, 10 April 1870.

38. Central Commission of Immigration, *The Standard*, 11 April 1870.

39. MacDonell to Clarendon, 14 April 1870, PRO, FO 6/293, pp. 105–109.

40. MacDonell to Clarendon, 30 May 1870, PRO, FO 6/293, p. 174.

41. Varela to MacDonell, 20 May 1870, published in *The Standard*, encl. in MacDonell to Clarendon, 22 May 1870, PRO, FO 6/293, p. 152.

42. MacDonell to Clarendon, 28 May 1870, PRO, FO 6/293, pp. 162–63.

43. Varela to MacDonell, 21 May 1870, PRO, FO 6/293, pp. 172–73.

44. See above, pp. 34–35.

45. Stuart to Eliot, 25 May 1870, PRO, FO 6/300, pp. 185–90.

46. MacDonell to Clarendon, 22 June 1870, PRO, FO 6/293, pp. 212–14; *The Times*, 29 April 1870.

47. R. G. Herbert to Foreign Office, 11 Jan. 1871, PRO, FO 6/305, pp. 247–48; Platt, "British Agricultural Colonization in Latin America," 9.

48. MacDonell to Clarendon, 23 July 1870, PRO, FO 6/292, pp. 66–67.

49. MacDonell to Clarendon, 8 May 1870, PRO, FO 6/293, p. 138.

50. Murdoch to F. Rogers, Foreign Office, 16 July 1870, PRO, FO 6/294, pp. 358–64, 365–66.

51. Pfeil to Bailey, secretary ECAC, 29 July, 17 Oct. 1870, Pfeil to Duke of Manchester, 31 Oct. 1870, PRO, FO 6/306, pp. 43–64.

52. Murdoch to Rogers, Foreign Office, 28 Nov. 1870, PRO, FO 6/306, pp. 67–87. Rogers wrote to Baily, secretary of ECAC, 21 Jan. 1871, informing him that Lord Kimberley (Colonial Secretary) felt that the ECAC did not have the elements of success, and he had no wish to prolong the correspondence; FO 6/306, p. 85.

53. Murdoch to Herbert, 19 June 1871, PRO, FO 6/303, p. 286.

54. Ibid.

55. MacDonell to Clarendon, 12 July 1870, PRO, FO 6/294, pp. 88–89.

56. MacDonell to Clarendon, 23 July 1870, PRO, FO 6/292, pp. 61–71.

57. Letter from "A River Plate Merchant," 23 Feb. 1871, *The Times*, 27 Feb. 1871.

58. Balcarce to Granville, 18 March 1871, PRO, FO 6/306, p. 8.

59. MacDonell to Granville, 22 Oct. 1871, PRO, FO 6/303, pp. 127–37.

60. See above, pp. 31–37.

61. Notice dated 5 April 1872, PRO, FO 6/312, p. 96.

62. MacDonell to Granville, 14 May 1872, PRO, FO 6/309, pp. 256–68.

63. *The Times*, 22 July 1872.

64. Franco Torrome, Letter, *The Times*, 31 July 1872.

65. Balcarce to Granville, 16 August 1872, PRO, FO 6/318, pp. 127–32.

66. Holland, Colonial Office, to Under-Secretary of State, Foreign Office, 26 Sept. 1872, PRO, FO 6/318, pp. 197–200.

67. Walcott to Herbert, 5 Oct. 1872, PRO, FO 6/318, pp. 207–209.

68. *The Times*, 11 Oct. 1872, p. 10; Balcarce to Granville, 15 Oct. 1872, Granville to Balcarce, 29 Oct. 1872, PRO, FO 6/318, pp. 202–203, 220.

69. *The Times*, 16 Oct., 4 Nov., 15 Nov., 25 Dec. 1872.

70. Robertson to Herbert, 4 March 1873, PRO, FO 6/318, pp. 292–300.

71. See below, Chapter 9.

72. St. John to Granville, 30 June 1873, PRO, FO 6/315, pp. 59–70.

73. Sackville-West to Granville, 3 Sept., 13 Sept. 1873, PRO, FO 6/314, pp. 352–53, 375; Sackville-West to Derby, 1 Oct., 13 Dec. 1874, FO 6/321, pp. 123, 156, 223.

74. R. G. Herbert to Under-Secretary of State for Foreign Affairs, 20 August 1874, PRO, FO 6/324, pp. 297–302; Sackville-West to Derby, 28 August 1874, FO 6/321, pp. 83–84, 123.

75. Sackville-West to Derby, 13 Oct. 1874, PRO, FO 6/321, pp. 152–58.

CHAPTER 9

1. Mitre, *Los Debates*, 22 Oct. 1857, in Halperín, *Proyecto y construcción de una nación*, 338.

2. Phipps, "Report," in MacDonell to Granville, 15 July 1871, PRO, FO 6/304, pp. 125–96.

3. For modern statistical evidence for the province of Buenos Aires, see Sábato, *Agrarian Capitalism*, 99–104.

4. MacDonell, "Remarks," 14 March 1872, in MacDonell to Granville, 16 May 1872, PRO, FO 6/318, pp. 5–66.

5. See Hennessy and King, *The Land That England Lost*, 159–64, 172, 295, who conclude that British culture and values "held an important position in the largely immigrant society" of Argentina.

6. Seymour, *Pioneering in the Pampas*, 88–89.

7. Ferns, *Britain and Argentina in the Nineteenth Century*, 368. See also Míguez, *Las tierras de los ingleses*, 28–29.

8. Balcarce to David Robertson, 30 August 1872, PRO, FO 6/318, pp. 182–85.

9. MacDonell to Granville, 2 Sept. 1872, PRO, FO 6/318, p. 155.

10. See above, pp. 138–45.

11. *La Tribuna*, 10 Sept. 1872; MacDonell to Granville, 14 Sept. 1872, PRO, FO 6/309, pp. 452–53.

12. MacDonell to Granville, 28 Nov. 1872, PRO, FO 6/309, pp. 504–505.

13. F. R. St. John to Granville, 21 Jan. 1873, PRO, FO 6/314, pp. 3–5.

14. Balcarce to Granville, 7 April 1873, PRO, FO 6/318, pp. 317–20.

15. Thomson and Bonar, undated, PRO, FO 6/318, pp. 301–16.

16. *The Standard*, Buenos Aires, 5 April 1873.

17. St. John to Granville, 12 April 1873, PRO, FO 6/314, pp. 93–94.

18. Sarmiento, "Mensaje de Apertura del Congreso," 2 May 1873, *Obras* 51:270; St. John to Granville, 14 May 1873, PRO, FO 6/314, pp. 141–62; "Answer to Mr. MacDonell's Remarks on the Argentine Republic," by M. R. Garcia (1873), copy in FO 6/318, pp. 328–63.

19. St. John to Granville, 8 May 1873, PRO, FO 6/314, pp. 120–24.

20. Sackville-West to Granville, 18 Oct. 1873, PRO, FO 6/314, pp. 381–84.

21. Sackville-West to Granville, 8 Nov., 29 Dec. 1873, PRO, FO 6/314, pp. 402–403, 439; Sackville-West to Granville, 12 March 1874, PRO, FO 6/320, pp. 29–36.

22. On Mansilla and his views see above, Chapter 1.

23. Sackville-West to Granville, 28 Oct. 1873, PRO, FO 6/314, pp. 388–92.

24. Sackville-West to Derby, 30 March 1874, PRO, FO 6/320, pp. 51–52.

25. Sackville-West to Derby, 9 March 1875, PRO, FO 6/326, pp. 65–68.

26. Sackville-West to Derby, 10 May, 13 June 1875, PRO, FO 6/326, pp. 181, 205–11.

27. Hernández, *El Río de la Plata*, 30 Sept. 1869, in Halperín, *Proyecto y construcción de una nación*, 357.

28. Barros, "Actualidad financiera," *Indios, fronteras y seguridad interior*, 145–46, 259.

CHAPTER 10

1. Weber and Rausch, *Where Cultures Meet*, xiv–xvi; see also David J. Weber, *The Spanish Frontier in North America*, 11–13.

2. León Solis, *Maloqueros y conchavadores*, 200–206; Carlos A. Mayo and Amalia Latrubesse, *Terratenientes, soldados y cautivos: La Frontera (1736–1815)*, 43–58.

3. McLynn, "Consequences for Argentina of the War of the Triple Alliance," 83–86, 90–91.

4. Seymour, *Pioneering in the Pampas*, 179–80.

5. *La Nación*, 14 September 1872.

6. Richard W. Slatta, "Rural Criminality and Social Conflict in Nineteenth-Century Buenos Aires Province," *Hispanic American Historical Review* 60, no. 3 (1980): 465.

7. John Charles Chasteen, "Fighting Words: The Discourse of Insurgency in Latin American History," *Latin American Research Review* 28, no. 3 (1993): 83–111; on the millenarians of Tomochic see Vanderwood, "'None but the Justice of God': Tomochic, 1891–1892," in *Patterns of Contention in Mexican History*, ed. Jaime E. Rodríguez, 227–41.

8. Richard W. Slatta, "The Gaucho in Argentina's Quest for National Identity," in *Where Cultures Meet*, ed. Weber and Rausch, 151–64.

9. On standards of policing in Buenos Aires, recorded by a French observer, see Armaignac, *Viajes por las pampas argentinas*, 29–30; on the relative leniency of sentencing, see Slatta and Robinson in *The Problem of Order*, ed. Johnson, 38–39.

10. Ferns, *Britain and Argentina in the Nineteenth Century*, 359.

11. D. C. M. Platt, *Latin America and British Trade, 1806–1914*, 126–28, 131.

12. Sarmiento, "Mensaje de Apertura del Congreso," 2 May 1873, *Obras* 51:270.

13. Platt, "British Agricultural Colonization in Latin America," *Inter-American Economic Affairs* 18 (1964): 15, and 19 (1965): 39–42; Hennessy, "Argentines, Anglo-Argentines and Others," in *The Land That England Lost*, ed. Hennessy and King, 20.

14. Míguez, *Las tierras de los ingleses*, 35–58, 304–305, 310–21.

Glossary of Spanish Terms

alcalde de campaña.   Mayor of a rural district.

alsinismo.   Policy or party of Alsina.

alsinista.   Follower of Alsina.

aparcero.   Sharecropper.

barrio.   Quarter, district, neighborhood.

banda fanática.   Gang of fanatics.

bandido.   Bandit.

cacique.   Indian chieftain, chief, boss.

capataz (pl., *capataces*).   Foreman of estate or ranch.

capitanejo.   Captain of a band of Indians, subordinate to a cacique.

caudillo.   Leader, whose rule is based on personal power rather than constitutional form.

chacra.   Small farm.

changador.   Porter.

china.   A native woman of the pampas, a gaucho's wife or girlfriend.

chiripá.   Gaucho garment in place of trousers.

cholo.   Person of mixed race (sometimes used pejoratively).

comisario.   Police or military official.

comisión municipal.   Municipal committee.

conchavador (Mapuche). Merchant, Indian frontier merchant.

conventillo.   Tenement.

corporación municipal.   Town council.

criollo.   Spanish American, native Argentine.

curandero -a.   Folk healer, medicine man or woman.

degollador.   Cutthroat.

estancia.   Cattle or sheep ranch.

estanciero.   Owner of an *estancia*.

facón.   Long gaucho knife.

fuero.   Right or immunity conferred by membership of a profession or community.

gaucho.   Mounted nomad, free cowboy, inhabitant of the pampas of Argentina.

gaucho de caballería.   Mounted gaucho.

gringo.   Pejorative term for foreigner.

hacendado.   Owner of a hacienda.

hacienda.   Large landed estate.
jornalero.   Rural day-laborer.
lazo.   Lasso.
malhechor.   Malefactor, criminal.
malón.   Indian raid.
mayordomo.   Manager of estate or ranch.
mitrismo.   Policy or party of Mitre.
mitrista.   Follower of Mitre.
montonera.   Irregular forces under a caudillo.
montonero.   Guerrilla fighter.
paisano.   Countryman.
pampa.   Grassy plain, prairie.
partido.   Administrative unit, county or parish.
patrón.   Patron, master, boss.
peon.   Rural laborer, ranch worker.
peonaje.   Occupation of a peon.
porteño.   Of Buenos Aires, inhabitant of Buenos Aires.
puestero.   Worker in charge of a *puesto*.
puesto.   Work station, pasture.
pulpería.   General store and bar.
pulpero.   Storekeeper.
recado.   Saddle.
rosismo.   Policy or movement of Rosas.
rosista.   Follower of Rosas.
sereno.   Night watchman.
terna.   Short list of three candidates.
toldería.   Indian camp.
toldo.   Indian tent or hut.
vago.   Vagrant.
vagos y mal entretenidos.   Vagabonds and idlers.

Bibliography

PRIMARY SOURCES

Archives

Archivo Histórico de la Provincia de Buenos Aires, La Plata. Ministerio de Gobierno, Tandil 110, 1871–74. Juzgado de Crimen.
Archivo General de la Nación, Buenos Aires. Sala X.27.3.1.
Banco de la Provincia de Buenos Aires. Archivo y Museo Históricos. Copiador de Correspondencia, Tandil, 1872.
Public Record Office, London. Foreign Office, General Correspondence. FO 6, Argentina, 1865–75.

Published Documents and Contemporary Works

Alberdi, Juan Bautista. *Las "Bases" de Alberdi.* Ed. Jorge M. Mayer. Buenos Aires, 1969.
——, *Obras completas.* 8 vols. Buenos Aires, 1886.
Argentina. *Primer Censo de la República Argentina.* 1869. Buenos Aires, 1872.
——. Ministerio del Interior, Dirección Nacional de Migraciones. *Estadística del movimiento migratorio, 1857–1956.* Buenos Aires, 1956.
Armaignac, H. *Viajes por las pampas argentinas: Cacerías en el Quequén Grande y otras andanzas, 1869–1874.* Buenos Aires, 1974.
Barros, Alvaro. *Indios, fronteras y seguridad interior.* Ed. Pedro Daniel Weinberg. Buenos Aires, 1975.
Dirección General de Inmigración. *Resúmen estadística del movimiento migratorio en la República Argentina, 1857–1924.* Buenos Aires, 1925.
Echeverría, Esteban. *Dogma Socialista.* La Plata, 1940.
Fugl, Juan. *Memorias de Juan Fugl: Vida de un pionero danés durante 30 años en Tandil, Argentina, 1844–1875.* Trans. Alice Larsen de Rabal. Buenos Aires, 1986.
Halperín Donghi, Tulio. *Proyecto y construcción de una nación (Argentina 1846–1880).* Caracas, Venezuela, 1980.
Latham, Wilfrid. *The States of the River Plate.* 2d ed. London, 1868.

Mansilla, Lucio V. *Una excursión a los indios ranqueles.* Ed. Julio Caillet-Bois. Mexico City and Buenos Aires, 1947.

Parish, Sir Woodbine. *Buenos Ayres and the Provinces of the Rio de la Plata.* 2d ed. London, 1852.

Rosas, Juan Manuel de. *Cartas del exilio, 1853–1875.* Ed. José Raed. Buenos Aires, 1974.

Sarmiento, Domingo F. *Facundo.* Edición crítica y documentada. Prologue by Alberto Palcos. La Plata, 1938.

——. *Obras de D. F. Sarmiento.* 53 vols. Santiago, Chile, and Buenos Aires, 1866–1914.

Seymour, Richard Arthur. *Pioneering in the Pampas; or, The First Four Years of a Settler's Experience in the La Plata Camps.* London, 1869.

United Kingdom. "Correspondence Reporting the Treatment of British Subjects in the Argentine Republic, 1870– 1872," *Parliamentary Papers,* 1872, vol. 70, pp. 87–120.

——. *Hansard Parliamentary Debates,* 3d ser., vol. 213. London, 1872.

——. "Remarks on the River Plate Republics as a Field for British Emigration," by H. G. MacDonell, Chargé d'Affaires, Buenos Aires, 14 March 1872, *Parliamentary Papers,* 1872, vol. 70, pp. 1–85.

Newspapers

Buenos Aires
    La Nación
    El Nacional
    La Prensa
    La República
    The Standard
    La Tribuna
    La Verdad
Montevideo
    The River Plate Times
London
    The Times

SECONDARY WORKS

Academia Nacional de la Historia. *Historia Argentina Contemporánea, 1862–1930.* Vol. 2, parts 1 and 2. Buenos Aires, 1964–66.

Adelman, Jeremy. *Frontier Development: Land, Labour, and Capital on the Wheatlands of Argentina and Canada 1890–1914.* Oxford, 1994.

Amadasi, Enrique, et al. *Estructura y dinámica de la población, evolución económica y empleo en el partido de Tandil.* Tandil, 1981.

Anderson, Benedict. *Imagined Communities: Reflections on the Origin and Spread of Nationalism.* 2d ed. London, 1991.

Baily, Samuel L. "Sarmiento and Immigration: Changing Views on the Role of Immigration in the Development of Argentina." In *Sarmiento and His Argentina,* 131–42. Ed. Joseph T. Criscenti. Boulder, Colo., 1993.

Baines, Dudley. *Migration in a Mature Economy: Emigration and Internal Migration in England and Wales, 1861–1901.* Cambridge, 1985.

Bejarano, Manuel. "Inmigración y estructuras tradicionales en Buenos Aires (1854–1930)." In *Los fragmentos del poder,* 75–149. Ed. Torcuato S. Di Tella and Tulio Halperín Donghi. Buenos Aires, 1969.

Bethell, Leslie, ed. *The Cambridge History of Latin America.* Vols. 3 and 4. Cambridge, 1985–86.

Brown, Jonathan C. *A Socioeconomic History of Argentina, 1776–1860.* Cambridge, 1979.

——. "Revival of the Rural Economy and Society in Buenos Aires." In *Revolution and Restoration: The Rearrangement of Power in Argentina, 1776–1860,* 240–72. Ed. Mark D. Szuchman and Jonathan C. Brown. Lincoln, Nebr., 1994.

Brown, Richard Maxwell. *Strain of Violence: Historical Studies of American Violence and Vigilantism.* New York, 1975.

Campobassi, José S. *Sarmiento y su época.* 2 vols. Buenos Aires, 1975.

Carril, Bonifacio del. *El gaucho a través de la iconografía* Buenos Aires, 1978.

Castro, Donald S. *The Development and Politics of Argentine Immigration Policy, 1852–1914: To Govern Is to Populate.* San Francisco, 1991.

Chasteen, John Charles. "Fighting Words: The Discourse of Insurgency in Latin American History." *Latin American Research Review* 28, no. 3 (1993): 83–111.

——. "Violence for Show: Knife Dueling on a Nineteenth-Century Cattle Frontier." In *The Problem of Order in Changing Societies: Essays on Crime and Policing in Argentina and Uruguay,* 47–64. Ed. Lyman L. Johnson. Albuquerque, N.M., 1990.

Chiaramonte, José Carlos. *Nacionalismo y liberalismo econímicos en la Argentina, 1860–1880.* Buenos Aires, 1971.

——. "El federalismo argentino en la primera mitad del siglo XIX." In *Federalismos latinoamericanos: México, Brasil, Argentina,* 81–132. Ed. Marcello Carmagnani. Mexico City, 1993.

Cohn, Norman. *The Pursuit of the Millennium: Revolutionary Millenarians and Mystical Anarchists of the Middle Ages.* London, 1993.

Criscenti, Joseph T., ed. *Sarmiento and His Argentina.* Boulder, Colorado, 1993.

Cunninghame, Graham R. B. "La pulpería," in *Thirteen Stories.* London, 1900.

Curran, Thomas J. *Xenophobia and Immigration, 1820–1930.* Boston, 1975.

De la Fuente, Ariel Eugenio. "Caudillo and Gaucho Politics in the Argentine State-Formation Process: La Rioja, 1853–1870." Ph.D. diss., State University of New York at Stony Brook, 1995; University Microfilms, Ann Arbor, Mich., 1996.

Del Valle, Antonio G. *Recordando el pasado: Campañas por la civilización.* 2 vols. Buenos Aires, 1926.

Díaz, Benito. *Juzgados de paz de campaña de la provincia de Buenos Aires (1821–1854).* La Plata, 1959.

Ferns, H. S. *Britain and Argentina in the Nineteenth Century.* Oxford, 1960.

Fontana, Osvaldo L. *Tandil en la historia.* Tandil, 1944.

Garavaglia, Juan Carlos, and Gelman, Jorge D. "Rural History of the Río de la Plata, 1600–1850: Results of a Historiographical Renaissance." *Latin American Research Review* 30, no. 3 (1995): 75–105.

Gorraiz Beloqui, R. *Tandil a través de un siglo*. Buenos Aires, 1958.

Gould, J. D. "European Inter-Continental Emigration, 1815–1914: Patterns and Causes." *Journal of European Economic History* 8, no. 3 (1979): 593–679.

Halperín Donghi, Tulio. *José Hernández y sus mundos*. Buenos Aires, 1985.

———. "¿Para qué la inmigración? Ideología y política inmigratoria en la Argentina (1810–1914)." In *El espejo de la historia: Problemas argentinos y perspectivas latinoamericanas*, 189–238. Buenos Aires, 1987.

———. et al. *Sarmiento, Author of a Nation*. Berkeley, Calif., 1994.

Hanisch, W. "Manuel Lacunza S. I. y el milenarismo," *Archivum Historicum Societatis Jesu* 40 (1971): 496–511.

Harrison, J. F. C. *The Second Coming: Popular Millenarianism 1780–1850*. London, 1979.

Hennessy, Alistair. *The Frontier in Latin American History*. London, 1978.

———. and King, John, eds. *The Land That England Lost: Argentina and Britain, a Special Relationship*. London, 1992.

Hernández, José. *El Gaucho Martín Fierro*, bilingual ed., trans. Walter Owen. Buenos Aires, 1964.

Hudson, W. H. *Far Away and Long Ago*. London, 1967.

———. *Tales of the Pampa*. London, 1916.

Instituto Panamericano de Geografía e Historia, Comisión de Historia. *Bibliografía sobre el importe del proceso inmigratoria masivo en el Cono Sur de América: Argentina, Brasil, Chile, Uruguay*. Vol. 1. Mexico City, 1984.

Ivereigh, Austen. *Catholicism and Politics in Argentina, 1810–1960*. London, 1995.

Jacobsen, Joel. *Such Men as Billy the Kid: The Lincoln County War Reconsidered*. Lincoln, Nebr., 1994.

Johnson, Lyman L., ed. *The Problem of Order in Changing Societies: Essays on Crime and Policing in Argentina and Uruguay*. Albuquerque, N.M., 1990.

Jones, Kristine L. "Civilization and Barbarism and Sarmiento's Indian Policy." In *Sarmiento and His Argentina*, 35–43. Ed. Joseph T. Criscenti. Boulder, Colo., 1993.

———. "Indian-Creole Negotiations in the Southern Frontier." In *Revolution and Restoration The Rearrangement of Power in Argentina, 1776–1860*, 103–123. Ed. Mark D. Szuchman and Jonathan C. Brown. Lincoln, Nebr., 1994.

Jones, Maldwyn Allen. *American Immigration*. 2d ed. Chicago, 1992.

———. *El Reino Unido y América: Emigración Británica*. Madrid, 1992.

Korol, Juan Carlos, and Sábato, Hilda. *Cómo fue la inmigración irlandesa en la Argentina*. Buenos Aires, 1981.

León Solis, Leonardo. "Alianzas militares entre los indios araucanos y los grupos indios de las pampas: La rebelión araucana de 1867–1872 en Argentina y Chile." *Nueva Historia* 1, no. 1 (1981): 3–49.

———. *Maloqueros y conchavadores en Araucanía y las Pampas, 1700–1800*. Temuco, Chile, 1990.

Lewis, Colin M. *British Railways in Argentina, 1859–1914: A Case Study of Foreign Investment*. London, 1983.

Lynch, John. *Argentine Dictator: Juan Manuel de Rosas, 1829–1852*. Oxford, 1981.

McGrath, Roger D. *Gunfighters, Highwaymen and Vigilantes: Violence on the Frontier*. Berkeley, Calif., 1984.

McLean, David. *War, Diplomacy and Informal Empire: Britain and the Republic of La Plata, 1836–1853.* London, 1995.

McLynn, F. J. "The Argentine Presidential Election of 1868." *Journal of Latin American Studies* 11, no. 2 (1979): 303–23.

———. "Consequences for Argentina of the War of the Triple Alliance, 1865–1870." *The Americas* 41, no. 1 (1984): 81–98.

Maeder, Ernesto J. A. *Evolución demográfica argentina de 1810 a 1869.* Buenos Aires, 1969.

Mandrini, Raúl, ed. *Los Araucanos de las pampas en el siglo XIX.* Buenos Aires, 1984.

———. and Reguera, Andrea, eds. *Huellas en la tierra: Indios, agricultores y hacendados en la pampa bonaerense.* Tandil, 1993.

Mayo, Carlos A. *Estancia y sociedad en la pampa, 1740–1820.* Buenos Aires, 1995.

———. ed. *Pulperos y pulperías de Buenos Aires, 1740–1830.* Mar del Plata, 1996.

———. and Latrubesse, Amalia. *Terratenientes, soldados y cautivos: La Frontera (1736–1815).* Mar del Plata, 1993.

Míguez, Eduardo José. *Las tierras de los ingleses en la Argentina (1870–1914).* Buenos Aires, 1985.

———. "La expansión agraria en la pampa húmeda (1850–1914). Tendencias recientes en sus análisis histórico." *Anuario IEHS* (Tandil) 1 (1986): 89–119.

———. "Política, participación y poder: Los inmigrantes en las tierras nuevas de la Provincia de Buenos Aires en la segunda mitad del siglo XIX." *Estudios Migratorios Latinoamericanos* (Buenos Aires) 6–7 (1987): 337–79.

Miller, Rory. *Britain and Latin America in the Nineteenth and Twentieth Centuries.* London, 1993.

Mulhall, Michael G. *The English in South America.* Buenos Aires, 1878.

———. and Mulhall, E. T. *Handbook of the River Plate.* 6th ed. Buenos Aires, 1892.

Nario, Hugo. *Los crímenes del Tandil, 1872.* Buenos Aires, 1983.

———. *Mesías y bandoleros pampeanos.* Buenos Aires, 1993.

———. *Tata Dios: El Mesías de la última montonera.* Buenos Aires, 1976.

Oszlak, Oscar. *La formación del estado argentino.* Buenos Aires, 1982.

Panettieri, José. *Inmigración en la Argentina.* Buenos Aires, 1970.

Platt, D. C. M. "British Agricultural Colonization in Latin America." *Inter-American Economic Affairs* 18 (1964): 3–38; 19 (1965): 23–42.

———. *Finance, Trade, and Politics in British Foreign Policy, 1815–1914.* Oxford, 1968.

———. *Latin America and British Trade, 1806–1914.* London, 1972.

Poggi, Rinaldo Alberto. "Derrotado pero no vencido: Calfucurá después de San Carlos." *Nuestra Historia* 21 (1978): 134–57.

Recalde, Héctor. *La iglesia y la cuestión social, 1871–1910.* Buenos Aires, 1985.

Rock, David. *Authoritarian Argentina: The Nationalist Movement, Its History and Its Impact.* Berkeley, Calif., 1993.

Rodríguez Molas, Ricardo E. *Historia social del gaucho.* 2d ed. Buenos Aires, 1982.

Sabato, Hilda. *Agrarian Capitalism and the World Market: Buenos Aires in the Pastoral Age, 1840–1890.* Albuquerque, N.M., 1990.

Sáenz Quesada, María. *Los estancieros.* Buenos Aires, 1980.

Salvatore, Ricardo D. "Reclutamiento militar, disciplinamiento y proletarización en la era de Rosas." *Boletín del Instituto de Historia Argentina y Americana "Dr. E. Ravignani,"* 3d Series, 5, no. 1 (1992): 25–47.

Scobie, James R. *Revolution on the Pampas: A Social History of Argentine Wheat, 1860–1910.* Austin, Tex., 1964.

Shumway, Nicolas. *The Invention of Argentina.* Berkeley, 1991.

Slatta, Richard W. *Cowboys of the Americas.* New Haven, 1990.

——. *Gauchos and the Vanishing Frontier.* Lincoln, Nebr., 1983.

——. "The Gaucho in Argentina's Quest for National Identity." In *Where Cultures Meet: Frontiers in Latin American History,* 151–64. Ed. David J. Weber and Jane M. Rausch. Wilmington, Del., 1994.

——. "Rural Criminality and Social Conflict in Nineteenth-Century Buenos Aires Province." *Hispanic American Historical Review* 60, no. 3 (1980): 450–72.

——. ed. *Bandidos: The Varieties of Latin American Banditry.* Westport, Conn., 1987.

——. and Robinson, Karla. "Continuities in Crime and Punishment: Buenos Aires, 1820–50." In *The Problem of Order in Changing Societies: Essays on Crime and Policing in Argentina and Uruguay,* 19–45. Ed. Lyman L. Johnson. Albuquerque, N.M., 1990.

Solberg, Carl E. *Immigration and Nationalism: Argentina and Chile, 1890–1914.* Austin, Tex., 1970.

——. *The Prairies and the Pampas: Agrarian Policy in Canada and Argentina, 1880–1930.* Stanford, Calif., 1987.

Súarez García, José María. *Historia de la parroquia de Tandil.* Tandil, 1954.

Szuchman, Mark D. *Order, Family, and Community in Buenos Aires, 1810–1860.* Stanford, Calif., 1988.

——. and Brown, Jonathan C., eds. *Revolution and Restoration: The Rearrangement of Power in Argentina, 1776–1860.* Lincoln, Nebr., 1994.

Thompson, Damian. *The End of Time: Faith and Fear in the Shadow of the Millennium.* London, 1996.

Torre, Juan Carlos. "Los crímenes de Tata Dios, el mesías gaucho." *Todo es Historia,* No. 4 (1967): 40–45.

Utley, Robert S. *High Noon in Lincoln: Violence on the Western Frontier.* Albuquerque, N.M., 1987.

Vanderwood, Paul J. "'None but the Justice of God': Tomochic, 1891–1892." In *Patterns of Contention in Mexican History,* 227–41. Ed. Jaime E. Rodríguez. Wilmington, Del., 1992.

Walther, Juan Carlos. *La conquista del desierto.* 3d ed. Buenos Aires, 1970.

Weber, David J. *The Spanish Frontier in North America.* New Haven and London, 1992.

——. and Rausch, Jane M., eds. *Where Cultures Meet: Frontiers in Latin American History.* Wilmington, Del., 1994.

Williams, Glyn. *The Desert and the Dream: A Study of Welsh Colonization in Chubut, 1865–1915.* Cardiff, Wales, 1975.

Yans-McLaughlin, Virginia, ed. *Immigration Reconsidered: History, Sociology, and Politics.* New York, 1990.

Index

DATE DUE

OCT 23 1998	

UPI   PRINTED IN U.S.A.